Transforming PR

This book introduces the concept of the Picnic Society – a society which we all belong to today because social media has given us unlimited opportunities to create or destroy our own and our circle's (our bubble's) realities, possibilities, and reputations.

In today's world every organization is integrated into society, and the people belonging to organizations are integrated into various continually interacting communities. Social media has – or soon will – erase any remaining boundaries between organizations and the world's social fabric. It is increasingly pointless for organizations to try to establish relationships with society, because these already exist – 24 hours per day, 7 days per week, and all 365 days of the year. This is what I mean when talking about the transformation of the field of PR – from Public Relations to People Relations. This book discusses the challenges facing public relations professionals working in a contemporary society that is flooded with information, offers endless channels of communication, gives rise to true and false leaders, and is marked by both openness and mistrust, by real and fake news.

This book will appeal to professionals who already have a solid grasp of public relations technologies but would like to review their skills and develop their own model of public relations know-how without being limited by the strict boundaries of traditional PR theory.

Andrius Kasparas is a consultant, managing partner at KOKO PR, lecturer, and author with more than 25 years of experience in public relations. He has created, managed, and participated in more than a hundred public relations projects in the business and NGO sectors; has extensive experience consulting in the energy sector; has lectured in PR and marketing communications at the university level; has given talks at various PR conferences and seminars; and has participated in numerous professional contest juries. Andrius Kasparas was director of the Lithuanian Communication Association in 2016.

Transforming PR

Public Relations to People Relations

Andrius Kasparas

Routledge
Taylor & Francis Group
LONDON AND NEW YORK

Designed cover image: Jason Hawkes Photography

First published 2025
by Routledge
4 Park Square, Milton Park, Abingdon, Oxon OX14 4RN

and by Routledge
605 Third Avenue, New York, NY 10158

Routledge is an imprint of the Taylor & Francis Group, an informa business

British Library Cataloguing-in-Publication Data
A catalogue record for this book is available from the British Library

ISBN: 978-1-032-73937-3 (hbk)
ISBN: 978-1-032-68709-4 (pbk)
ISBN: 978-1-003-46680-2 (ebk)

DOI: 10.4324/9781003466802

Typeset in Galliard
by Apex CoVantage, LLC

I dedicate this book to the most important and loyal ones – Giedrė, Vilius, Adelė, and Grytė. Without you, there wouldn't have been the desire or purpose to start this book. Therefore, you are its foundation, meaning the most important ones.

Contents

Figures

Tables

Introduction

> Communication is a skill that you can learn. It's like riding a bicycle or typing. If you're willing to work at it, you can rapidly improve.
>
> Brian Tracy – motivational public speaker and self-development author.

This book is intended for students who already have some knowledge of the field of public relations but have not yet mastered the profession's tools and are preparing to do so. It is also suitable for professionals with experience of public relations technologies but who would like to organize their skills, rethink them, and create their own public relations know-how model. It should encourage one not to limit themselves within strict theoretical frameworks of public relations but to create an acceptable structure for themselves. This book, while not overly academic and full of public relations terms understandable only to professionals, could also be suitable for someone reading about public relations for the first time but would like to learn more about the profession. It should also attract marketing specialists who want to step out of their comfort zone and rethink their activities.

I hope that the majority of readers of this book already know how to write a press release, organize a conference, create and manage a Facebook profile, and present good news to the media.

This book is not about technology. However, if you would like to learn the basics that I have mentioned, I believe there have been many excellent books written on these topics so far, and various trainings are organized as well.

Although I have never worked for a corporation, I have often worked as their insider – an internal public relations person. Sometimes I just consulted those who were the public relations people of the companies. This has allowed me to gain a comprehensive view from both the outside and the inside. Over more than 25 years of practice, I have consulted or participated in more than a hundred public relations projects.

For this reason, since I have never worked for any corporation, the term "client" is more familiar to me than "manager". However, readers who have worked within corporations for a more extended period can easily replace

DOI: 10.4324/9781003466802-1

"client" with "manager": every mention of "client" here is well thought out and can be replaced with "manager" appropriately.

In 2009, Erik Qualman's book *Socialnomics: how social media transforms the way we live and do business*[1] was the first stimulus for me to review my attitude towards traditional public relations. I had felt something similar before, but after reading the book, everything began to fall into place. Later, I visited a PR agency in Helsinki, where I heard the word "picnic" from a colleague. She said that everything that was happening now was a big picnic. Imagine your social media account as a picnic blanket – you spread it out, start loading it with food, friends start gathering, and communication begins. Now imagine that there are many such picnic blankets around – you can approach each one, share your thoughts, go to the next one, come back, and continue constantly.

And then I unconsciously decided that before I could write about it, I first needed to talk and communicate with a larger circle of public relations specialists to form a wide-ranging view of today's public relations activities as well as with a smaller group of like-minded people, with whom it would be possible to discuss even the most minor details.

So began my period of collecting knowledge and opinions. Over a year, I tried to participate in at least four to five very different public relations events. This led me to attend global public relations festivals in Trieste, London, and Madrid, participate in Eurocom and Worldcom member meetings, teach at university, and follow and read reports at various conferences. Many international thoughts and practices came from clients. I communicated with public relations specialists from Estonia, Belarus, Belgium, Great Britain, Italy, Spain, Latvia, Poland, Norway, Russia, Finland, Sweden, Ukraine, Hungary, Germany, and other countries. I visited public relations associations in Great Britain, Italy, Latvia, Finland, and Sweden, actively participated in creating and developing two professional organizations for Lithuanian public relations specialists, and everywhere I "brewed" ideas for this book.

The entire activity led to the creation of a book, which you now hold in your hands.

My book aims to tell the story of the challenges a public relations professional faces in the modern, information-saturated world filled with various communication channels, real and fake leaders, openness and distrust, and honest and fake news.

My book aims to show that public relations specialists are navigators in the stormy sea of information. They are the captains – strong, honest, uncompromising in terms of ethics, and flexible and adaptable when it comes to finding the key to the hearts and minds of different people waiting for various types of information.

My book aims to show that a public relations professional is not a robot coldly calculating how to deceive the community, but rather a human constantly searching for ways to provide the most information to those who need it.

My book aims to support those true public relations professionals who work in a constantly emotionally-demanding profession, to help them not break down when emotional exhaustion makes it seem like they want to disappear.

Although the level of stress caused by the profession of public relations is lower than that of soldiers, firefighters, pilots, or police officers, it still appears in many top ten lists of the most stressful professions. It can be confidently said that out of all "office" professions, this is one of the most stressful. By the way, it is hardly possible to call this profession completely office-based: the main work of a public relations specialist is done not in their own office, but in other people's offices, in conference rooms, halls, or any other necessary places. Public relations specialists must constantly be where they are most needed, so a true professional in this field is constantly on the go, meeting someone, continually communicating with people, and continuously being where dialogue and understanding are needed.

Finally, this book aims to reveal the unique world we live in today and how we are the first people in human history to have such difficult-to-grasp communication opportunities. This is a fantastic time, and we are fortunate to live in it. We can no longer feel time and geographic boundaries when communicating, even at the most remote points in the world. So please take a few seconds to pause next time you edit a document on your computer screen with a colleague from another country and think about how incredible and, at the same time, simple it is! At least half of this book is about that.

This book is divided into five main parts: People Relations, Transformation, Social Picnic, Practicing a Picnic, and Future. It is a coherent narrative about the fundamentals of this profession, moving towards a change that shapes a new concept, describing the application of that concept, and reflecting on the future.

Over the past 20 years, the possibilities for applying our profession in public relations have fundamentally changed. It can be said that if 20 years ago public relations specialists were riding bicycles, today they are flying on the fastest planes and are soon preparing to enter space. The reason for this change is the transition of the world community to a new stage of development in public relations, which I have called the "Network" stage in later chapters, and the transformation of public relations activities. You will learn about these processes as you continue reading.

However, there is one aspect related to the title of the first chapter of this book that I would like to clarify immediately. The chapter is called "People Relations". This is not a mistake. I believe that alongside the other changes that have taken place in recent years, it is time to change the profession's name, as "Public Relations" no longer reflects the spirit of the times. This name implies an inaccurate relationship between an organization and society as if suggesting that organizations are some separate part of society and they need to find ways to communicate with it, as if organizations were one world and society another. That may have been true 20 or more years ago, but today, all organizations are integral parts of society, and the people within organizations are fully integrated into various communities. Furthermore, social media has erased – or will soon erase – the boundaries between organizations and society. Therefore, there is no longer much point in organizations seeking to establish a relationship with the community – it already exists. It is uninterrupted 24 hours a day, 7 days a week, and 365 days a year. Therefore, it is worth considering that Public Relations has changed into People Relations. I call this the transformation of PR into PR.

In this book, I will continue to use the abbreviation PR. It is familiar to us and can remain so. However, when I use PR, I will use it to shorten the words "people relations" instead of "public relations". This is because I believe that in the long run, "people relations" could become the new name of our profession.

Chapter 1, "People Relations", is divided into five sections.

In the first section, "History", I divide the history of PR into four stages: Fire, Book, Television, and Network. I believe that the emergence of books and traditional and social media have had the most significant impact on changes in PR. Knowing the main historical facts creates a foundation for building the "house" of any field.

In the second section, "PRofession", I attempt to reveal the essence of PR activities through five essential skills: Hearings, Feelings, Explanations, Truths, and Relations. These five skills are interconnected and form a circle.

The third section, "Reputation", is about the primary goal of PR activities – assistance in creating a reputation. In this section, the relationship between PR and reputation is revealed, factors affecting reputation are described, and a reputation complex is constructed. At the end of the section, I identify ten benefits for which it is worth managing reputations. Any PR specialist, even those less experienced, can use these benefits when arguments are needed to defend the necessity of their activities.

The fourth section, "Let's Think About the Terms a Bit", is dedicated to the confusion between PR and marketing terminology. I do not claim to resolve this confusion. Still, I wanted to draw attention to the fact that incorrect and incompetent use of terms can do significant harm to PR activities and distort their essence.

At the end of this chapter, in the fifth section, "His Majesty the Client", I focus on clients and their desires, which are often overvalued in an attempt to please them. My goal here is to emphasize that the client is, first and foremost, a partner to the PR professional and that results are always a shared achievement. Client desires are essential but not absolute. The client must allow freedom of action, understand the essence of PR activities, evaluate the consultant's experience, follow the same ethical principles, be reliable, and the client and consultant must trust each other.

Chapter 2, "Transformation", is dedicated to the change that began with the emergence of social media and which is still ongoing.

The first section, "Two Eras", is about the end of the third stage of PR, "Television", and the beginning of the fourth stage, "Network", which is about the transition from one-way mass communication (traditional media) or the "Marketing era" to two-way mass communication (social media) or the "PR era". This transition is a significant change in PR because, for the first time in human history, we have mass communication that works in two directions: we can not only spread one message to millions but also present millions of messages sorted and categorized by priority to one person. I highlight six flaws of the "Marketing era" that were solved by six advantages of the "PR era". The goal of "Two Eras" is not to reflect each era objectively, but to highlight the things that were missing in the "Television" stage and, therefore, naturally emerged in the "Network" stage.

The transformation from one era to another, like any change, revolution, or modification, had its reasons. They are revealed in the second section. The things that remain the same, regardless of which PR stage we are in and what transformations are taking place, also caught my interest. The overall conclusion is straightforward: technologies, their speed, accessibility, and platforms change, while the needs of humans remain fundamentally the same, as is precisely arranged in Maslow's Hierarchy of Needs.

The end of this chapter describes the transition from hierarchical to picnical communication.

Chapter 3, "Social Picnic", is dedicated to presenting the Social Picnic. The Social Picnic is a modern communication model, an idea of how communication should work in today's world, where we have all the tools to implement mass two-way communication.

The first section of this chapter introduces readers to the seven elements of the Social Picnic model, which are named after things or phenomena that can be observed in a simple picnic in nature: Sun (quality and well-functioning information technologies), Meadow (boundaries that separate one picnic from another), Plaid (a community that unites one or more interests), Sharer (a person who directly or indirectly participates in a Social Picnic), Food (conversations and data), Vase (a positive and visual Plaid identity), and Concert (a temporarily dominant theme).

In the second section, I discuss the four successful elements – or the ConCrEtE formula – of a Social Picnic. These elements were identified in *The social media bible: tactics, tools, and strategies for business success*[2] by Lon Safko and David K. Brake in 2009. These elements are communication, collaboration, education, and entertainment.

In the penultimate part of this chapter, the rules that are often unwritten but recommended to follow when participating in a Social Picnic process are summarized.

This chapter ends with a reflection on what constitutes "Success and Value" and how these concepts differ for different participants in the Social Picnic. For example, suppose the success of Creators is their achieved popularity, and the value is the content they create. In that case, the success of Ignorers is their resistance to the Social Picnic and their ability not to be a part of it. Still, through this, they become valuable participants in the Social Picnic by providing a different, offline perspective on what is happening around them.

Chapter 4, "Practicing a Picnic", is a practical section, a brief guide on organizing your activities for a Social Picnic. It is divided into ten steps, stages through which it is best to proceed consistently and without deviation. Of course, it is not you or anyone else who starts the Social Picnic; however, it is ongoing, so it is worth knowing the basic rules that govern it before arriving at it.

The goal of the fifth chapter of the book, "Future", is dreams. Of course, all of them are related to the future because that is where we are all heading. Some dreams should come true faster, while others are still very distant and not directly attainable for me or anyone reading this book. Still, our ancestors, I believe, put in much effort to ensure we can fly in airplanes and into space. For the sake of our future descendants, we can also make an effort, at least by dreaming. In this chapter, that's what I do: I present seven predictions in the field of PR.

Thank you, and I wish you good reading and new ideas!

Notes

1 Qualman, E. (2009). *Socialnomics: how social media transforms the way we live and do business.* New Jersey: John Wiley & Sons.
2 Safko, L. and Brake, D.K. (2009). *The social media bible: tactics, tools, and strategies for business success.* New Jersey: John Wiley & Sons.

1 People Relations

> Good communication is just as stimulating as black coffee, and just as hard to sleep after.
>
> Anne Morrow Lindbergh – author and aviator.

I have always wanted to look deeper into PR activities, to define the sensations that every PR specialist experiences and try to express those states we go through. This is because while everything that has been written so far on the theory of this activity is essentially correct, I always felt they lacked the essence, depth, emotions, and, most importantly, the feelings, that, it is my profound conviction, make up the essence of PR activities. Only a strongly empathetic person can be a good professional in this field. It isn't easy to define and describe these things, but without them, this profession remains just a few dry words that are included in publicly used definitions of public relations.

Two of what I consider to be the most authoritative and globally recognized organizations which have made the most progress in terms of PR branding define this activity as follows:

1. Public relations is about reputation – the result of what you do, what you say, and what others say about you. Public relations is the discipline which looks after reputation, with the aim of earning understanding and support and influencing opinion and behavior. It is the planned and sustained effort to establish and maintain goodwill and mutual understanding between an organization and its publics.[1]
2. Public relations is a strategic communication process that builds mutually beneficial relationships between organizations and their publics.[2]

The first definition is from the Chartered Institute of Public Relations, and the second is from the Public Relations Society of America.

But, as I mentioned earlier, the term "public relations" – or my proposed term "people relations" – hides much more. This section is about the "more".

So what is PR in the broad sense, or if you will, in the more profound sense? What is this profession about? Let's start with its history.

DOI: 10.4324/9781003466802-2

1.1. History

> The history of PR is . . . [the] history of a battle for what is reality and how people will see and understand reality.
>
> Stuart Ewen – author, historian, and lecturer.

It is common to divide PR history into two periods: the time before Ivy Lee published his first press release – or "Declaration of Principles" – and Edward Bernays published his famous works *Crystallizing public opinion*[3] and *Propaganda*[4] and the time after. It is often argued that what began with these two intelligent and undoubtedly influential figures was modern PR. At the same time, everything that came before had PR manifestations even if it was not systematized in the same way as PR in the 20th century.

I think such a division is correct, but here I would like to look at PR from a slightly different angle. Such an approach seems necessary to me to define the concept of the Picnic Society, which I will discuss in Chapter 3. I want to understand whether what is happening in the PR field today is systematic and we are naturally moving towards a specific goal, and what that goal is, or whether we are wandering in a fog.

So I have looked at the history of PR not in terms of people, books, or concepts, but in terms of the technical abilities to disseminate information throughout human history. Humans are social beings, and PR is one of the essential conditions for their existence. Let's imagine that Homo Sapiens constantly wanted, could, and had to communicate. Therefore, we can divide PR according to the means that humans had to communicate, and the spread that those means could ensure for them.

1.1.1. Fire

The first stage of PR, which began with the advent of humanity approximately 2 million years ago, ended when the first portable written materials appeared in the world. While not made of paper, clay tablets and papyrus scrolls played an essential role in the development of PR, namely, the dissemination of information beyond the local community to a wider geographic area. Thus, the "Fire" stage ended around the 3rd millennium BCE.

In this stage, humans had only the means they could find around themselves or were born with: writing on rocks, smoke signals, voice, and community gatherings. Based on this, I have named this stage "Fire". At that time, communication on a global scale was very fragmented and limited by geography. There were many local community interactions, but they were very limited or unrelated to each other. I believe that PR existed back then – there were technologies for spreading good or bad news, there were PR specialists, and communication was probably very active. At that time, people did not have mass media tools. Still, they actively communicated with each other.

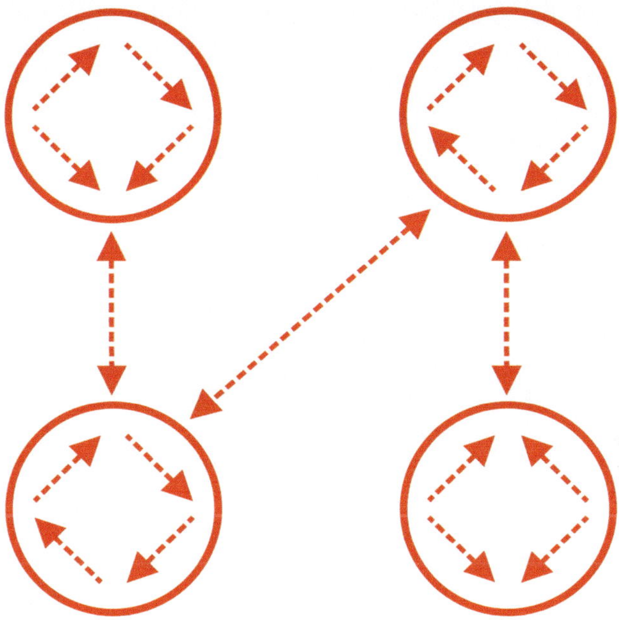

Figure 1.1 The first stage of PR history – "Fire". There were many community relationships and much two-way communication in this stage.

Figure by the author.

In our time, mass media tools are weakening, and we are sharing more actively – albeit indirectly, using technology – but are relatively closed in our communication circles.

PR specialists of that time are probably referred to today as wizards, shamans, or other assistants in spreading knowledge and influence. Their goal then, as it is today, was to be able to disseminate information and, along with that, help manage the community and influence its decisions.

So, in summary, the characteristics of the first "Fire" stage are as follows: active local communication, weak globalism, and an absence of mass media tools and technologies.

The predominant nature of communication was local two-way communication.

1.1.2. Book

The second PR stage involves the emergence of writing and, eventually, paper. Starting from the minimal use of writing tools in the 3rd millennium BCE and ending with the emergence of newspapers in the 17th century CE, this PR stage opened up new geographic horizons for communication specialists – it became possible to communicate in much broader areas than just local communities.

This stage is the beginning of mass communication, but not mass media. With the help of books, it became possible to spread information in wider geographic areas, such as throughout a country or even a religious community. The information recorded in books became the basis for uniting societies. Since books were only accessible to a tiny segment of society, the power to control the masses was concentrated in the hands of those who could write and read. In this stage, brilliant PR specialists wrote all the most crucial PR works of that time, which served as the basis for managing societies: the Quran, the Old and New Testaments, and the Torah.

In this stage, even though ordinary citizens still communicated relatively locally, the most potent means of communication emerged – information media. Based on them, dominant (usually religious) information appeared in society. I have named this stage in PR history "Book".

The most important thing is that this stage began the dominance of one-way communication, as there were not effective technical means to provide feedback.

During this time, PR specialists were probably the writers, interpreters, and disseminators of the Holy Scriptures, priests, and many other representatives of religious communication. Their goal, then as now, was to be able to disseminate information and, at the same time, help manage the community and influence its decisions. Here I want to draw attention to the fact that as

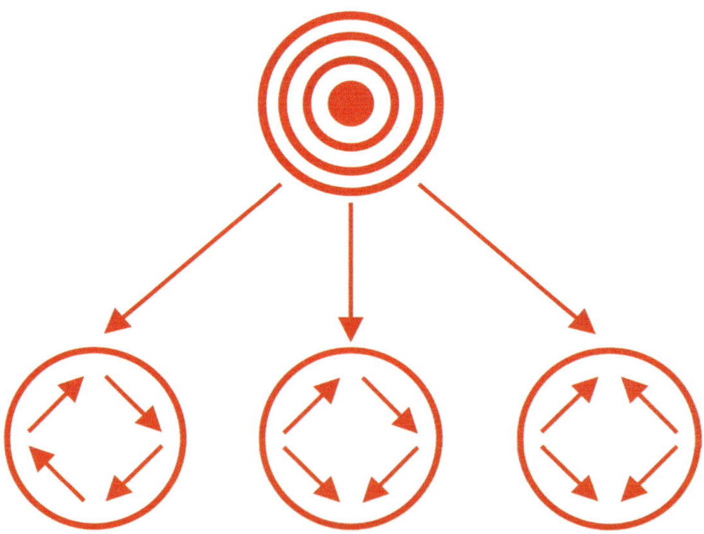

Figure 1.2 The second stage of PR history – "Book". Vital one-way communication centers emerged and began to dominate, based on books, especially those with religious content.

Figure by the author.

we moved from one stage to another, the tools changed, but the PR specialist's function remained the same – to help the client (ruler) communicate with the public.

The characteristics of the second stage are as follows: dominant public opinion, growing globalization, active local communication, and the absence of mass media tools and technologies.

The general nature of communication was global one-way communication.

1.1.3. Television

The third stage of PR development is the era of mass media. Although there were attempts to publish something similar to newspapers as far back as ancient Rome, the mass media proper can probably be said to have begun after the first newspaper, *Relation aller Fürnemmen und gedenckwürdigen Historien*, was published in Strasbourg in 1605.

This stage, which began in the 17th century, peaked in the 20th century when television became the primary communication tool – a media outlet capable of reaching hundreds of millions of people. That's why this stage is called "Television".

During this stage, media outlets and their owners became monopolists in spreading information, and one-way communication reached unprecedented heights, as mass media could disseminate a message to millions of people

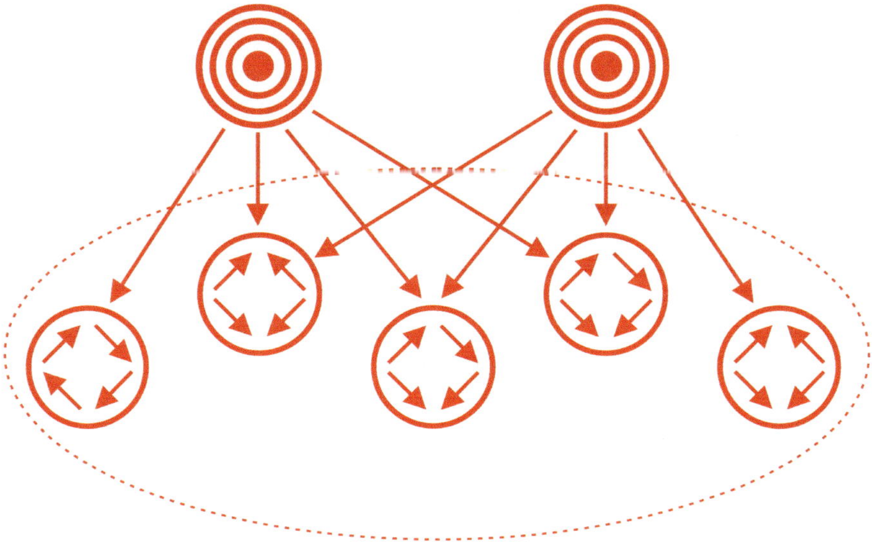

Figure 1.3 The third stage of PR history – "Television". The world community receives information from several oligopolistic centers.

Figure by the author.

worldwide. Advertising also experienced its golden age in this stage, as it was a perfect one-way communication tool for selling goods and services.

Although this stage is the golden age of one-way communication, in democratic countries, oligopolistic relationships between information disseminators and recipients were formed instead of monopolistic ones. Newspapers and television stations, driven by competition, represented different opinions and competed for readership and viewership and tried to appeal to these readers and viewers.

The main task of PR specialists became the ability to convince the media, while the goal remained the same – to disseminate information and, at the same time, help manage the community and influence its decisions.

The characteristics of the third stage are as follows: dominant multiple public opinions, high globalism, low local communication, domination of mass media, and developing technologies.

The general nature of communication was global one-way communication.

This stage ended when the main drawback of the "Television" stage – one-sidedness – was eliminated. Although television could reach millions, that is, transmit one piece of information to millions of people, it could not gather millions of opinions back, that is, transfer many pieces of information to one person. This scarcity was the reason why social media was born.

1.1.4. Network

The fourth stage of PR development, which we are currently in and which I have named "Network", began when the world saw the first social network. The path to this started in the 1970s, and the main factor that led to the emergence of the first social network was the Internet, which appeared in 1983. However, this stage began to take its most important steps in 2004 when people heard the word "Facebook". In 2005, Facebook had 6 million users; today, it has 3.01 billion[5] users worldwide. Facebook, on average, grew by about 160 million users yearly!

Where does this rapid growth in popularity come from? Why did people need it so much that they rushed to create accounts on this and other social networks around the world?

I would argue that the answer seems quite obvious – the ability for two-way communication provided by social media.

From the first stage of PR development, humanity has long longed for two-way communication, i.e. such a form of information dissemination where one can simultaneously be both consumer and creator as well as distributor and information updater. Humanity has grown tired of one-way communication and has moved towards two-way communication. The oligopoly of traditional media has collapsed, and if global society continues to progress, it will never return.

Today's children no longer understand what a newspaper is and why news programs should be watched precisely at 8 pm and children's programs at 10 am on Sunday. Moreover, newspaper publishing essentially no longer seems logical – to use expensive resources to report outdated news while hot events are broadcasted simultaneously.

In the new millennium, humanity has entered a two-way, pluralistic, democratic age in which information is formed anywhere, everyone has the right to destroy and create, and no information center has exclusive rights anymore. It is an entirely different world in which new yet poorly described and examined but already involving and enticing communication opportunities apply.

In this fourth stage of PR development, there are fewer dominant opinions or information centres. Rather, opinion leaders rise and fall every day, each of them has their circle of supporters, and people actively communicate with each other in those circles. This time is a very democratic stage of PR. The world has become incredibly diverse. If we compare it to colors, we have moved from the six primary colors to a world with a full spectrum of shades. If an economic comparison is more acceptable to you, communication has shifted from an oligopolistic market to a free one.

Of course, like any new thing, the new stage has also brought negative changes, but compared to how much people have become more accessible, all negative changes are insignificant.

The most significant change that, in my opinion, happened in the PR field is that reputation has started to play a more important role.

The PR tools have expanded incredibly, and the task has changed significantly. If, in the third stage, the media and the ability to persuade it had the most significant influence on public opinion, today, it is no longer as important. PR specialists finally communicate effectively with communities: they can create them, communicate directly with leaders, join ongoing dialogues, share important information, quickly reach the highest individuals, update events, and much more.

However, the goal of PR professionals remains the same – a good PR specialist can effectively and adequately disseminate information to the target audience.

The characteristics of the fourth stage are as follows: there is no dominant public opinion, high globalization, very active local communication, a decrease or even disappearance of mass media influence, and almost everyone has access to technology.

The dominant nature of communication is global two-way communication.

In summary, the PR history briefly described here clearly shows how PR goals and tools have evolved. It is clear that in ancient times, both in governance and communication, other moral norms and ethical understanding prevailed. However, the main goal of PR activity has remained the same throughout history – to help spread information.

After briefly discussing the historical stages of PR, I would like to move on to the essence of this profession and at least try to reveal what is inside and often remains unsaid or unexpressed in some other way. For example, what settles inside you after finishing work for one or another client, and it

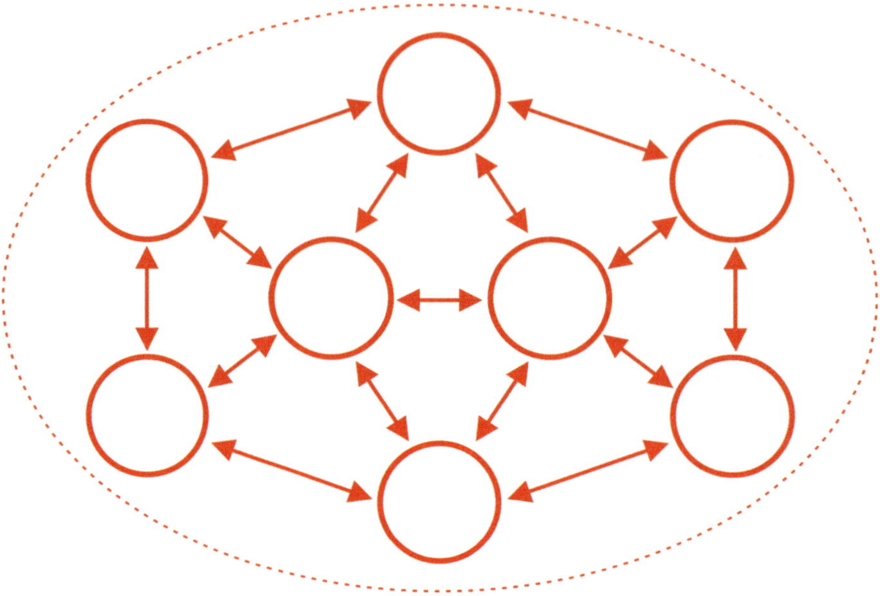

Figure 1.4 The fourth stage of PR history – "Network". No single information dissemination center exists. There is much direct communication.

Figure by the author.

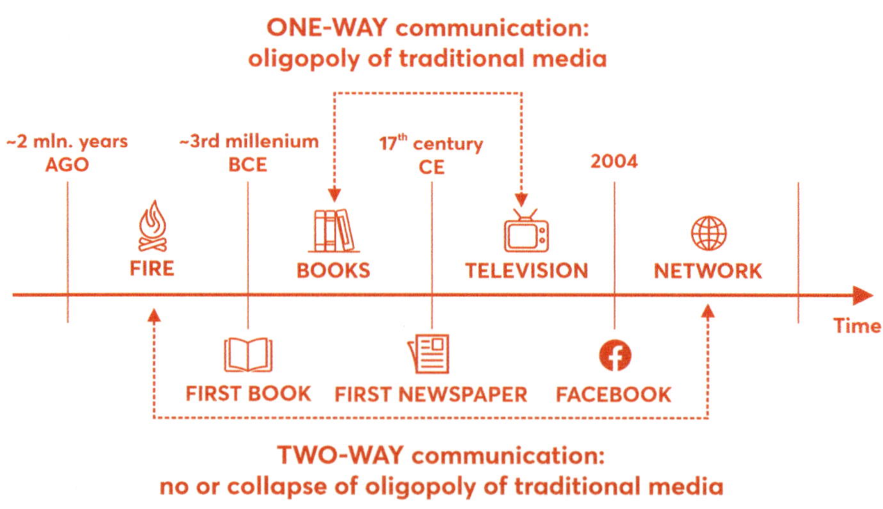

Figure 1.5 PR timeline. We return to the natural era of two-way communication, where there are no oligopolistic centers for information dissemination.

Figure by the author.

is almost impossible to find time to talk about it. Not only is time scarce, but also the interlocutor: the next day brings new tasks, clients, and assignments. Therefore, I have listed here what I believe lives not only with me but also with many experienced PR specialists. I want them to read it and feel professional solidarity.

1.2. PRofession

> The ability to express an idea is well-nigh as important as the idea itself.
>
> Bernard Baruch – financier, stock investor, philanthropist, statesman, and political consultant.

While immersed in your professional bubble, it's easy to forget that what you do may not be so apparent to others. Many politicians, journalists, and even some PR professionals have only a vague understanding of the essence of PR. Edward Bernays, the founder of modern PR, and the concept of propaganda formulated in his book of the same name[6] at the beginning of the 20th century have added confusion to the discussion. Although we cannot deny his contribution to creating the foundations of PR, Bernays spoke of the communication of one ultimate truth, which is not the case in modern PR.

Figure 1.6 The wheel of PR skills is constantly spinning: building relationships is the primary goal of the PR profession.

Figure by the author.

Since then, much time has passed, but people often confuse the terms and imagine PR activity as unfavorable. Statements like "This is his political PR", "He is doing PR", and the like have negative connotations.

Students who plan to become PR specialists, when coming to their first lectures, often expect to be immediately introduced to the technologies and tools that they can immediately take and use, and that by using them, they will become tough PR aces in a few years, usually invisible, lurking in the shadows, but ruling the world. Many imagine that their job will be to direct and juggle clients, more or less as seen in the movies, where a brutal and infallible PR specialist plans everything so that all that remains is to follow the plan and the masses will follow you.

However, telling people about tools when they don't yet know how and why to use them is not meaningful. Moreover, it can even be dangerous. For example, a fork in one person's hands can be a tool for comfortable eating, while for another can be a weapon for killing someone. So if we think of a fork as information, it can be equally helpful, valuable, and necessary but also deadly.

People say that a cobbler's shoes are often without soles. Doctors are often not the healthiest people, restaurant kitchen workers are not necessarily the best eaters, and a computer technician's computer may not function perfectly. These misunderstandings are because when a person is doing something all day long in one field, they become tired of it and put their own

Figure 1.7 The fork can be used in various ways.

Figure by the author.

needs last. A doctor will first rest after work, and even after that, they may not necessarily prioritize their health.

It is the same with PR specialists. I know many colleagues for whom the best rest is solitude and silence. This discrepancy happens because constant communication, contact, and talking can be exhausting, just like any other job. Therefore, the PR profession often maintains an inappropriate reputation. Even though all PR activities are aimed at reputation building, the importance of the PR profession itself is usually not that great. Only a tiny circle of people understand that it is a beneficial and good activity.

Once, I met a classmate whom I hadn't seen for many years, and we had a sincere conversation about the old times, friends, and the time when we hadn't seen each other. Then the conversation turned to what each of us was doing. "I became a paediatrician," she said. "Well, nothing surprising, considering how well you studied," I replied. "And I became a PR specialist." From her expression, I could easily read disappointment. That disappointment perfectly reflects the reputation of our profession.

I have been working in the PR industry for three decades, and my only job has always been to help some people understand others. So essentially, that's how I know my profession. And although the prevalent myth in society is that "all those PR guys are only engaged in brainwashing or trying to deceive someone", I sincerely don't believe that.

Of course, we, as PR professionals, are responsible for it. We are responsible for what the public thinks about us. However, while working with our clients, we often neglect to explain who we are, what we do, and what our goals and aspirations are. It's understandable – we have tight deadlines, little time, and the client's needs and problems are our top priority. Therefore, I am still surprised when long-time clients confuse PR with advertising or ask about sponsored articles. Then I realize that I have not paid enough attention to our profession's reputation.

Admittedly, we often create a negative reputation not only by not talking much about what we do but also by occasionally tarnishing the importance of our profession with our actions. It is common to encounter people who label their activities as PR when their actions have nothing to do with PR. Here's an example I managed to find among the services of one "PR" agency. As one of the solutions to the problem, they suggested organizing a hunger strike for their clients. They even proposed fasting on behalf of their clients. Calling such a service PR is absurd and should be identified as a deception of people.

Politicians and other public figures often use the term PR to describe harmful activities, completely misunderstanding its meaning. When criticizing an opponent, these individuals often claim they are "engaging in PR". A significant portion of the public believes that PR specialists are involved in some mysterious, difficult-to-understand activity whose essence is to deceive someone. Paradoxically, what is commonly thought about PR usually has nothing to do with it.

I wonder where the roots of such a misunderstanding of this profession lie. It seems this profession is good, positive, and respected, and my colleagues have never engaged in anything resembling manipulation or theft. I am convinced that PR is the foundation of a socially and communicatively functioning society – community trust. In a world where the need for information exchange is growing exponentially, the role of a PR specialist is vital. Under such conditions, the number of people who want to communicate constantly increases. Along with it, the need for people who are good at doing it also grows.

Sometimes it's amusing to hear statements like, "One politician is good because they speak for themselves, while another has speeches written by a PR specialist." However, the truth is that there is no significant difference in who writes speeches, be it for one politician or another. The quality of the speeches' profile matters as long as they are delivered on behalf of the politician. It is akin to whether you should solve the need to clean your clothes by doing it yourself or by taking them to a laundry service. It is merely a matter of approach or technique, and it does not make the politician or the owner of the clothes any better or worse.

Whether politicians write their speeches or social media messages or have an assistant who does it for them is no different. In both cases, it is direct communication with that person and reading their thoughts. It is about engaging with someone ready to communicate directly with you. And if they cannot do so, if they are incapable of expressing their thoughts clearly, they hire someone with that skill or more resources to allocate towards it.

Ultimately, not every doctor or entrepreneur is inherently a good communicator. However, the definition of reputation states that one must communicate to have a proper reputation. So here comes a PR specialist to clearly articulate what the doctor or entrepreneur would like to convey to the public. A doctor has to treat people, an entrepreneur has to earn money and create jobs, and a PR specialist has to help them express their thoughts. It would seem simple, like two times two equals four, but the PR profession is shrouded in secrecy and rumors. A PR specialist has to tell the public about the beneficial work that the doctor or entrepreneur is doing because neither of them has the time, skills, or ability to do so. Therefore, a PR specialist helps someone unable to present information about themselves to do just that effectively.

Professionals from various fields, excellent experts in their areas but with little interest in PR, claim that social media is not attractive to them. They rarely use the media, they are introverted, and communication is not their forte. Perhaps. However, it doesn't mean it's not attractive to others if it's not interesting to you. And ignoring a particular media channel doesn't mean someone else isn't working there on your behalf. And that someone else may not necessarily have a positive attitude towards you.

And often, these people who negate the meaning of PR only start thinking about it when they encounter the negative consequences of their attitude: someone writes falsehoods about them or defames them. However, taking action to communicate at that point is already too late.

I believe that PR, more than any other profession, is often transparent and built on trust. It is pretty tricky to measure, but one wrong step, false fact, or PR deceit can lead to unpleasant consequences. The mathematics here are quite simple. If you take that wrong step, for example, to deceive someone, you immediately become vulnerable, and your reputation is at risk. And that step can be tiny, but it will be brought up precisely when you least expect it and when you think you have achieved outstanding results. The shadow of your negative reputation will fall upon your client, and any fact you distribute, even if it is correct, may be doubted.

Therefore, PR specialists, prioritizing their reputation, must evaluate every step they take, as it can come back to haunt them even after a long time and in the most inappropriate place. But, first and foremost, like in any profession, we should act honestly and speak about our job.

Each PR consultant is familiar with this situation. You find yourself in the company of new, unfamiliar people. Perhaps long-lost relatives. Maybe you were invited to talk about your profession at your son or daughter's school. And well, you come out with "I help people express their thoughts" or "I'm a communications specialist, and I help others be heard." "Oh, so it's like advertising, isn't it . . . " is the most common conclusion you hear.

So we all understand well among ourselves what we do, but how can we explain it concisely and clearly to others?

Who is this mysterious PR specialist: a secret agent, manipulator, a silent and secretive gray cardinal? What is this profession, and what constitutes its essence? Why is it so valuable that even one of the wealthiest people in the world, Microsoft founder Bill Gates, says, "If I were down to the last dollar of my marketing budget, I'd spend it on PR!"?

My colleague is straightforward and concise in this matter: PR is one of the most effective technologies in the world, based on truth, transparency, and informed communication.

PR solves all communication problems, regardless of the nature of your work or the tasks you are addressing, whether at a state level or fish aquarium projects. If you don't communicate about your activities to people or do them inaccurately, people will never know about them, and you won't have their support.

Another colleague says that PR helps society live without shocks and disasters, address problems as they arise, and avoid accumulating offences and misunderstandings. PR, of course, is not a panacea for all troubles, but it is an effective technology that can ensure the interests of all parties.

The primary mission of a PR professional is not too big or too small – it is to save the world. No, these are not just empty words. Perhaps individually, this mission may seem overwhelming, but remember – "And the truth shall set you free."[7] A professional PR specialist can only communicate the truth. In this profession, there are hundreds of thousands of professionals, and the essence of all their work is to free people. And free people are the only logical condition for the world's survival.

Open communication and dialogue lead to understanding and unity, a saved world. If all PR professionals worked with this mindset as their foundation, the plan for salvation would not take long to unfold.

Therefore, for a person who wants to connect their life with this profession, it is vital first to understand the essence of this profession. And the nature of this profession, perhaps one of the most beautiful and positive professions, is honest communication and open dialogue. And it is essential to talk about this with colleagues, clients, and students.

Of course, PR tools can also be easily manipulated to work in the opposite direction. It is possible to harm the competitor, spread negative information, and deceive. However, this path leads to a dead end. Spreading lies destroys while truth builds.

Throughout all my years of practice in this profession, the following five skills have appeared to be the most important:

1. Listening (hearings).
2. Intuition (feelings).
3. Explaining (explanations).
4. Being truthful (truths).
5. Building relationships (relations).

Strong bonds interconnect these skills; none of them is possible without the others. Start ignoring one, and you will quickly weaken the entire chain. For example, if you can listen and hear, it will help you develop intuition. If you can hear and intuit, it will help you explain. If you define and don't lie, it will help you build solid and long-lasting relationships. Relationships will allow you to hear and intuit even more, enabling professional growth.

Next, let's delve a little deeper into each of them.

1.2.1. PRofession of Hearings

> When people talk, listen completely. Most people never listen.
>
> Ernest Hemingway – journalist, novelist, and short-story writer.

A professional PR specialist is, first and foremost, a listener before being a speaker. Listening, observing, and understanding the environment and context are crucial tasks in this profession. Only by comprehending these aspects can one take action, convey the context to their client, and propose the most appropriate PR actions.

"To understand everything is to forgive everything," says a French proverb. And understanding is impossible without listening. Therefore, before engaging in proactive activities, a PR specialist should first listen and thoroughly understand their target audiences, grasping the reasons behind their behaviors. If we can truly listen, we often accomplish half of the work and sometimes even the entire task. Therefore, I suggest never skimping time for conversations, meetings, presence, and communication. During these moments, we can hear a person, observe their reactions to problems and ideas, and learn about their attitudes and expectations. Communicating blindly, attempting to persuade a particular group without understanding them, is akin to shooting blindly. The better we know our target audience, the more we engage with them, and the more we learn from them, the more purposeful and, most importantly, sensitive our communication can be. Buddhist monk and teacher Shunryu Suzuki says, "Only when you understand people, they may understand you. So even though you do not say anything, if you understand people, there is some communication."

When you spend a long time solving a single problem, you often lose sight of the bigger picture and only see that one problem. It starts to seem like your perspective is the only correct one. This problem usually happens to people with narrow expertise. Still, it can happen to anyone who works on a single issue for a long time, meaning they only hear themselves or the people around them. The same problem can also happen to PR professionals who work on a single issue for an extended period. The mind is limited and cannot hold multiple perspectives simultaneously.

Therefore, it is often worth taking a step back and looking at everything from a different perspective, which means engaging in communication and listening. Only by constantly listening, observing, and analyzing the situation can a PR specialist understand it themselves and advise others on how and when to communicate effectively.

My colleague emphasizes another aspect at this point – emotional and analytical audiences. These audiences could be related to the feminine and masculine approaches, but some men possess more of the feminine path, while some women exhibit more of the male course.

My colleague states that communication worldwide adheres to these two types of audiences, which means it encompasses the entire world. Each of these audiences has its distinct language. Deborah Tannen, an American academic and linguistics professor at Georgetown University in Washington, states that, "Male-female conversation is cross-cultural communication."[8]

The language of an emotional audience naturally contains more emotions, and conversations need to be longer. For an analytical audience, brevity and calculations are required: e2, e4, forward, backwards, left, and right. We will always face defeat if we try to convince one type of audience using a different language. Not because our intentions were wrong but because we couldn't speak in a language acceptable to the specific audience. First and foremost, we must listen, and only then can we use one of the techniques to reach an agreement. We can create dialogue effectively if we can hear, understand, and translate from one language to another.

Due to the inability to listen and know what to do after hearing, reaching agreements within a family can often be challenging. In general, being in a family is a complex endeavor. However, such a situation is an opportunity for growth. If a couple wishes to live together for a long time, they must continually develop those relationships. It requires constantly listening and, once heard, engaging in discussion and reaching agreements. It is impossible without it. It is effortless for all of us to argue, but agreeing is challenging. And that's where the essence of PR lies – listening, negotiating, and continuously developing relationships.

If you can listen and hear, it will help you to sense.

1.2.2. PRofession of Feelings

> There are no problems, only solutions.
>
> John Lennon – singer, songwriter, and peace activist.

The ability to sense another person, understand, and empathize are indispensable for this profession to exist. However, in this line of work, there is always another side, always a need to establish a connection, and always a need to consider the other party's motivations. Only then will you find the key to the doors behind which there are communities, authorities, the media, or anyone else important to your client.

Once, I participated in a government meeting with local community representatives. The community representatives had a critical and even slightly aggressive attitude. They questioned why the government officials didn't listen to their arguments and why the people in the government apparatus didn't like or accept them. In reality, this wasn't the case – the people in that city had a fairly decent connection with the government and were involved in the decision-making process. However, a few community groups felt ignored.

So, during that meeting, after listening for a while, a former city leader, an older person, requested the floor. He stood up and politely addressed the dissatisfied community representatives. He said:

> My dear friends, I understand your arguments very well, and we could discuss them, but I would like to draw your attention to the fact that behind every door in this building, there are people. I agree that they may not be perfect. They may sometimes be irritable or in a bad mood. But they are just as human as you are. And just like you, they react differently depending on their approach. In my many years of experience, a respectful attitude, kind words, and a polite request always worked much better than forcefully kicking the door open, making demands, or shouting.

So, the former city leader asked the community representatives to empathize with how the people working in the city administration feel when shouted at. He encouraged them to change their way of behavior if they wanted to achieve something. Of course, there are various situations and different officials, but those who can empathize with the official's feelings, approach them, and genuinely interest them with their questions – these consistently achieve more than those who demand.

The ability to intuit, sense, and empathize with a situation, scent, or anticipation is one of the essential qualities of a professional PR specialist.

A PR specialist is constantly in search of solutions. There are no problems, only solutions waiting to be found. It just requires a strong desire to find them. All my colleagues and partners are like that – they constantly seek and propose solutions because this profession is closely related to the field that finds solutions the most – human communication. My colleagues are the ones for whom the word "impossible" barely exists. It is through communication that people find answers, and it is only through a lack of communication that problems arise. If there is a problem somewhere, we will immediately see a lack of communication nearby. And most often, by eliminating the lack of communication, we will solve the problem. Or if the pain and lack of communication become so deeply rooted that simply restoring communication won't be enough, the communicating parties need to be changed. However, we will still solve the problem through communication even after changing them.

This profession is particularly empathetic. If we don't understand the other person's motives, we will only be superficial PR specialists, even if highly skilled in using various PR tools.

People in this profession often experience panic attacks, emotional exhaustion, and burnout. They may need the help of a psychologist and sometimes even a psychiatrist. Why is that? It's because this profession encompasses almost all other areas of work and is strongly connected to one's conscience. People in this profession don't know the word "no" and must be aware of everything happening around them, within the organization or with clients. We have an atomic cocktail if we add in the multi-functionality of working in a PR agency. These individuals are constantly building relationships, which means they first need to learn to detach themselves from their work, switch off their minds, and stop thinking about work matters outside of working hours. Then, they need to know how to rest. However, when it comes to building relationships and being the conscience of an organization, this is very challenging, especially when one is not yet mature enough to do so. Therefore, a sincere, empathetic, and sensitive person entering this profession risks becoming responsible for everything. At a certain point, it may start to feel like if they don't do something, then, a crisis will arise that will sweep away everything. And that is a direct path to "burnout".

And a significant portion of my colleagues (in many cases, I probably don't even know) go through this, and either they don't cope and change the nature of their work, or they become highly resilient and professional, able to remain detached when necessary, capable of switching off. But, unfortunately, a panic attack in our profession, in many cases, signifies "initiation into knighthood". If that doesn't happen, there are two possible conclusions: either the person hasn't reached that level yet, or they have mastered the art of managing their emotions perfectly.

It is challenging to explain this to someone who hasn't experienced it, but even now, I consciously restrain myself from reacting to work-related issues outside of working hours. Today, I am adept at managing my time well. If necessary, I can quickly switch into work mode and start tracking when I would have started working. I wouldn't say that the number of urgent tasks has decreased. However, no job can throw me off balance anymore. If I work during my designated rest time, I know precisely how much time I have spent working and how much I need to compensate for that time with rest later on.

Sometimes, accidentally, I catch a glimpse of something on social media related to my clients, and thoughts start racing, suggesting that I should take specific actions or delve deeper into something. However, if I start doing that, I will quickly lose control of my time and start drowning in it. Now, I have a system where I can make a note, mark it as necessary, or forward it to someone if needed without diving into the depths myself.

When the sinking becomes overwhelming, you can no longer control it. It is a terrifying and utterly uncontrollable feeling. At that point, you are taken to doctors or manage to go to them yourself. It's a very unpleasant sensation, scary, and utterly unmanageable. I remember riding a bus with colleagues, the journey lasted for several hours, and I couldn't utter a word. I could only force a smile, and I don't know why I was so intensely afraid of something. What? I can't explain. Perhaps the fear of an abyss opening up, of uncontrollably falling or being thrown out of the bus while it was still moving. That's just an approximate description of that feeling. I wouldn't want to experience it again. I hope that experience will prevent it from happening again in the future.

Strange, but I haven't heard that it would be written about or told to future PR specialists at university. I keep hearing about technologies, strategies, planning, campaigns, relationships, and networking, but I rarely hear that this profession is primarily about emotions. True PR professionals work with emotions – they build trust in themselves and others. The further I advance on my professional path, the more I understand that.

"The most important thing in communication is hearing what isn't said," stated Peter Ferdinand Drucker, a management consultant, educator, and pioneer of modern business corporations. It's not so difficult to track down what has been said, written, or broadcast. This task can usually be accomplished by ordering monitoring services. However, to hear what hasn't been said, what has been implied or planned but not yet expressed requires many more subtle qualities. To listen to what hasn't been said or at least directly said, to intuit or anticipate, one needs:

a) To read a lot. And it doesn't necessarily have to be professional literature. An experienced PR specialist must constantly read a wide range of literature. This literature includes the most mundane romance novels or children's books, classics, and works by little-known local authors. Literature shapes one's perspective, allows for understanding, and enables the intuition of mentality. In other words, the more one reads, the more one develops the skill to sense what is left unsaid.
b) To take an interest in diverse topics. This is because the combination and understanding of various subjects allows one to be a good consultant. Let's imagine we are working for an energy company. It might seem enough to be interested in what is happening in the energy sector. However, that is not sufficient. Energy is produced for people, and everyone uses it. Therefore, it is necessary to understand how they perceive energy, why people feel they are paying too much, what shapes their opinions, and why they don't know where the electricity comes from that is in their power outlets.

If you can listen and intuit, it will help in explaining.

1.2.3. PRofession of Explanations

The relationship is the communication bridge between people.
Alfred Kadushin – social work practitioner and academic.

In September 2014, in sunny Madrid, the eighth World PR Forum organized by the Global Alliance for PR and Communication Management was attended by 800 PR professionals from 65 countries. During the forum, the role of a PR specialist was wonderfully described as akin to that of a window cleaner for an organization. It was explained that if one imagines an organization as a large glass building, those working inside can become so engrossed in their activities and outcomes that they might overlook the gradual accumulation of dirt on the windows, obstructing their view of the outside world.

Therefore, the task of a PR specialist is to clean those windows and show the people inside that if they look through the windows on the first floor, the world will appear one way, if on the eleventh floor, another way, and if they climb onto the roof, a different way altogether. A PR specialist must be well acquainted with what is happening externally and internally and be capable of continuously informing internal employees about the external world and vice versa. They must help the organization see the external world through the eyes of various target audiences.

It can indeed be referred to as a translation from an organization's internal language to the external world's language and from the external language to the internal language of the organization. Although a PR specialist may have relatively limited knowledge compared to professionals working in specific fields within the organization, their understanding is significantly greater than that of people on the street. At the same time, by continuously staying informed about what is happening externally, they can explain a lot to the employees of the organization:

- What are people talking about?
- What are other organizations doing?
- What prevailing opinions exist in various communities on matters important to the organization?

My colleague provides the following example. In a kindergarten, children are seated facing each other and asked to draw a cup that is placed between them. Later, they are asked to draw the cup as Mary or John sees it while sitting across from them. Often, a five-year-old child doesn't realize that Mary and John know the cup differently – the handle is on the right for them, not on the left. The strangest thing is that even after people grow up, they still don't understand that a person sitting in front of them can see the same problem from a completely different perspective.

My colleague argues that we often disagree not because we are against each other but because we see a particular problem differently. It's simply because some of us already have experience in that area while others do not. As a result, some people have formed stereotypes, while others have a completely different perspective.

The work of a PR specialist with company employees is just as important as their work with external audiences. And that work doesn't necessarily have to involve delivering information to employees. Information delivery, especially today, is not the main task. Much more important is the result of the explanation, the translation, if you wish. The PR specialist serves as a conduit for external information to be presented comprehensibly in various forms: through personal meetings, media relations, social media, and more. And the more dialogue, the better.

Conversely, company employees should receive information presented in a comprehensible manner through the PR specialist in various forms as well. On the other hand, internal support for the PR specialist from the employees is also crucial, enabling quick action, the obtaining of information, and deciding whether to share it with the outside.

I see the PR specialist as a facilitator, a router, a translator, an explainer, and a window cleaner positioned between the organization and the public, whose primary goal is to ensure a smooth flow of information.

Indeed, modern technological advancements allow for the excellent implementation of this role.

In one company, we implemented a simple solution – we created an internal Facebook group for employees. The company was spread across five cities, making it quite challenging for a communicator to sense the moods and understand what is happening at each location.

So, during one of the meetings with the employees, I announced that we would create a closed employee group on a social network to exchange information. Like in many companies, employees were used to mainly receiving information from PR-generated newsletters or through the company's intranet rather than actively sharing it. I asked employees to share things that people typically share on social media: celebrations, photos on the way to work, current events – anything that came to mind. Of course, I assured them that this information would stay within the closed group, and if we wanted to share it more widely, we would always seek permission from the author.

At first, there wasn't much activity, as I expected. However, as a few employees started sharing information and gained popularity among their colleagues, things began to pick up. Nowadays, the company's main website proudly displays a sunrise photo taken by an employee, and colleagues greet each other on various occasions, exchange information, and engage in natural and informal dialogue. In addition, there's a memorable story about employees from different offices collectively "caring for" a blooming cactus in one of the offices.

Employees have grown accustomed to and understand the importance of sharing informal internal information. It helps create a friendly and secure organizational climate where we learn more about each other and respond to each other's inquiries. This way, a friendly atmosphere of trust is established. As PR specialists, we also benefit because we miss fewer opportunities to communicate information externally. We can also sense the company's mood and, most importantly, provide explanations. If we cannot do it ourselves, we can request that the manager or another responsible person comment on some issues.

A PR specialist is no longer just someone who secretly does something in another city and communicates only with company executives. Instead, they become close, familiar, and friendly, constantly commenting, consulting, helping employees understand processes, and responding to questions.

The internal and external audiences must be equally important to a modern PR specialist because they constantly feed each other, like an hourglass where information flows from one side to the other, and both sides cannot exist without each other. Moreover, today, practically every person, which means every employee, has a mobile device in their pocket, and therefore can be seen as a potential medium of information.

Sometimes it needs to be planned, thought out, and created; other times, it happens spontaneously.

For example, one company actively engages with members of the local community on social media regarding waste incineration plants. The action takes place on a community page on social media, and efforts are made to respond to community questions as accurately as possible. However, emotional discussions are avoided because it is known that any wrong word can be used against the company in the future.

One of the community leaders posts something along these lines of, "It's a shame, but it seems like this summer I won't be able to go to my garden, pick an apple from the tree, and eat it unwashed." Following this post, an intense discussion ensues about the destruction of nature, accusations are directed towards the company, and everyone laments that nature will never be the same again.

Suddenly, an employee of the company who is also a member of the community interrupts the discussion.

He writes, "Could I come and pick the ripe apples from your garden?" The post's author immediately responds, clarifying that she meant only unwashed apples and that she will conduct research. The discussion immediately shifts from focusing on how things will go wrong to questioning whether something will be as bad as anticipated.

If the company's PR specialist or manager had written such a post, it would have been received differently. However, when written by an employee from within the community, the effect was completely different.

Today, when every individual, both inside and outside the company, has the potential to be a media outlet, the entire society becomes one large targeted audience. Therefore, the main task of a modern PR specialist has changed significantly. While in the past, messages were often formulated to be received and understood by the recipients, essentially ending their journey there, today, they need to be prepared, explained, disseminated in various forms, and then clarified and commented upon, as each person understands them differently. Thus, a PR specialist today must be prepared to engage in constant dialogue. And in that dialogue, they must constantly explain, refine, and assist.

You must explain – without lying.

1.2.4. PRofession of Truths

> One thing you can't hide – is when you're crippled inside.
>
> John Lennon – singer, songwriter, and peace activist.

In PR practice, a simple rule applies – the one who speaks first, even if it's a lie, always wins. So they win the battle, but not the war. And as we know, it's often worth losing a battle to win the war.

No one pays as much attention to the truth as an experienced PR specialist because no one else knows better the negative consequences of lying. Professional PR is about communicating the truth.

The theme of the Madrid forum I already mentioned, "Communication with Conscience," and the clear statement, that PR specialists must be the conscience of the organizations they represent may sound pompous to some. However, I wholeheartedly believe in it, and my entire professional activity relates to that principle.

Some people believe that all PR professionals are scheming to deceive and manipulate using black techniques. I can assure you that I don't want anything to do with such individuals. Indeed, many of the people I have encountered throughout my career have been precisely those who made every effort to bring the truth to light.

Some may argue that shaping public opinion, in other words, manipulating it, is necessary. However, the only correct path is dialogue, conversation, and explanation. It is impossible to spread falsehoods because the truth always comes to light in communication. It becomes apparent very quickly if a dialogue is being simulated, creating the illusion that it is taking place, while the interlocutor cleverly leads to a desired answer. Such manipulation is equivalent to lying, even though it may appear more appealing.

My colleague likes to demonstrate an example like this. He writes down the suit and number of a card on paper. Let's say it's the seven of hearts. Then he folds the paper and gives it to the interlocutor, asking them not to look at it for now. The answer the interlocutor should choose is hidden within that piece of paper. If we compare the cards to the simulation of dialogue, the deck of cards represents all possible options for the interlocutor's response, in this case, 36 options. The interlocutor holds the one correct answer they should choose in their hands, but at the beginning of the dialogue, they don't know it yet.

Then the "dialogue" begins, meaning my colleague starts questioning the interlocutor, and after each question, the interlocutor has to make a free choice. And indeed, the interlocutor chooses freely, but the essence lies not in what the interlocutor decides but in what my colleague does with those answers. However, the interlocutor focuses on selecting the answers and does not notice the manipulation.

"Now it's winter – gray, gloomy, and wet," my colleague continues. "The cards come in two colors: red and black. Which ones do you choose?"

The interlocutor chooses black cards, perhaps concluding that they should select that color if it's winter and wet. However, it has no significance.

Then my colleague says that red cards are left if the interlocutor chooses black. And red cards can be hearts and diamonds. The interlocutor chooses hearts. Then my colleague asks them to choose from hearts, which can be numbers and pictures. Numbers are chosen. Then from the numbers, the interlocutor chooses odd numbers, which are two, seven, and nine. Finally, the interlocutor chooses nine, leaving seven behind.

The interlocutor unfolds the paper and finds written there – the seven of hearts. And after thinking for a while, almost everyone realizes they were manipulated with their answers. However, while focusing on choosing the answers during the conversation, almost no one notices it. In reality, my colleague would choose the opposite response to what the interlocutor chose.

Let's imagine that the 36 cards represent 36 products, and you are a buyer to whom the seller wants to sell, specifically, the seven of hearts. And in the end, the buyer ends up purchasing precisely that after the "dialogue" between the buyer and the seller. Why? Because they were manipulated.

Indeed, nobody forced the buyer to choose what they chose. However, was that the choice the buyer wanted? Was it a conversation where the buyer figured out why they needed one product over another? No, the clever and cunning seller actually led the buyer to this particular answer. The person chose the only correct answer that the seller desired. There was no honest dialogue here.

That is indeed a perfect example of manipulation. Manipulation is a technique, but it belongs to spreading falsehoods rather than disseminating the truth. If we employ it repeatedly, people will stop believing in us. We need to be honest, open, and transparent to prevent that from happening. We need genuine dialogue, which can be ensured by PR professionals whose goal is truthful communication.

Therefore, I refer to my profession as the profession of truthful communication. I can help build relationships and expect a proper reputation only by communicating the truth.

My colleague says that professional PR results in the feeling that you are not just a buyer to whom the seller wants to sell something but a participant in the overall process: your opinion matters and is considered. But unfortunately, PR never yields immediate results for the business, and investments in this area do not quickly pay off.

In PR practice, honesty, openness, and trust are crucial, just like in a family. When there is a lack of communication, secrets, or lies within a family, rumours, misunderstandings, and, eventually, relationship breakdown occurs. And as a rule, each person blames their partner without paying attention to the fact that were both involved in the process. Actress, screenwriter, activist, author, and comedian Dame Emma Thompson says, "Any problem, big or small, within a family always starts with bad communication. Someone isn't listening."

A PR specialist teaches clients to look at the world openly, just as we all learned in childhood but later forgot. There is truth, and there is falsehood. There is black or white. Or, as I like to say, there is black and colorful because the truth is always colorful.

Indeed, once we realize it, PR no longer seems so confusing and complex. We can take any example and see that if we lie, we paint the entire communication that arises from that lie with black. But, on the other hand, if we speak the truth, we have unlimited colors to express it.

Let's say we have a simple regular financial statement for the press, in which we need to announce that the company's revenue decreased in the last quarter. If we lie, that is, write that it increased, all other communication will have a black, deceptive color, and everything will turn black when the lie is revealed. However, if we decide to tell the truth, we will have a range of explanations to explain why the revenue decreased.

If we claim that homosexuality is an illness, we would be lying. Scientists and life itself have long and repeatedly proven that being gay or lesbian is as natural as not being one. So, those who claim otherwise are lying. Moreover, they often try to justify their lies with various vague arguments or numbers. In other words, they engage in shady practices. Denying, prohibiting, or somehow restricting the presence of gays or lesbians is wrong, just as lying is. However, the truth about gays and lesbians is very diverse. There can be various opinions – whether we should equate their relationships to those of traditional families or whether it should be any other form of family, whether we need parades or not, whether we should teach children to be boys or girls or let them naturally develop and choose. And there are countless other truths, all of which are true, but they are based on one fundamental truth: these people exist and are just as much inhabitants of the world as everyone else.

We would be lying if we claimed that a polluting company does not pollute. But, if we acknowledge that it pollutes, we can discuss how little or how much it pollutes and what can be done to reduce pollution further. And it applies to every example because lies are monochromatic and black, while the truth is colorful.

A communicator should be well aware that if they spread lies or half-truths, they undermine the foundations of the PR profession and harm society. Spreading lies or half-truths is manipulation and deception. People get lost in the fog of information, authorities disappear, and what is true and false becomes unclear. Moreover, half-truths are just as much a lie and even more dangerous because the truth is mixed with falsehood. Knowing that part of it is genuine, a recipient of information may assume the same about another piece. One of the black technologies is precise: taking accurate facts, mixing them with speculations, and presenting them to readers or viewers. An uncritical recipient of information then "consumes" the complete information as truth. Russian propaganda channels are particularly fond of this technique.

The only correct solution is complete transparency in communication. Of course, there is the possibility of errors being made or trade secrets being exposed. All of that can exist, but it can also be clearly stated that a particular fact cannot be disclosed because it is stipulated in an agreement between two organizations, or it would violate principles of competition, or another specified reason. That is already truthful communication if we do not disclose something and publicly explain why we did not disclose it.

The life of a PR specialist often involves ongoing discussions or even conflicts with clients regarding the amount of information to be disclosed. However, this only highlights the role of a PR specialist. The PR specialist must try to convince the client that it must be revealed if they believe a particular fact should be made public. That is why the PR specialist serves as the conscience or window cleaner of the organization.

Clients often prefer that less is better and that it's safer to withhold information and refrain from speaking about certain things. However, the role of a PR specialist should involve constant persuasion that transparency is one of the most crucial conditions for building reputation and trust.

Some organizations are reluctant to open up and engage in dialogue, partly because they perceive it as a daunting and meticulous task. Indeed, it is a fact, and this task falls within the realm of a PR professional's work. However, speaking the truth is beneficial to society, beneficial to employees of the company, and beneficial to everyone. Openness, transparency, and the avoidance of secrecy foster solidity, confidence, and pride. They build a reputation while leaving the silent ones behind as losers.

A public organization that openly communicates and spreads the truth shapes its present and future, with no room for deceit and fabrications.

It is possible to draw the opposite conclusion – if you want to remain unclear and mysterious, and these elements create fear and mistrust, then you isolate yourself completely. Such a strategy is also possible. However, this strategy always results in defeat when an organization faces a crisis. Isolation will then reveal its destructive force. There are only a small portion of organizations for which isolation is the right strategy. Without exception, they are state or internationally significant closed organizations protected by laws or international agreements. In all other cases, openness is a long-term winning strategy. And openness is inseparable from truth.

In PR practice, truth encompasses essential characteristics such as honesty, transparency, openness, two-way communication, and the ability to ask questions and provide answers.

In PR, organizations or individuals cannot afford any lies. It is not permissible to disseminate false facts and figures because lies erode relationships. Long-term relationships cannot be built on deceit. The best way to remember everything is never to lie. If you've lied somewhere, you have to remember it. If you do it frequently, you have to remember a lot. Eventually, it is easy to get confused because remembering whom you lied to and whom you told the opposite to becomes almost impossible. And for the person you lied to, it may be the only phrase that reminds them about you. If we send a press release with false information to the media, we will quickly lose the trust of journalists or editors because, by trusting us, they can easily deceive their readers. It becomes challenging to expect the dissemination of your information a second time. Trust is built by consistently and honestly telling the truth, and trust is shattered by lying even once.

A trust-based relationship between the media and a PR specialist develops over time. If that trust is broken even once, it becomes tough to work in this field.

A PR specialist must verify all the facts. However, in practice, it is often impossible to verify everything, so it is necessary to rely on authoritative sources and trustworthy individuals. Here the word "trust" arises again. You must be reliable, and your reference must be reliable as well. A PR specialist aiming to disseminate the truth must have sources they trust, and those sources must understand the harm that spreading falsehoods can cause.

Although the truth is one, there are many shades of fact. Therefore the world of truth is diverse. On the other hand, lies are only one, and it is black, dull, and empty. It is essential to understand that when we spread the truth, we constantly have a wide range of colors to choose from, but when we start spreading lies, we have only one black choice. The world of truth allows us to argue, prove, and discuss, while lies only allow manipulation.

If you explain and don't lie, it will help establish strong and long-lasting relationships.

1.2.5. PRofession of Relations

> Count your age by friends, not years. Count your life by smiles, not tears.
>
> John Lennon – singer, songwriter, and peace activist.

The foundations of this profession are truth, transparency, and being well-informed. PR builds honest, open, and trust-building long-term relationships on these foundations. Investing in these foundations, my colleague says, is the best investment for anyone: a brand, a country, or an individual.

Relationships in business activities (as well as in any other activity) do not have a clear, specifically defined goal. Therefore, attempting to evaluate their effectiveness is quite a challenging task. Nevertheless, I like the comparison to firefighting tools in this context.

Indeed, more than once, you may have noticed a fire extinguisher that almost always stands in the corner and often seems completely unnecessary. However, it only takes a fire to break out for the presence and knowledge of how to use that extinguisher to become a matter of life or death.

It's the same with relationships. They are created not when they are most needed but when they seem not to be needed at all. So basically, the relationship is entirely mutual.

Relationships must be continuously built with all target audiences. Those audiences are employees, suppliers, media, government, and the community. Of course, there must be priorities here, but no target audience, even that with the slightest interest in our company's activities, should be forgotten. Why? Because their opinion might be needed tomorrow, or maybe a year from now, or they will perhaps give their opinion exactly when it is needed and in exactly the right circle of people. And the more global the space we live in, the greater this need.

It often seems that lunch and meetings with various people are unnecessary, as if the people you meet are essential, but it is a waste of time. However, this is not the case. You need to build relationships when you don't need them directly because they will help when you do need them. It is a mistake to think you can create relationships just when they are needed. Therefore, people in this profession must constantly build relationships, which is a big part of our work.

A good client understands that the more the PR specialist working for him communicates, organizes various meetings, talks, tells about the company's activities, and meets with an increasingly diverse circle of people – the better he does his job. A good customer does not expect a return from this activity the next day or month. A good client understands that an investment in a relationship is a long-term investment and that returns can usually only be expected in the long term.

More than once, I have received calls from potential clients when they are already in crisis. Unfortunately, in almost all such cases, I give them a negative answer, or I only start work after explaining very well what they can expect a result. Of course, some understand this while others refuse the services offered. But it is better not to earn than to create unfounded illusions and damage a reputation.

Putting out a fire without a fire extinguisher is impossible, so there is no need to promise it. And usually, that's what the customer wants during a fire. Without a fire extinguisher, the best thing to do is to minimize the damage of the fire and, once it's over, prepare for a new fire so that it doesn't happen again. It's the same with relationships. If there is a crisis and we did not create a relationship before it, we will not suppress it, we can only reduce the damage, and it will end by itself. And when it's over, you need to start building relationships.

PR is all about building relationships. And that's true for any area of PR, whether it's community affairs, media relations, or social media communications. Relationships are constantly being created, and this process cannot be final unless we choose to end that relationship.

It's easy to understand when we take relationship building to a personal level. If we start communicating with a person, we always have some purpose for that communication – it may not be expressed consciously, but it is always there.

A young guy trying to start a conversation with a girl he likes, even if he does not fully realize it, in his subconscious has a clear goal. And although far from every such conversation ends in marriage, the plan can be that. If the relationship is successful, the goal is being approached. When the goal is reached, the relationship continues, and the whole of family life is a confusing long-term relationship building exercise, with compromises, defeats and victories, disappointments and discoveries. In a family, building relationships is a continuous and never-ending process, the result of which is not final, never achieved, but very important. A family with good relationships enjoys peace, laughs, feels good, and lives a fulfilling life.

The same processes take place outside the family. The same processes occur in the lives of companies, politicians, and communities. Suppose a company, politician or community can create a relationship with their environment. In that case, they get the same as a family – they enjoy comfortable work and have the opportunity to carry out their activities calmly. The employees of such a company feel good and receive many benefits that would not exist if such relationships did not exist.

Having and nurturing good relations with your environment is the main goal of the PR profession.

My colleague says perfect public relations are possible but not perfect marriages. Marriage is a form of agreement, a union. You need to build a relationship in PR, not a marriage. PR helps form relationships, by listening, understanding, taking pauses, and creating common values.

For example, creating a romantic evening or weekend is similar to working with a large audience, say, organizing a large celebration. It's not enough to buy tickets, wine, and candles. You also need to decorate the room nicely and create an atmosphere of anticipation. It is essential to do this together. PR is about building mood and suspense and working to create a miracle.

Only by doing so can romantic relationships last for many years, but this is not enough either. It would be best to light the fire constantly and keep adding firewood. Do not pour gasoline, but carefully and delicately stoke the fireplace by placing a twig under it. It is a two-person process and property. That's PR.

Honest and trusting relationships cannot be built by hurting someone. Therefore, every PR professional must disseminate comprehensive information about the subject they represent: both positive and negative. However, this only applies to the represented entity, not third parties.

Nevertheless, harming another to benefit one's principal client is just as wrong a strategy as lying. Maybe it is possible to achieve some results in the short term, but in over the long term, such activities will always backfire on you. People to whom you spoke ill of others will remember you as a destroyer, not a relationship builder. Harm, as well as spreading lies, is one of the black technologies that should have nothing to do with PR.

However, such temptations are not uncommon. Such requests can come from both customers and dirty media. For people not very good at PR, such instant "solutions" to situations can be beneficial.

I apply strict standards of non-falsehood and non-harm in my practice. However, this is not necessarily the case with all colleagues. It must be admitted that you will meet people with different thinking and careers. The most intriguing thing is that those who do not apply such standards think others are just pretending.

I once worked with an organization whose ethical principles completely matched my own. That organization was attacked by competitors who, to put it mildly, were not very scrupulous in choosing the means to prove their truth: they bought self-serving media, spread lies through community members, and actively harmed in other ways. Our response to such actions was the only possible one – ignoring them. And one day, a detailed journalistic investigation appeared in the media about our competitors, revealing all the dirty schemes they used. That information had long been obscure, but journalists gathered information from various sources, systematized it, and made it public. Later, a book was even published about it. Our long-term strategy worked – we never responded to the attacks of our competitors. When the material about our competitors came out, we could enjoy the public victory we had achieved by ignoring them.

But something else was the most exciting and fun thing for me in this situation. I learned from reliable sources that the competitors were 100% convinced that we bought the journalists, and that this led to those articles and then the book. They could not believe journalists did this in the name of interesting material for readers. And I can put my hand to my heart and not flinch in my sleep because I know 100% that we did not touch it in any way.

Since there are no laws in PR activities, an important place is occupied by the code of ethics. Every PR professional must have and follow their code of ethics and understand its importance for themselves, without any penalties. If there is such a code, there are never any questions about what can and can't be done.

Consistently and patiently building relationships allows you to hear and sense even more and to develop professionally.

1.3. Reputation

> It takes 20 years to build a reputation and five minutes to ruin it. If you think about that, you'll do things differently.
>
> Warren Buffet – investor, business tycoon, and philanthropist.

Chairman Neville Bain of the Institute of Directors (UK) emphasizes the significance of one's professional assets in the "Guidance for PR Consultants and Board Directors"[9] issued by the Chartered Institute of PR (UK). While some may prioritize their education or unique skills, Bain underscores that a good reputation surpasses all. He defines reputation as a reflection of ability, consistent performance, and adherence to personal values, distinguishing individuals from their peers. Moreover, Bain highlights the importance of reputation for companies and organizations. Employees and executives are keenly aware of their organization's reputation, and how it influences their ability to attract top talent and foster positive relationships with stakeholders. Bain suggests that a strong reputation leads to greater efficiency, better customer and supplier relations, and increased societal legitimacy. Conversely, a poor reputation severely limits a company's ability to create value. Bain also notes that, like trust, reputation takes time to build but can be easily tarnished.

Interpersonal relationships form the foundation of personal reputations, and genuine, trust-based relationships can only be developed over an extended period.

Building a reputation is a long-term and continuous process. It requires time, trials, and trust for a reputation to form.

We create our reputation every day, sometimes consciously and often unconsciously. Whether we want it or not, our reputation follows us every day. Reputation is like a tail that always trails behind us. As the Dakota Indians said, "We will be known forever by the tracks we leave."

Footprints in the sand make for a fantastic visual description of reputation. However, in real life, especially in the virtual realm, that sand is more like wet concrete, where footprints get imprinted and solidified permanently.

Every newborn child already has some reputation. Unless that child is left on an uninhabited island, where nobody knows about them, and they somehow manage to survive, only under those conditions can we say that a person does not have a reputation. In all other cases, they do have a reputation.

Every newborn child immediately creates a reputation even without being able to speak or do anything initially except for crying, smiling, or even remaining silent. What does this mean? Building a reputation does not require any proactive, conscious actions. For example, a newborn baby can cry a lot and gain a reputation for being fussy. As a result, their parents can spoil them excessively, making them appear spoiled to others. Another child can be without parents at all. However, all children have a reputation. All people have a reputation.

Before we delve into a detailed explanation of what reputation consists of, let's take a moment to enjoy, in my opinion, the best lyrical definition of reputation. So put on your headphones, find Jason Mraz's song "Life Is Wonderful", and sing along together. It's a beautiful song, and I believe it could serve as an informal anthem for our profession.

1.3.1. Relations Help With Managing Reputation

> There are four ways, and only four ways, in which we have contact with the world. We are evaluated and classified by these four contacts: what we do, how we look, what we say, and how we say it.
>
> Dale Carnegie – writer and lecturer.

The PR profession builds relationships, and interpersonal relationships help manage reputation. Here, I emphasize "manage" rather than "create". Reputation forms on its own, even if we do nothing. Reputation begins when something significant happens. We can only manage it, meaning we can guide its development in the desired direction.

For a long time, the market was dominated by the belief that organizational communication is necessary primarily to maximize sales. Unfortunately, this perspective can still be observed in some organizations today. Consequently, there is a peculiar attempt to evaluate the effectiveness of PR activities based on sales results or establish criteria for assessing PR effectiveness through sales. However, reputation does not sell anything, so I am always surprised when encountering such opinions.

The goal of this section is to explain how reputation is managed.

Let's return to the definition of reputation provided by CIPR.

PR is about reputation – the result of what you do, what you say and what others say about you. PR is the discipline which looks after reputation, with the aim of earning understanding and support and influencing opinion and behavior. It is the planned and sustained effort to establish and maintain goodwill and mutual understanding between an organization and its publics.

This definition is excellent and fully reflects the essence of PR activities. However, while reading and reflecting on it, I couldn't help but have the urge to: a) add a few words to it; and b) illustrate the transformation of PR activities into reputation schematically.

I have made numerous attempts to present it schematically to students and listeners, but whenever I tried to show "what you do", "what you say", and "what others say about you" on the same level, something didn't quite fit together. It wasn't until recently that I understood what it was.

The first two factors are actions, while the last is the result. "What others say about you" is the outcome. We take steps, and in the minds of others, a result forms which they talk about and think about, i.e. reputation. Our reputation is the result of our actions in other people's minds.

Is there something missing here?

In my opinion, one more crucial factor is missing here – appearance. Like actions and speech, appearance is also a significant aspect of reputation. "How you look" is the third reputational factor. When this thought crossed my mind, I eventually found confirmation in the quote by Dale Carnegie, which you read at the beginning of this section.

In my country, there is a saying: "Your appearance initially judges you, but your character melts or solidifies through your intellect." People have perfectly and independently captured how reputation is formed in these few words. I found a schematic representation of this folk saying in the book *Marketing communications.*[10] In a diagram, called the "PR mix", the foundation of the PR complex consists of two main words: CREDIBILITY and VISIBILITY. Comparing this diagram to the folk saying, CREDIBILITY represents intellect, while VISIBILITY represents appearance.

So we have three factors that shape reputation:

- What you DO? I named this factor – ACTION.
- What you SAY? I named this factor – TONGUE.
- How you LOOK? I named this factor – STYLE.

These three factors shape two main elements of the reputation complex:

- CREDIBILITY, which is the result of ACTION and TONGUE.
- VISIBILITY, which is the result of TONGUE and STYLE.

Our credibility depends on what we do and how we communicate about it, while our visibility depends on what we say and how we appear.

Finally, both elements of the reputation complex, CREDIBILITY and VISIBILITY, form a derived element of the reputation complex called NOTABILITY, which corresponds to the "what others say about you" mentioned in the CIPR definition. The connection between NOTABILITY and "people's minds" is bidirectional, as just as our actions influence others' opinions, those opinions also affect our visibility.

I will return to the folk saying I mentioned and add a little: "By appearance, they meet; by intellect, they get along; but by emotion, experienced together, they are remembered for a long time." "I have learned that people will forget what you said, people will forget what you did, but people will never forget how you made them feel," said Maya Angelou.

NOTABILITY is indeed the feeling that remains after actions, words, and images come to an end.

The relationship between the main elements of the reputation complex, CREDIBILITY and VISIBILITY, and the derived element, NOTABILITY, is revealed in Figure 1.8. High credibility and high visibility form an appropriate reputation with high notability (Leaders' reputation), and high credibility and low visibility create a proper reputation with low notability (Professionals' reputation). Similarly, low credibility and low visibility form an inappropriate reputation with low notability (Frauds' reputation) and low

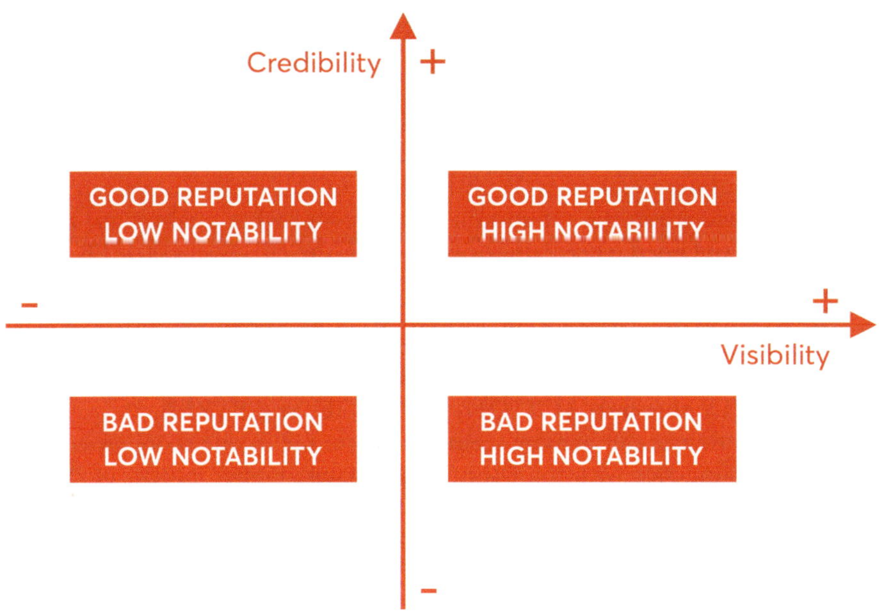

Figure 1.8 The relationship between the main and derived elements of the reputation complex.

Figure by the author.

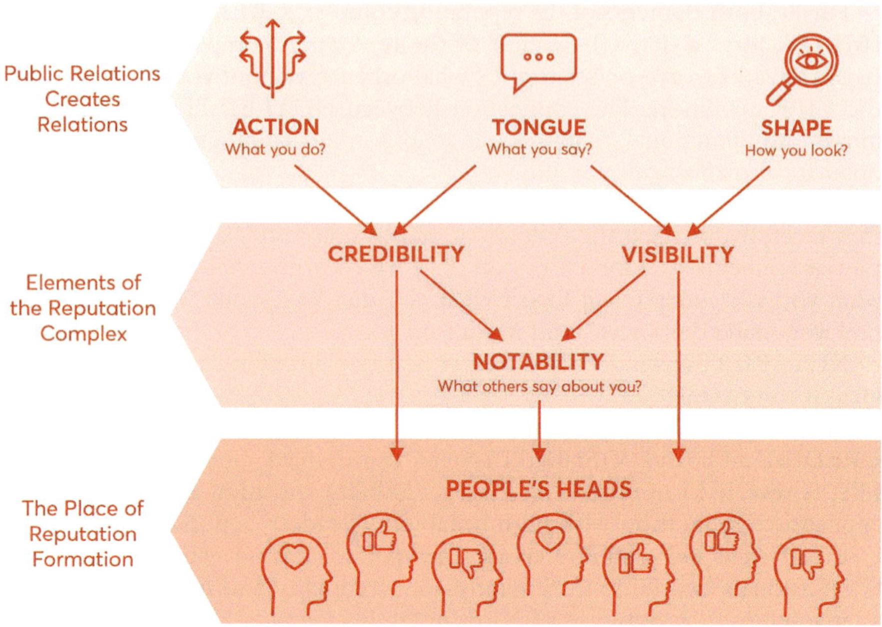

Figure 1.9 The relationship between reputation and PR. PR creates relations between people to manage reputation.

Figure by the author.

credibility and high visibility form a hard reputation with high notability (Populists' reputation). Therefore, we have four basic types of reputations and four reputation extremes. With the help of this diagram, we can determine where we are in the reputation complex and what goal we are aiming for. We have obtained a diagram for evaluating the effectiveness of PR activities, which can be easily applied in practice.

In summary, in this section I have obtained a new definition of PR activity.

PR creates RELATIONS between people to manage REPUTATION. Management is done by creating CREDIBILITY, VISIBILITY, and NOTABILITY through ACTION, TONGUE, and STYLE.

This definition of our activity seemed close to me in one more aspect, due to its correspondence with the enormously changed environment of PR and our life in the "Network" stage of PR development. This definition is based on people relations, not organization-to-people relations (PR). There will be more about this is in the "Transformation" section.

1.3.2. Factors and Complexes

> When the trust account is high, communication is easy, instant, and effective.
>
> Stephen Covey – educator, author, businessman, and keynote speaker.

In the previous section, we discovered that reputation is shaped by three factors (ACTION, TONGUE, and STYLE) and three elements of the reputation complex (CREDIBILITY, VISIBILITY, and NOTABILITY).

Every individual or organization is constantly taking action, speaking, and presenting themselves in some way. Every person or organization is continuously influenced by the three reputational factors – ACTION, TONGUE, and STYLE. These reputational factors, in turn, constantly shape the three elements of the reputation complex – CREDIBILITY, VISIBILITY, and NOTABILITY. Therefore, the process of reputation formation is ongoing, whether we intend it or not.

This section aims to provide a more detailed discussion of each of the reputational factors and each of the elements of the reputation complex, as well as to explore the extent of influence that PR activities have on each of them.

Here are five examples of different reputations:

- Reputation No. 1: a cheerful and well-cared-for newborn baby.
- Reputation No. 2: a lazy and idle person spending empty days on the couch.
- Reputation No. 3: an active entrepreneur.
- Reputation No. 4: a famous surgeon.
- Reputation No. 5: the best teacher in town.

Next, let's talk about the three reputational factors (ACTION, TONGUE, and STYLE) that shape the three elements of the reputation complex, as well as the three elements themselves (CREDIBILITY, VISIBILITY, and NOTABILITY), which we use to assign a reputation to individuals.

Factor 1: ACTION
Quality First; or What You DO?

> Words should be used as tools of communication and not as a substitute for action.
>
> Mae West – actress, singer, playwright, screenwriter, comedian, and sex symbol.

The first and, in my opinion, the most crucial reputational factor is the actions a specific person, organization, or entity does or is engaged in. This factor is vital because the other two factors, TONGUE and STYLE, are meaningless without it. We can speak eloquently and appear impressive, but if we lack a foundation of meaningful actions to support our words and appearance, our façade will quickly unravel, and the emptiness will be revealed. Attempting to build a reputation solely through communication methods has no long-term prospects. The credibility of our actions comes first, and only then can the credibility of our communication follow.

It is important to emphasize this fact because it dispels illusions that a PR specialist can create anything out of nothing. It is not valid. A PR specialist can only help build a reputation when there is a solid foundation of meaningful and quality actions.

Here's how ACTION works in practice. The child with the first reputation rarely cries and often laughs. The owner of the second reputation, a lazy person, can be found at home on the couch daily. The owner of the third reputation, an entrepreneur, is wealthy and manages a successful business that creates excellent food products. The owner of the fourth reputation, a surgeon, performs surgeries successfully and professionally. Finally, the owner of the fifth reputation, a teacher, prepares students well for exams and has been one of the most popular teachers for several years.

If someone were to perform their actions inappropriately, differently from what they have done before, their reputation would immediately change. Therefore, the foundation of every reputation is primarily based on a person's actions that justify the reputation they have built.

Here, I would like to emphasize the word "built" because only the individual themselves can build their reputation through their actions, and it cannot be created for them by someone else.

The same applies to organizations. The foundation of every organization is its actions. If an organization is reliable, high-quality, professional, and beneficial to society, even without doing anything more, it will almost certainly have a positive reputation. However, only a few people may be aware of it. Contrary to popular belief, reputation is primarily a matter of quality rather than communication. It starts with high-quality actions, and then good communication comes into play to showcase them.

Naturally, the question arises as to whether PR influences the ACTION factor or if this is solely a matter of individual or organizational activities.

PR plays a significant role in developed organizations, even during product development. The product must be created with PR in mind, and a PR consultant must be part of the product development team to foresee aspects that may go unnoticed by the product creators. For example, will the product be environmentally friendly? What are the ethical aspects of product creation? Also, while it may seem normal for a marketing specialist to use small, barely legible letters to disclose "additional" terms in a mobile service contract, a PR specialist must oppose such a practice, knowing the long-term reputational consequences it can have, regardless of the quick and high profits.

During the Madrid Forum (2014), it was highlighted that PR specialists must be the consciences of their organizations because PR is not just about what the organization says, it's about what the organization does.[11] An example was drawn from the marble mask in Rome known as "The Mouth of Truth" (Italian: La Bocca della Verità), where visitors boldly insert their hands into the open mouth.

So, truth is only possible when actions align with words. Therefore, PR is primarily about actions (product, quality) and only then about words (publicity).

It is evident that a PR specialist does not dictate business processes. However, the PR specialist must participate in all those processes and guide them in a direction that avoids potential quality and, at the same time, communication problems in the future. There are no communication issues when these processes within the represented organization are fair and transparent.

Through the interaction of ACTION and PR activities, another exciting aspect emerges, which I first heard about in 2011 at the "Communication on Top" forum in Davos. Standing on stage, the speaker pondered which term – "PR" or "communication" – was broader. Which is a part of the other? And he demonstrated that communication is a part of PR rather than vice versa, as is commonly assumed.

The relationship between ACTION and PR activities also perfectly demonstrates this. Therefore, PR must first and foremost prioritize ACTION, meaning product quality, and only then its communication.

A PR specialist must participate and, with the product creators, be directly responsible for product quality and ensure that the represented organization does not harm the environment and creates value for society.

The keywords describing the ACTION factor are: **QUALITY, PROFESSIONALISM, INTEGRITY, and THOROUGHNESS.**

Factor 2: TONGUE
It Ain't Selling; or What You **SAY**?

> Lying is done with words and also with silence.
>
> Adrienne Rich – poet, essayist, and feminist.

An essential idea of this section is that reputation doesn't sell. Although, of course, it can assist in sales, it doesn't sell directly.

Therefore, any attempt to give to reputation a sales function is inappropriate and unprofessional. However, if the communication task in reputation management is not to sell, what is the task at hand?

The answer is quite simple – the main task of a PR consultant in communication is to prevent the organization from knowingly or unknowingly spreading falsehoods and to make the organization as transparent and open to the public as possible. For example, suppose a client has thoughts about restricting something, such as photographing their facilities. In that case, the PR specialist should always ask why and constantly discuss this with the client, showing that publicity brings more benefits than unnecessarily hiding behind a veil of commercial secrecy.

Of course, it does not mean commercial secrets cannot exist in principle. For example, confidential matters, protected patents, and specific "know-how" solutions are rightfully known only to a particular organization. However, ensuring that they are not abused and that there are as few secrets as possible is crucial.

PR and advertising have fundamentally different ways of communication. My colleague claims that advertising, in principle, has nothing to do with PR because often advertising is a beautifully wrapped lie, a desire to show something that is not true. We all know that a hamburger in an advertisement and the real thing are two different things, and thirst cannot be quenched by sweet fizzy drinks alone. Advertising can afford to do that, but PR cannot. Moreover, PR must ensure that this type of advertising is minimal in any organization's activities. There should be a constant discussion, and sometimes even a struggle, between PR and marketing specialists within an organization because their goals can fundamentally differ: one (the marketer) may be interested only in short-term plans, which are often difficult to reconcile with long-term reputation goals. These differences do not mean that marketing specialists are unnecessary. No. It means that there should be a constant effort to achieve a balance between short-term and long-term goals.

My colleague also says advertising is a strategy for shaping human desire: how to make people aware of and want to buy something. On the other hand, PR is a strategy for building trust, and trust is formed among people through dialogue and respect. PR involves company transparency, internal communication, working with opinion leaders, and building relationships with the media.

PR and advertising provide information to the public, but their presentation styles are fundamentally different. The style of advertising is one-sided. It is a game and flirtation. PR presents information differently, in a manner that allows the public to become more open, honest, and demanding at the same time.

In the case of PR, we first need to work on ourselves, our organization, and our reputation: to think about who we are in this life, what brings us joy, and what kind of circle of allies we need. By doing so, we enter an environment where we are heard and can also benefit others.

In PR practice, we strive for long-term relationships and mutual attention. PR is about the collective long-term work of building trust and creating the world and environment we need. The most important aspect of this work is continuous dialogue and openness.

The keywords describing the TONGUE factor are: **TRUTH, TRUST, DIALOGUE, OPENNESS, and LONG-TERM.**

Factor 3: STYLE
Beauty is Never Ignored; or How You **LOOK**?

> Fashion can be bought. Style one must possess.
>
> Edna Woolman Chase – editor.

Fashion is a marketing term, while style is reputational. Something can be unfashionable, but you will always have a style. Perhaps it will be refined, possibly very original, dull, and unremarkable, but it will always be there. And if you care about your reputation, you will always care about your style. If you care for your reputation, your STYLE will always correspond to your ACTION and TONGUE. Style is the visual expression of action and speech and an essential and equal component of reputation.

In practice, we often see attempts to create a style disconnected from action and speech. The result is always lamentable.

These words were written when the residents of Belarus were striving to overthrow the last dictator of Europe, Alexander Lukashenko. My attention was drawn to two excellent examples: one where the style completely corresponds to the actions and speeches, and the other where it is the opposite. In the first case, the style follows the actions and speeches, while in the second case, an attempt is made to create a style of mockery, which always leads not to an improvement of reputation but to further deterioration.

In Belarus, in the summer of 2020, everything related to Alexander Lukashenko and the green-red color became old, disliked, Soviet-like, and non-modern after the pseudo-elections. To make matters worse, the unelected president was beating people, torturing them in prisons, and the people took to the streets. There were hundreds of thousands of people, smiles shining on everyone's faces, everyone singing and chanting, and it seemed like the air began to tremble, and a fresh gust of wind suddenly swept through all the cities of Belarus.

Social media was filled with memes on various topics of that time. Many of them were created by professional artists and designers who wholeheartedly aimed for the changes to happen as quickly as possible in this country that had been ruled by a dictator for 26 years. Therefore, people willingly shared and diversified the information with various images and videos.

Rufina Bazlova, a Belarusian artist living in the Czech Republic, decided to capture the events happening in her country at that time through her works, embroidered in the old Belarusian style. Each piece is carefully planned, drawn, and meticulously embroidered for long hours. Every artwork exudes love, empathy, and sincerity. Each piece is stylish and perfectly expresses the protesters' actions and words.

Another example is the supposedly modern images distributed by Alexander Lukashenko's press service, intended for individuals supportive of the regime. The images were meant to be created in a youthful style that resonated with the protests against the government. However, it was forgotten that these images' target audience was disconnected from the internet and social media and primarily relied on regime-controlled newspapers. Also, the designer tasked with this work lacked the desire, sensibility, and understanding of how it should be done. As a result, it was an attempt to create a style that did not align with the actions and speeches, and it did not work. Not

Figure 1.10 DJ of changes, 2020.
Artwork by Rufina Bazlova.

only did it fail to become famous and voluntarily spread, but it also contributed to the regime's already poor reputation.

Another critical and often overlooked aspect of style is what I term communication hygiene. It is often overlooked because many consider it a common and natural thing that doesn't require particular attention. Perhaps that is true, and it's great if it is. However, in practice, many individuals and organizations prioritize their style but ignore the basics of effective communication. As a result, their employees struggle to write an email without errors, and when they answer the phone, their voice sounds tired and indifferent.

I consider these seemingly simple but collectively important details for overall reputation as communication hygiene. Just as a modern individual should maintain personal hygiene and not walk around in dirty or foul-smelling clothes, organizations should ensure that their employees answer the phone with a sharp and courteous voice, that information on their website is easily accessible, and that provided email addresses exist and give prompt responses. But, again, these details are matters of style.

Therefore, a PR specialist working on a specific organization's reputation needs numerous assistants from various fields: design, information technology, training, and many others. They can achieve excellent results by having reliable partners and managing a specific reputation.

The main words describing the STYLE factor are: **CORRESPONDENCE TO THE ESSENCE, STYLE, and COMMUNICATION HYGIENE.**

Three further connected factors are: credibility, visibility, and notability.

CREDIBILITY

> If you can build a powerful brand, you will have a powerful marketing program. If you CAN'T then all the advertising, fancy packaging, sales promotion, and PR in the world won't help you achieve your objective.
>
> Al Ries – marketing professional and author.

Credibility is built on two reputation factors: ACTION and TONGUE. Out of these two, undoubtedly, priority should be given to ACTION. Without it, reputation-building is meaningless. ACTION is like the foundation of a house, the legs of a table. Without quality ACTION, it is impossible to create a long-term reputation, and all attempts to do so lead, at best, to an empty image that crumbles over time and, at worst, to a crisis that can destroy the entire organization. If we were to create a reputation pyramid, credibility would be the foundation of that pyramid.

A well-executed operation, a successful business deal, secure political steps, a fully functioning phone, or the successful launch of a spacecraft to the International Space Station are the foundation of CREDIBILITY.

In whatever activity we engage in, we should always strive to ensure that it is performed with high quality, on time, and provides the utmost satisfaction to the customer.

When we have quality ACTION, we can then talk about quality TONGUE. This means speaking about our actions professionally, tailoring our communication to the appropriate audience, preparing high-quality presentations, knowing which channels to choose, going back to the fundamentals, writing press releases effectively, organizing press conferences, or giving interviews.

Quality ACTION and professional TONGUE work hand-in-hand in building CREDIBILITY. To be trusted by their patients, skilled surgeons must perform surgeries well and communicate with patients, understand their feelings, and conduct themselves in a polite and reassuring manner. For a successful entrepreneur aiming to be reliable, it is not enough to achieve business deals but also to be able to explain what those deals bring to the company, its employees, the community, and society at large. A trustworthy politician should be good at public speaking or posting self-promoting photos with a raised thumb on social media and have a clear, consistent, and long-term program or idea that guides them in leading and representing their constituents.

Such duets of ACTION and TONGUE must be present everywhere we seek CREDIBILITY.

ACTION without TONGUE can exist, but only within a narrow circle of professionals who understand each other without needing words. To appear credible in a broader society, we must professionally care for our TONGUE.

TONGUE without ACTION can only exist for a very short time, and once that time is up, TONGUE can even become harmful. Empty talk without taking action can only work until everyone realizes it is empty talk. We can say that a person or an organization that starts with TONGUE without ACTION receives time credit, during which they must start taking action. Failing to do so risks acquiring a reputation as someone who talks a lot but doesn't follow through on promises for a long time.

The best and most beneficial situation for CREDIBILITY is to execute ACTION and TONGUE simultaneously – acting and explaining one's actions simultaneously.

VISIBILITY

> Music is the greatest communication in the world. Even if people don't understand the language that you're singing in, they still know good music when they hear it.
>
> Lou Rawls – singer, songwriter, actor, voice actor, and record producer.

VISIBILITY is created by two reputation factors: TONGUE and STYLE. Unlike CREDIBILITY, there is no clearly expressed primary factor without which the other would be impossible, but the primary factor undoubtedly is TONGUE. It is easy to imagine professional communication without a deliberately created style, but style without communication is only possible in exceptional cases.

Once again, we need to talk about periods – short-term and long-term. It cannot be denied that style can be created and maintained while remaining silent in the short term, but in the long term, it is impossible. Sooner or later, one has to speak up, and how it is done can significantly impact the direction of the entire reputation.

It is not only me who has encountered well-presented individuals who can confidently maintain their appearance. However, the opinion about them can drastically change upon hearing them speak or seeing their written text.

Prominent cases are often encountered in professions where extensive communication is not required, such as sports. For example, a basketball player who excels in shooting three-pointers may often have a good athletic appearance. We can see their excellent photos, hairstyles, and even a new way of chewing gum. In our minds, an image of an almost perfect person is created and persists until that person speaks. In most cases, reputation changes significantly in such situations.

During my practice, I have seen many professionals who excel in managing ACTION and STYLE but struggle with their TONGUE. Such individuals can be found in various professions, and in the case of organizations, there are organizations like that in every field.

TONGUE is involved in the creation of both CREDIBILITY and VISIBILITY. And since NOTABILITY is a derivative of these two components, TONGUE is necessary for all elements of the reputation complex.

Suppose a surgeon performs surgeries excellently but fails to communicate with patients, constantly uses uncensored language, and has bad breath. In that case, it is unlikely that we can expect a satisfactory reputation because this surgeon ignores one element of the reputation complex – VISIBILITY. The same applies to an entrepreneur or a CEO of a large company.

And here, I would like to emphasize that it's not about having a "right" appearance but a sense of style. The choice of language, manner of dress, and manners themselves can be unexpected, different, or original, but they must be consciously controlled. Only in such cases will VISIBILITY be a beneficial element in reputation building.

It is also worth noting that both VISIBILITY factors, when combined, significantly reinforce each other. For example, a well-delivered speech will be much more impactful if the audience remembers the speaker's original appearance and something surprising done in a new and exciting style will always enhance that impression when accompanied by timely and contextually appropriate words.

And once again, like all PR principles, this applies to individuals as well as organizations. For example, a modern company that creates technology-driven products will significantly enhance its reputation if its leader consistently participates in various conferences and youth gatherings, not just those limited to their field, and freely engages with the audience and becomes a leader everyone listens to with bated breath. If we add to that their informal style of dress and the ability to appear as a "person from the street", we will steer the company's reputation in the right direction at full speed.

In creating VISIBILITY, TONGUE and STYLE do not have clear boundaries and often overlap. Therefore, we can discuss a speaking style encompassing TONGUE and STYLE.

NOTABILITY

> The fundamental way of getting public approval is to deserve it.
>
> Arthur W. Page – vice president and director at AT&T, the father of corporate PR.

Finally, we have the derived reputation component, or what is no longer within our control based on our actions – NOTABILITY. We have done good work (CREDIBILITY) and presented it effectively to the public (VISIBILITY), and now we can observe the impact it has generated.

It is worth noting an exciting aspect of PR activities that some may find appealing but which others may dislike – the element of uncertainty or lack of complete control.

For example, we cannot accurately predict the outcome of a press release (which depends on factors such as the day, other events happening, and the mood of the editor). Nor can we precisely determine the exact response our actions will receive from the public. Moreover, the same activities performed in different countries can result in different notability levels. Again, notability is a mirror – our image may appear unfavorable because we present ourselves poorly. Still, it can also be distorted due to a curved mirror, dirt, poor lighting, excessive magnification, or reduction.

Unfortunately, we do not really have the power to change the mirror – perhaps only to a small extent. We need to understand how the mirror works and strive for the desired result based on those principles.

Summary

As I mentioned earlier, three reputation factors (ACTION, TONGUE, and STYLE) form two main elements of the reputation complex:

- CREDIBILITY, which is the result of ACTION and TONGUE.
- VISIBILITY, which is the result of TONGUE and STYLE.

Our credibility depends on what we do and how we talk about it, while our visibility depends on what we say and how we appear.

Finally, both elements of the reputation complex, CREDIBILITY and VISIBILITY, combine to form a derivative element of the reputation complex – NOTABILITY, which corresponds to the CIPR definition of "what others say about you".

So, every individual or organization's reputation complex or reputation consists of three parts: CREDIBILITY, VISIBILITY, and NOTABILITY.

These interrelated and mutually influencing elements form a solid foundation for any reputation.

1.3.3. Benefits

> There is only one thing in life worse than being talked about, and that is not being talked about.
>
> Oscar Wilde – poet and playwright.

And finally – the last question about reputation: why is reputation important if it doesn't sell? What specific benefits does reputation provide? I often hear this question asked openly and, even more frequently, left unspoken. Still, I feel how it usually hangs in the air when the company's financial personnel look at a report describing the work done by the PR specialist in a month. It is often filled with “meetings”, “consultations”, “discussions”, “planning”, and similar “soft” tasks that are often not even considered as work but rather as idle talk. And is it worth paying money for that?

This section aims to explain what that money is being paid for, that is, to highlight specific benefits that an organization receives by prioritizing its reputation.

Let’s start by acknowledging that any attempt to quantify PR effectiveness using quantitative measures is fundamentally flawed. Various quantitative methods for evaluating the effectiveness of PR activities are unnatural. Why is that? It’s because the strength of relationships and reputations cannot be measured using quantitative indicators.

The most successful and impactful PR projects have never been and will never be recognized during lavish ceremonies. PR work is not a campaign, project, or event – it is a monotonous daily effort that is either very challenging or impossible to showcase publicly.

Advertising agencies are accustomed to measuring metrics such as impressions, reach, frequency, and similar indicators for their clients. This approach is fully justified in the case of advertising because its direct function is to sell. However, as I mentioned before, PR has often been confused with advertising, leading to a desire to quantify the results of PR activities.

However, what works for activities focused on generating sales is unsuitable for PR, which is about building relationships.

PR activities, such as press releases, articles, meetings, conversations, care, monitoring, and others are used to build relationships. However, the quantity or frequency of those activities does not determine the quality of those relationships. Sometimes, it is even the opposite – sending frequent press releases on insignificant topics can often disrupt relationships rather than build them.

Quantitatively assessing the effectiveness of a conversation is challenging. Should it be based on its duration? The number of words spoken? Unfortunately, that is not possible. However, some of the most important relationships are often built during those conversations. Just as we do not evaluate the effectiveness of a marriage based on the size of the family home or the number of children, we cannot assess the effectiveness of PR based on the number of articles published.

In the following sections, I highlight ten benefits of reputation that answer why it is essential even if it doesn’t sell.

First benefit: foundation for smooth operations (trust)

> Communication leads to community, that is, to understanding, intimacy, and mutual valuing.
>
> Rollo May – existential psychologist and author.

Internal and external PR professionals create relationships, an atmosphere, and trust, which serve as the foundations for various specialists, including marketing professionals, to carry out their activities smoothly.

In my practice, I have worked in the waste management sector for quite a long time. Specifically, I was responsible for the PR of the first two waste-to-energy plants in the country. These plants utilized waste as fuel, were modern, clean, and posed no environmental threat. However, this industry evokes strong emotions and controversies worldwide. When people hear "waste incineration", they immediately envision a large pile of burning trash emitting toxic fumes and a foul odor. No one wants to have such a neighbor, and rational arguments often struggle to make an impact. People either don't hear them or, even if they do, the imagery of burning waste overshadows logical reasoning.

Protests, outrage, letters to governing bodies, and various other forms of discontent are familiar to representatives of this industry. Even if they are entirely justified, have organized their operations effectively, and responsibly manage the waste of all residents by converting it into electricity and heat, owners of such facilities can never be at ease. Politicians often listen more to society's emotions than rational arguments. The public usually makes decisions based on emotions rather than logical arguments. Many politicians are more likely to seek to restrict or even halt the operation of such facilities rather than try to persuade their constituents through dialogue.

The importance of PR is incredibly significant in this context. While high-quality ACTION is necessary, as always, it is not sufficient. Converting waste into heat in a high-quality way is not enough; it requires substantial and long-term explanatory work with the public to demonstrate that such operations are not harmful to them.

The emphasis on the importance of dialogue and open communication in modern public relations aligns with the principles outlined in "Demonstrating the value of public relations"[12] by the Chartered Institute of Public Relations (CIPR), published in January 2013. The text underscores the necessity for organizations to engage in transparent communication with stakeholders to build strong relationships and maintain a positive reputation, echoing the insights provided in the CIPR publication:

- In the modern world, with increased access to information, everyone is an "expert" and a cynic: no one takes what you say at face value. Saying you provide the best service or product, or that you are a good employer or business partner, isn't enough.
- People are going to ask questions and they are going to want answers before making up their own minds. In order to survive you need to enter into a dialogue with your stakeholders. Through open and honest communications you will build sound relationships and a good reputation – the type of relationships and reputation that will ensure your success.
- This is where PR comes in, as it is about managing communications and the relationships upon which reputations are based. PR best practice is also concerned with the concept of "dialogue" – representing your organization to your stakeholders and your stakeholders to your organization.

Efficiency:

The effectiveness criterion of such activities may appear unreliable in activity reports. The best result of such work is zero. We must monitor the environment (media, social media groups, and conduct surveys among residents). The fewer mentions of our company we find while observing, the better. If the public is calm, constantly receives the necessary answers, is well aware of the company, and has interacted with it before, they forget about it. The company exists and carries out its work; the public does not raise questions to politicians, and politicians do not take any initiatives. The company operates calmly. Silence and smooth operations, in this case, are the significant outcomes of PR work.

Second benefit: environmental monitoring and crisis prevention

> I suspect in most companies, the PR person is down at No. 20 in the pecking order. But here, he is fighting incredibly important battles. If a negative story starts running away with itself in the press and is not dealt with fast, it can badly damage the brand, and so we put enormous weight on our PR people.
>
> Richard Branson – business magnate, investor, author, and philanthropist.

The importance of PR is comparable to that of a psychologist or a mediator in a couple's relationship. The main goal of a mediator is to preserve the relationship and minimize the losses for both parties involved if that's not possible. However, when the relationship is going well, the mediator observes the situation passively and may offer occasional advice but not much more. Similarly, PR ensures that the "relationship" between an organization and society succeeds, benefiting the company and the public. If the organization's and society's relationship is strong, PR monitors the situation to identify potential crises as early as possible and resolve them before they escalate. In the case of a crisis, PR strives to minimize damage, provide information, and gradually rebuild trust.

Creating a purposeful reputation always helps in crises. This fact is often difficult to explain to salespeople and others who think in marketing terms and are solely focused on selling faster and increasing sales. However, it is crucial.

A crisis usually occurs when it is least expected, and it is not the time to start worrying about one's reputation. However, that is when the desire to "do something" arises. I have been asked to help during crises on multiple occasions. However, I rarely take on such work and limit the expectations. If a potential client showed little concern for reputation matters before the crisis, it is not worth expecting their attitudes to change significantly during the crisis. Yes, they may ask for help. I have even encountered individuals who appeared sad and were pleading with me during a crisis, despite having arrogantly claimed that their reputation was fine and not worth spending money on.

It is possible to start working with a client during a crisis, helping to manage the situation. However, before undertaking such work, it is essential to precisely define the expected outcome with the client. In these cases, the PR consultant often has minimal thoughts in mind, while the client has maximal ones. And as soon as the crisis eases, often due to significant efforts by the consultant, the client regains confidence and starts thinking that PR activities were not as necessary after all.

Organizations that have consistently built their reputation before a crisis find it much easier to weather crises than those that have not. It is much easier to communicate during a crisis with those who have already established relationships with journalists, community representatives, government authorities, and other interest groups. Why does this happen? It's pretty simple.

For many years, the organization has been building its reputation by engaging with the media and opinion leaders, opening its doors, demonstrating transparency, and engaging in discussions. If such an organization faces a crisis, it is unlikely that people will say, "With them, everything has always been murky and suspicious." The arising problems will most likely be viewed as temporary setbacks and may evoke sympathy and understanding from customers and the public.

Regarding a "gray" organization that was not well known before, it is likely to be said that, "Some unclear matters were taking place there, and what happened was to be expected." In such a case, rehabilitating the organization will be much more challenging than the first scenario.

By the way, from my experience, I know that many clients perceive crises as something significant (an explosion, a fire) but often forget that in everyday business, many minor crises silently but consistently do their destructive work. Perhaps strict PR theorists may disagree with me and argue that these are not crises, but I call them crises or perhaps precursors to crises. Poor customer service, for example, may not immediately cause significant consequences. Still, when accumulated over a long period, it can erupt and create a crisis that is no less impactful than a fire.

The work of a PR specialist here is silent and invisible: other employees often lack time to notice it, or they don't consider it essential. A PR professional must constantly observe and identify even the most minor assumptions that can cause crises, clarify their importance to clients, and ensure that those assumptions do not persist.

Hotel Creating a Reputation

There is one hotel in my mind that successfully built its reputation over a long period. After visiting their hotels several times, I started to like them. Occasionally, while traveling, I would stay at different hotels within the same network in one country or another. Our friendship was solidified in France when, upon arriving with my family of five, this hotel combined two rooms into a spacious apartment with a separate entrance and provided our children with backpacks and coloring supplies. After that, I acquired a loyal customer card for this hotel network, and whenever I traveled, I would choose hotels from the same network. I primarily enjoyed their services, and each stay earned me loyalty points. I became a truly loyal supporter of this hotel network, and if I couldn't find a hotel of the desired service level from this network in any city, I would opt for a lower-tier hotel, as long as it was from the same network.

This love affair lasted for about two years. I believe I left a decent sum of money within that network because I stayed there, dined, organized business meetings, and occasionally chose this network for more significant events. In my mind, a flawless reputation for this hotel was formed, which influenced many of my choices. No one directly sold me anything; the reputation worked its magic silently in the background.

And here's what happened one evening. I arrived at one of the hotels I already knew well. It was so familiar that I knew many of the employees by name and, I believe, recognized all of them by face. They knew me too. I arrived pretty late in the evening, and as often happens, I realized upon entering the room that I didn't have any toothpaste. I went down to the reception and asked for a toothpaste kit. After paying one euro, I received it and returned to my room. However, as I started brushing my teeth, I realized that the toothpaste was old or improperly stored, or maybe something else had happened because I couldn't squeeze it out of the tube. I was slightly annoyed, but not enough to make a significant fuss about it, so I went down to the reception again. In a very calm and natural manner, I mentioned that I would still like toothpaste that I could use. The hotel staff member told me that toothpaste was supplied to the hotel by some company, and he couldn't do anything about it. Since it was late, it was evident that the staff member was eager to get rid of me as quickly as possible and go to sleep. So, I asked if there was a 24-hour store nearby to buy toothpaste. He didn't know that either.

I took out my phone, found a store, bought toothpaste, and returned to my room. However, as I walked to the store, I felt the love had ended. I wasn't angry; I didn't demand anything; I realized I didn't want to return here anymore, and I didn't. I have not stayed at hotels from that network ever since. I wouldn't say that I was somehow offended or angry. I quietly, maybe even without fully understanding it myself, started avoiding that brand.

To this day, I can't decide whether incredibly improbable coincidences happen in life or if nothing is truly random. I think it's the same here. However, the next day I was supposed to travel to another city and then give a lecture on modern communication to the directors and employees of tourism information centers from across the country, who had gathered for their annual conference. Did I refrain from mentioning anything about my experience to them? No, I didn't hold back. And not because I wanted to criticize the hotel I didn't like. This example was a crucial detail missing from my lecture, demonstrating the importance of reputation. So why should I have missed the opportunity to use it? I revealed the hotel network's brand to the tourism information center employees. Here, I'll refrain from mentioning it because if, by chance, this book becomes popular, I believe the hotel network would pay a high price for it. Let's assume they have already paid it.

Here, this example is particularly relevant. Warren Buffett said that reputation is built over decades but can be lost quickly. Is the gradual loss of reputation through such means a crisis? I believe it is the prelude to a crisis.

This example shows that nobody sells anything to anyone; reputation works its magic silently in the background, either attracting or repelling.

Efficiency:

What is the effectiveness of monitoring and crisis prevention? The answer is obvious: either the absence of crises or well-managed crises. How can this be quantitatively measured? It is likely possible, but the result would still be 0. Zero crises. Perhaps we can measure how many assumptions capable of causing crises are found. However, the most crucial aspect is not the reports but rather the fact that such work is taking place. And it should be ongoing. The best criterion of effectiveness for the client should be their peace of mind and the knowledge that a professional is working in this field.

All individuals who care about their reputation must understand that the more robust their reputation is, the more opportunities they will have to survive a crisis and come out of it with minimal losses. Therefore, it is worth investing in continuous PR activities and not expecting immediate results.

The value created by PR specialists lies in understanding the expectations of clients and partners, maintaining constant communication with them, monitoring and identifying crises, and providing timely alerts to clients.

The client and PR specialist must communicate constantly, and the latter should be involved in all decision-making processes to monitor, evaluate, and compare the information with their knowledge. In doing so, there is a high likelihood that many crises can be prevented from developing. Clients need to understand that while the continuous presence of a PR specialist may not necessarily provide immediate relief and comes at a cost, being relatively more comfortable during a crisis and the costs saved by timely reputation management are valuable assets that do not require further justification.

One of the best alternatives to formal reports is continuous communication between the client and the PR specialist. Each PR specialist must secure their place in board meetings and employee briefings and allocate specific time for direct communication with the client.

Clients who understand the essence of PR activities will always find time in their schedule for such interactions.

Indeed, such communication should not be limited to mere conversations and should have specific formal frameworks. The PR specialist should define their indicators of effectiveness, which do not necessarily have to be quantitative.

A PR specialist, for example, can strive to initiate a dialogue with the community, government institutions, and other influential groups. The dialogue and its progression can be considered a result in and of itself if that is the intended goal. During conversations with the client, it is possible to show the client how the dialogue unfolds, what was discussed during meetings, and the topics communicated through social media.

Suppose a PR specialist actively participates in company meetings and engages in conversations with clients, presenting their work in such a way by providing explanations and directly answering various questions. In that case, there is a high likelihood that questions such as "Is the PR specialist working?" and "Are they doing their job correctly?" will not arise due to the benefits generated by their activities.

PR should serve as a connecting link between the company and the external world and between the company's executives and its employees. The PR specialist should present their work not by focusing on measuring durations or quantities but by engaging in communication and doing what they excel at. They should continuously and directly showcase their activities, not solely through reports but by actively participating in various processes taking place within the company.

One could even suggest a rule that the success of a PR specialist, in the eyes of the company's employees, directly depends on their ability to understand every process happening within the company and their skill in finding the appropriate form of communication for those processes.

When PR activities are well integrated, and there is a general understanding within the company of each function's role, everything falls into place.

It is crucial to emphasize that not only should the client know what activities the PR specialist engages in, but the PR specialist should also have a substantial understanding (rather than just surface-level knowledge) of every detail of the company's operations. It is essential to have an in-depth knowledge of ongoing processes and constantly deepen and update one's knowledge. Such knowledge includes:

- Regular communication with company specialists.
- Keeping up with market news.
- Participating in seminars and conferences.

These and many other knowledge-expanding measures contribute to the professionalism and influence of the PR specialist. Furthermore, they are beneficial for the specialist and the company since the PR specialist shares the acquired knowledge with the company's staff.

For those who have already experienced crises, these words should not be unfamiliar, and the cost of reputation is entirely clear. For those who have not experienced or experienced only minor crises, it is worth listening to and reconsidering their attitude towards reputation. While it is said that we learn from our mistakes, the least painful and most effective way is to learn from the mistakes of others.

Third benefit: assistance to sales

> The two words "information" and "communication" are often used interchangeably, but they signify quite different things. Information is giving out; communication is getting through.
>
> Sydney J. Harris – journalist.

This profession cannot help sell a bad product. However, it can help build relationships. Relationships create reputation, and reputation helps with sales.

It is clear how to measure the effectiveness of an advertising campaign: in the short term, the campaign is implemented, and sales either increase or do not. However, relationships are much more complex and nuanced than an advertising campaign.

During their lectures, students, who are future PR specialists, often encounter the question of what the goal of a PR strategy is when creating it for an imaginary organization. Most immediately respond by saying the goal is to increase sales. However, increasing sales cannot be the sole goal of a PR strategy because increasing sales is the overall business objective, which depends on various factors such as product quality, novelty, the work of salespeople, market conditions, demand, the supplier network, and many other factors. A significant part of increasing sales is attributed to a successful marketing strategy.

I often find PR industry awards puzzling, where participants are awarded for . . . increasing sales. In my opinion, PR activities, by their nature, are not well aligned with words like "campaign", "promotion", "sales", or "awards". These terms belong more to the field of marketing.

If someone asks you to create a PR campaign to increase sales, I suggest reconsidering that approach. If PR activities aim solely to increase sales, it will likely undermine the building of relationships in almost all cases rather than fostering them.

The CIPR emphasizes[13] that public relations is an inherent aspect of communication, occurring whenever individuals engage with others. Without proactive management, these interactions can lead to positive or negative relationships. However, by effectively employing PR strategies, organizations can consistently nurture strong relationships and uphold a favorable reputation across all circumstances.

Interestingly, investing in PR becomes particularly crucial during challenging economic periods, when organizations face difficulties and contemplate cost-cutting measures. Customer, supplier, employee, and regulatory decisions regarding engagement with an organization are heavily influenced by its reputation, especially compared to competitors. PR is pivotal in shaping and differentiating this reputation, offering organizations a competitive advantage.

In times of economic downturn, when consumer spending becomes more selective, investing in robust communication strategies becomes essential.

While prosperity may allow for more flexible spending, tighter financial conditions necessitate strategic communication efforts to maintain market share and stand out amidst competition. Thus, the argument for increased, rather than reduced, investment in communication during downturns is compelling, ensuring organizations can effectively navigate challenging economic landscapes and maintain their competitive edge.

In Dale Carnegie's book *How to win friends and influence people*[14], he presents an example of how he argued with a hotel manager about how it was his choice whether to receive less for renting a room that was used for lectures but attracted an intellectual audience that would associate the hotel with the venue and attract a specific type of clientele over time, or to rent the same room for weddings, receiving more in the short term but gaining a reputation as a place for such festivities in the long run.

Having accumulated significant financial resources, a well-known entrepreneur decided to invest a portion of them in real estate and create a separate recreational town. The whole project was established on a 200-hectare plot with millions of dollars invested. The creation looked truly impressive. One day, I decided to visit there. The weather was nice, so I took my family, and we decided to spend a day or two there. Everything seemed like a fairy tale: well-built cottages, a private lake, tranquillity, and peace, almost like paradise. That's how it seemed until we fell asleep. During the night, we were awakened by the songs and curses of drunken wedding guests. Looking out the window, I realized we were right in the center of a group of recently returned, rowdy men in revealing sports attire who were essentially letting loose and doing whatever they pleased.

The children started crying, and we began calling the town administration because we felt genuinely unsafe and lacked comfort. It all ended with us being escorted out of the town by a police patrol. The town apologized to us, offering my wife and me a complimentary visit to the massage parlor. It's probably needless to say that we did not visit the massage parlor. We never visited again and would not recommend anyone to do so.

Why did this happen? Because the entrepreneur, who had successfully accumulated his initial capital and invested it in tangible assets, forgot about the intangible aspects. He forgot about reputation. Maybe he didn't forget. Maybe he just thought that if he invested a lot of money in tangible assets, reputation would automatically be built, salespeople would sell, and so on. Unfortunately, the mechanism of reputation works a bit differently. First comes ACTION, which was done, and then comes TONGUE and STYLE. But that aspect was forgotten. It was followed by a marketing and sales process, which did not create a reputation. Therefore, the sales managers rented out the property based on price and demand but not based on reputation. They ended up having a family and a loud wedding nearby. If a deliberate reputation for peaceful and luxurious family leisure had been created, the mafia wedding attendees wouldn't have shown up. If a deliberate reputation for wedding venues had been created, the family wouldn't have shown up either. However, reputation would have helped attract more families or more weddings. Neglecting its reputation, the recreational town remains half-empty to this day.

PR does not directly sell but dramatically assists sales and strongly influences the outcome and choice. The sales process will always be more successful when the seller has an understandable reputation. The reputation must be "understandable", as "good" may not suit every sales process. The buyer must clearly understand the seller's reputation, and the sales process proceeds much more smoothly. Sometimes, even when buying illegal or counterfeit products, the buyer trusts the seller they know as reliable. When purchasing a clear and branded item, reputation works without any doubts because the brand itself has a reputation. We can also recall those times in my country when the sellers and buyers of used cars became popular. I remember well the 1990s when buyers, even when purchasing 10- or 15-year-old cars for a few thousand dollars or even hundreds, sought connections among reliable sellers who were supposed to ensure the old wreck would be reliable.

In principle, labeling a reputation as "good" or "bad" is not entirely accurate because what may be considered good for one person can be entirely different for another. For example, the reputation of an expensive iPhone may be seen as good to someone who has a lot of money because they can afford to buy it. On the other hand, for someone with less money, the same iPhone's reputation may be seen as bad because it is expensive, and a significantly cheaper model from another manufacturer may offer the same or even broader features. Therefore, it is more meaningful to talk about an understandable reputation, where the seller's reputation aligns with the buyer's values. It signifies that the seller is reliable, allowing them to sell their products at a higher price.

Reputation assists with sales in the long run by creating a positive environment. Therefore, those sellers who do not actively cultivate their reputation still have one, but it forms spontaneously. I won't claim that this is always a negative outcome, but there is a significant risk that something undesirable may spontaneously develop in the seller's reputation. On the other hand, this risk is significantly lower for those who intentionally build their reputation.

Among sellers who offer very similar products, there will always be one who can provide additional knowledge and know-how about the product's unique features, which the customer may not even be aware of.

As we move closer to businesses that deal with fast-moving, less critical, or large-scale products, reputation plays a minor role. Emotions, transience, quick purchases, visuals, packaging, discounts, and other marketing tricks take precedence in this context. While it cannot be claimed that reputation is entirely irrelevant here, people rarely consider a company's reputation when buying chewing gum or soft drinks. That is, of course, until an incident occurs, such as a choking hazard with the gum or the revelation that the soft drinks contain more sugar than stated on the label or are allowed to be sold on the market.

If we were to try to figure out everything ourselves, it would be highly irrational, and we would be reinventing the wheel. Therefore, we form our opinions about many things and phenomena based on the opinions of opinion leaders. For instance, if we are not knowledgeable about the forest, we sometimes rely on the opinions of foresters when we want to go there or broaden our perspective. In the financial sector or economics, we listen to those individuals for whom it is their daily bread and then make decisions. We expect that these individuals present us with complex matters in a language we understand. If we were to try to figure out everything ourselves, it would be very time-consuming. Therefore, the reputation of opinion leaders is essential. And since opinion leaders today are not only traditional leaders but also media outlets, reputation is crucial to them. People trust reliable individuals and make purchases.

Even Gates Needs Reputation

In my experience, I have encountered a client who offered security equipment (gates) to stores. The gate signaled when someone tried to pass through without paying for the merchandise. Sometimes, of course, they also triggered when a person who had paid wanted to pass through.

So my client sold these gates and created an entire system to combat theft, gathering statistics and a wealth of information about thieves' habits. However, when the client wanted to sell such equipment, buyers were initially unaware of all those value-added things. They would first find the gates, see their price, and not learn about the additional value until they met with the gate seller, who could explain it. However, they might not even encounter the seller because, in the initial stage, it was decided that plenty of gates were already available at a significantly lower price.

Together with the client, we addressed how to communicate to the buyers, even before they started choosing from all the available products on the market, that our product was more than just gates. We discussed how to convey to potential buyers that we had more knowledge and expertise.

We decided that the client should start systematically building their expert reputation, providing knowledge to the market and indirectly to potential buyers, to convey that this company knew everything about thefts and ways to prevent them.

While analyzing the materials provided by the client, we noticed that they conducted annual global research about retail thefts. It examined and revealed theft trends worldwide and in each country. We found this research to be an ideal tool to start building the desired reputation. From the study, we learned that there is an undeniable global trend: if a product sells well, it is also frequently stolen. In other words, a popular product is not only favored by buyers but also by thieves. The latter often steal such items precisely because they are in high demand for resale.

We presented this information to the media by organizing a press conference. Since negative information is desirable to the media, we did not doubt that the word "theft" would be well-received. To emphasize the severity, we added the word "war" to theft as part of our overall strategy for this client, as we concluded that what retailers face in stores is nothing less than a "battle". Retailers engage in a daily battle against theft. It sounded compelling!

We had only to choose the date for the press conference. Following the rule "good sales mean good stealing", we decided that the most relevant time for such information would be Christmas, as December is known as the traders' golden month. I've heard that some stores make up to a quarter of their annual turnover during the Christmas season. For the press conference, we came up with the title "Wars in the Stores".

We have been organizing these press conferences for five consecutive years. The results are always the same – a frenzy. All national television stations, radio stations, newspapers, and even emerging online portals would come to us. In short, we had the entire media at these press conferences. Furthermore, after the first press conference, representatives from two major retail chains approached us and requested to share the data we had.

Our client did not directly sell anything after this press conference. However, we were not in the business of selling products. This action aimed to establish an expert reputation for our client, to show that they knew more than other gate sellers and that their gates were not just gates – they were created by analyzing thieves' habits and trends and comparing different countries. Existing and potential customers of this company learned that by engaging with it, they would receive much more than just gates – they would gain knowledge and expertise that is difficult to quantify but valuable.

So with this action, we didn't make direct sales, but we set our client apart from the crowd of other sellers and created a background for them to carry out their sales activities successfully. And indeed, they continued to do so successfully. Through interactions with the client, it became clear that this reputation brought many benefits – their salespeople became instantly recognizable, and they no longer had to introduce themselves or prove why their product was better and more expensive than others. The client told us that these actions gave them a significant competitive advantage they couldn't have achieved through marketing alone. The client also mentioned that buyers started contacting them much more frequently, not just for the gates themselves but also for consultations.

This example perfectly reflects the essence of PR activities. PR creates a background, a favorable atmosphere, and opinion, in short – relationships. Relationships themselves do not make sales, but relationships are the foundation of successful long-term sales.

There can be many examples like these. Lawyers, doctors, hairdressers, fashion experts, plumbers – anyone can consistently earn more if they have built a proper reputation. Lawyers work with the same laws and handle the same cases, doctors perform the same surgeries, hairdressers create the same hairstyles, fashion experts design the same clothes, and plumbers fix the same pipes. Still, those who have a better reputation receive higher fees. Those who are not only professionals but also manage to become experts in their field earn even more.

Efficiency:

Reputation itself does not make sales, but it assists salespeople. Since sales are about results, they are more tangible. Summarizing the assistance to sales, I have identified three criteria of effectiveness:

1. Interest from the desired market segment in the company's products, invitations to competitions, discussions, or surveys for the salespeople.
2. The ability to sell products or services at a higher price than the average market price.
3. Attracting the desired, not just any, customer base.

However, as a conclusion to this section, I would like to tell salespeople that all three criteria are achievable only in the long term. If quick results are expected, the term "PR" should be forgotten.

Fourth benefit: easy employee selection

> Success and profitability are outcomes of focusing on customers and employees, not objectives.
>
> Jack Ma – business magnate, investor, and philanthropist.

With PR association members, we visited various organizations and interacted with colleagues. Once, I received an invitation to visit a prison. The main thought that crossed my mind was: "What does a prison need PR for?" Now, the answer is evident to me, but until then, I had never considered that prisons required PR. Just like any other organization, PR is essential for prisons too.

During the meeting, the prison warden suggested that we consider whether attracting employees to work in prison is easy. Soon, he answered the question himself: it's tough. Why? Because of the reputation the institution holds. Prisons require specialists, although many assume that only inmates and their supervisors work there. Prisons need cooks, laundry workers, psychologists, lawyers, electricians, and many other types of specialists. Do you think a skilled electrician dreams of working in a prison? No.

So, even though you usually have to deal with somewhat simpler institutions than a prison in everyday life, all of them are nothing without employees. The amount you'll have to pay to attract good, maybe even the best specialists, directly depends on the organization's reputation. The efficiency of the organization's operations, and if it's a company, its profit, will depend on the kind of specialists you attract.

By acting, speaking, and creating the organization's style, its leader and other representatives constantly shape its reputation. People talk about it and exchange information. And if this is done systematically, the organization will continuously attract people who want to work there.

Efficiency:

Well, in this case, the effectiveness of PR activities directly depends on the number of people eager to join your organization. Mostly, this is a result of the organization's reputation.

Fifth benefit: employees' sense of pride

> Train people well enough so they can leave, treat them well enough so they don't want to.
>
> Richard Branson – business magnate, investor, author, and philanthropist.

The organization's reputation affects its employees and their motivation. Once, while talking with company employees publicly accused of untrue things, I heard this thought: "They think of us as a black box that pollutes, but no one understands that we work in it, and we create great things, providing benefits to society."

I picked up words from that conversation about a "black box" and a transparent company. The reputation of a black box, which any company can become, will naturally form if you do nothing about your reputation and smoke constantly rises from your building. People, not knowing what is happening inside, will quickly create many legends. Legends will emerge if your "box" is located near residential areas. Legends will be born, grow, sprout wings, and they will fly, carrying the reputation of the black box into society. Society will express dissatisfaction which will come back to your employees through their family members and various media channels. This dissatisfaction will decrease employees' motivation; they won't want to be the bad guys everyone dislikes.

So, reputation directly affects the organization's members, identity, and motivation. Therefore, we automatically raise employee motivation and self-esteem by taking care of it. Everyone wants to work in a clean, modern company and be respected and recognized.

Efficiency:

Here is another criterion for effectiveness – employee satisfaction with their current job. Often, various surveys are conducted in companies on these matters, so it is worth including several questions about what employees think about their employer and the employer's reputation beyond the company's boundaries.

Sixth benefit: changing stereotypes (traditions, opinions)

> Wikipedia was a big help for science, especially science communication, and it shows no sign of diminishing in importance.
>
> Aubrey de Grey – author and biomedical gerontologist.

Various stereotypes influence various communities, societies, or groups of people, sometimes referred to as beautiful traditions. Sometimes those traditions are beautiful and harmless, while others strongly hinder progress, investment, and the introduction of new products and services.

Stereotypes can vary widely, from everyday and domestic ones like "what's tasty and what's not" to complex social and political ones, such as gay marriage or women being allowed to drive cars.

In the presence of stereotypes, new product sales activities can be either highly ineffective or impossible. It may lead to hindered investments and, as a result, hinder progress in specific areas. Sometimes stereotypes even undermine vital areas such as organ transplantation because a society believes such practices contradict certain church teachings. Once, we had to address such an issue with an organization that aims to ensure potential donors reach the recipients eagerly waiting for organ transplants.

PR can change stereotypes by initiating a dialogue, which is essential in such cases. PR specialists know how to pique the public's interest in various topics. This curiosity leads to discussions, and discussions lead to understanding, which ultimately results in decision-making.

Many professionals in their respective fields, especially engineers, manufacturers, and others in areas that require deep expertise and education, often do not realize that only a few people know what they know. Therefore, they are often surprised when the public perceives their actions differently from what they expect. At first, they may be stunned, then they try to explain, and eventually, they often become angry and retreat to a "no comment" room. Often, such isolation and strict adherence to rules causes many problems for businesses, sometimes leading to their demise, because if a business does not communicate, rumors flourish in society. These rumors reach politicians, and the latter want to win over the public to get elected. And politicians in power already have the authority to restrict the activities of organizations.

PR consultants must be involved in the early stages of project development to prevent such situations. They can identify prevailing societal stereotypes, interact directly with community members and media, and warn clients about moods and beliefs while creating programs to change them. Engaging PR specialists can avoid many tensions, obstacles, investigations, and similar restrictive factors.

People are inclined to listen, learn, discover, and benefit. PR professionals can identify these aspects and ensure that an informal agreement is "signed" between the organization and the community: the organization receives the green light to operate, and the community knows that the organization's activities benefit them.

In a discussion among colleagues, we once debated the most important result of PR work when it comes to working with communities. The discussion revolved around plans, messages, transparency, and other crucial aspects. However, in the end, we unanimously agreed that the most critical result is the creation of trust. We can have excellent technologies, messages, and presentations, but if we don't know how to build trust, all other things become less important, and we will achieve only minimal results.

Efficiency:

Changing stereotypes and traditions is crucial for attracting investments, expanding, and introducing new products. In the case of non-business entities, it also helps to gain more followers and supporters. PR plays a vital role in accomplishing this. The best evidence of the effectiveness of such actions is changes in stereotypes, more accurate questions, fewer emotions, more discussions, requests to answer questions, and fewer contradictions. These are intangible aspects, although we can conduct public opinion surveys, monitor the reactions we receive on social media, analyze the questions asked, and compare them with other companies operating nearby.

Seventh benefit: the only available capital for opinion leader

> You can have brilliant ideas, but if you can't get them across, your ideas won't get you anywhere.
>
> Lee Iacocca – automobile executive.

The reputational capital of "opinion leaders" is their only capital. Opinion leaders (among them politicians and commentators) are directly worth as much as their reputation is worth. In the case of business, if companies' products and services are often talked about, then for an opinion leader, their products and services are indeed their reputation. For professions based on speaking, persuasion, and communication, reputation is the primary indicator of their value. In the case of politicians, this value manifests through recognition among other politicians and popularity among voters; in the case of other opinion leaders, this reputation is a direct monetary measure of their value.

The more renowned and better-reputed an expert is, the higher their remuneration and the less frequently negotiations are held with them.

Once a colleague from an association told me about how she had devised the idea to organize a meeting with a well-known political opinion leader for her organization's members. This individual wasn't a politician, but they commented on political events, and their opinion carried weight.

At that time, the leader was visiting the country and planning to attend a conference. She directly contacted him, as she had obtained his contact details through one of the association's members, and asked if he would be interested in having dinner with her association's members. He gladly agreed. My colleague was thrilled and informed everyone there would be an opportunity to have dinner with such a famous person. She said she was excited throughout the day until an unexpected and unsettling thought crossed her mind in the evening: what if they had to pay for the person's presence at this dinner? She began to contemplate whether an honorarium might be required, so she called the office of the political expert and posed this question to his administrator. And she immediately heard the response: dinner with the professor costs €6,000.

What do you think? Did my colleague dare to negotiate? No. She still decided that it would be better to apologize to the association members for her mistake and admit her incompetence to all of her employers rather than negotiate with this celebrity. And that's what she did – she apologized and asked if the association members would be willing to cover this amount and save her. The dinner took place, the money was paid, and no one even attempted to discuss it. That's how reputation worked its magic.

Opinion leaders can express themselves not necessarily in one field; in the future, the number of multifunctional opinion leaders will only increase. However, they should not forget that their activity in one area influences the activity and reputation in another. For example, a person who actively speaks against vaccines, even though all scientific research indicates that vaccines are the way to prevent epidemics (although we also know this from opinion leaders, just from different ones), will seem suspicious to me when they talk about finances. However, finances are the main area from which they earn a living. So their reputation, which will form when they talk about vaccines, will influence me in evaluating them as a financial specialist.

Efficiency:

In this case, effectiveness is measured very easily. Opinion leaders don't directly create any product whose sales we can count. They develop ideas, opinions, politics, and doctrines, which people either "buy" or not. This buying process is indirect through popularity, event invitations, and voting. However, we can certainly decide whether reputation management and PR activity are beneficial.

Eighth benefit: inexpensive

> Using yourself to get out and talk about it is a lot cheaper and more effective than a lot of advertising. In fact, if you do it correctly, it can beat advertising hands down and save tens of millions of dollars.
>
> Richard Branson – business magnate, investor, author, and philanthropist.

The golden age of advertising has come to an end. It ended because a) the market became saturated with advertising, and it became ineffective, unnoticed, it simply became too much; and b) many new dialogue-based methods of obtaining information emerged, and society transitioned into the "Network" PR stage, where recommendations are much more important than any other one-sided form of communication.

It might sound bold, but today it's fundamentally impossible to create a brand using advertising alone. These days, new brands seem to appear in our minds somehow. We could precisely say how in the past, but nowadays, it's challenging. Why is that? Because consumer choice has become complex, and it no longer suffices to call it simply a trend. Trends are disappearing alongside advertising and being replaced by more lasting aspects such as style and PR. An informed society that shares knowledge wants to know a lot before making a purchase: how a product is made, where it's made, the conditions of production, its ingredients, and much more. Advertising can't convey all of that.

The ability to convey that lies only in continuous communication and dialogue. And that already falls under the realm of PR.

In the 20th century, the marriage of advertising and media accustomed us to the idea that if you want a lot of visibility, you need a lot of money: you must buy advertising space and time. Traditional media set the price of publicity. The principle that someone aptly named "pay & play" was in action. If you want to play, act, or show up – pay.

However, the "Network" has brought about changes. Before the emergence of social media, it was unimaginable that one could reach an audience more significant than a few hundred people without paying money to a media outlet. But this situation has changed. Today, active and charismatic leaders, politicians, and public figures quickly gather millions of readers, viewers, or listeners. They can have those audiences almost daily if they remain attractive for a long time. Most importantly, they achieve this without paying the media a single cent.

Of course, creating good content comes at a cost – it requires a team, ongoing care, and effort. However, all of that was necessary before as well, but a mountain of money was also needed to spread that content. Today, the "play & play" principle created by Mark Zuckerberg and others allows anyone to become famous.

New brands are being created without advertising. They are formed through the word-of-mouth principle, which spreads faster and more effectively than even the most efficient advertising. People trust company leaders, follow them, listen to what they say, and willingly share information within their circles. These circles have their opinion leaders, who are trusted; this way, news spreads completely independently from paying information carriers.

Comparing PR to advertising, it is indeed less expensive. Less expensive doesn't mean free, but the former main component of its cost – payment to media outlets – has been eliminated from the information distribution chain. PR has continuously operated on the "play & play" principle; it never knew the people from the advertising departments of the media and never interacted with them because it had nothing to offer them. However, PR specialists had many journalists and editors on their phones with whom they consistently communicated. As the world transitioned to the "Network" stage, those names and skills didn't disappear; quite the opposite – the list expanded significantly. Most importantly, the circle of media outlets grew, working on the "play & play" principle.

Efficiency:

The effectiveness of these benefits is evident – all the publicity achieved through reputation-building is cost-free. Every public statement, conference announcement, and social media discussion comes at no cost. Any result, even the slightest, achieved through PR methods is much more effective than a similar result achieved through advertising.

Marketing professionals devise a very peculiar method to measure the results of PR work regarding advertising equivalence. For those unfamiliar with it, this involves taking an article published, for instance, in a magazine, measuring its space, and calculating how much such an article would cost if advertising money were paid for it. Then, these funds are compared to the expenses of PR activities. I understand some marketing professionals' desire to view the world through an advertising lens, but this method fundamentally lacks logic for two reasons.

Most often, an article in a magazine or a television interview appears not because the interviewee needed it but because the media outlet believed it would interest its readers or viewers. The fact that such material appeared in media indicates its significance, much greater than that of an advertising text or video of the same space. The latter might only be attractive to its creator. In many cases, no amount of advertising is as valuable regarding reputation as a substantial interview with a professional journalist.

Advertising and articles or reports are indeed incomparable entities. In the case of advertising, the content appears because the content provider desires it, while in the case of an article, it arises because the media outlet's editorial team chooses it and, ultimately, so does the reader.

An article or report can exist without direct efforts because the interviewee is a fascinating speaker or a personality contributing to innovation. Comparing advertising space to editorial content is illogical and inaccurate: all achieved publicity is cost-free because there's no need to pay a media outlet for it.

Ninth benefit: others will do it for you if you don't

> If you don't make a conscious choice . . . someone else will decide for you. It may be your boss, a family member, an advertiser, a collective social influence, or someone or something else, but it won't be something of your deliberate choosing.
>
> Steve Pavlina – self-help author, motivational speaker, and entrepreneur.

The most universal and widespread PR rule is "first come, first served". Therefore, when asked when it's best to start speaking or acting, I usually respond: "immediately".

Of course, it's a somewhat simplified view of reality: there are many situations when it's worth waiting, not rushing, and carefully considering things. However, the rule still holds – if we want to be heard, we must speak first. Because those who speak first set the rules, introduce innovations, and capture attention, while others are left with only repeating or adding to what has already been said.

If you have thoughts, know they are correct, well-founded, and backed by data – speak up. Because if you don't speak, others definitely will. We must constantly monitor our information space, observe which topics are prevailing when new ones emerge, and when events happen, and as soon as we have something to say – we must speak, discuss, present material, show openness, and substantiate our opinion with facts and figures.

Not too long ago, when the "Network" was taking its first steps, many clients looked at the new phenomenon of social media quite skeptically. Their arguments often centered around the idea that it wasn't their target audience there, that they were too important to engage in those childish games, and that the platform wasn't suitable for them. However, their opinions quickly changed when you showed them that there was already a wealth of information about them and their products on social media. The only difference was that the source of this information wasn't them; it was entirely unfamiliar people who, sometimes unfortunately, had many thoughts about the company and its product.

When thinking about the benefits of reputation, it's essential not to forget that reputation is not created. It forms on its own. And all we can do is influence its development in one direction or another. However, if we don't take

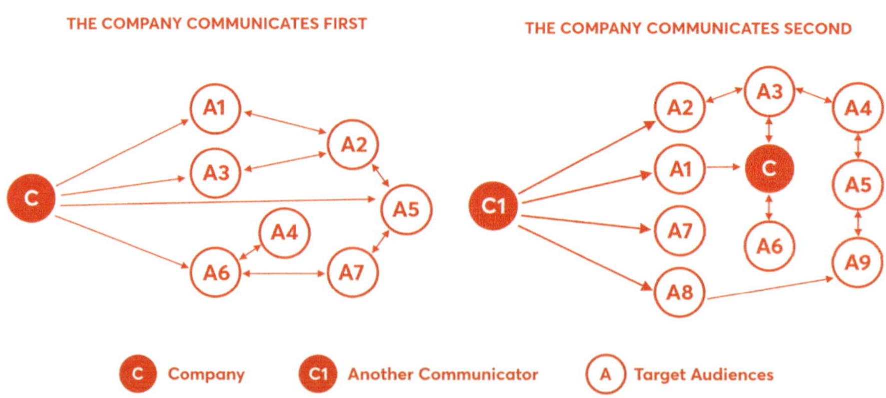

Figure 1.11 Differences between the first and second shots.

Figure by the author.

action, others will eagerly do so. Perhaps not intentionally, but they will still shape it. As we've discussed before, a part of our reputation depends on the opinions of those around us.

My colleague argues that it doesn't mean someone else isn't doing it if we don't manage our informational space. There's always someone active in the informative area. Informational space cannot tolerate emptiness.

Efficiency:

Taking care of one's reputation is valuable, as we steer the development of reputation in the desired direction:

- Ensuring the quality of our activities.
- Creating exciting and informative content about ourselves.
- Thus influencing the environment's opinion of us.

By building a reputation, we ensure that our informational space is not empty, and instead of rumors, it contains information created by us that corresponds to the truth.

To accurately measure the benefit of this action, it would be necessary to compare it to the situation that would arise if we didn't do it. This comparison can only be done theoretically. In practice, it should be understood that filling the informational space with authentic and reliable information, thus avoiding rumors and falsehoods, is inherently beneficial and eliminates many barriers that could arise otherwise.

Tenth benefit: connections

> There is a world of communication which is not dependent on words.
>
> Mary Martin – actress, singer, and Broadway star.

Conflicts arise on their own, while good relationships need to be built. Bad news emerges by itself and travels at the speed of light, while for good news – effort is necessary. It's always easy to complain, but it's much harder to admit that problems fundamentally don't exist and that they only exist in our minds. Destruction is much easier than construction. I believe you've heard these phrases more than once. However, why do negative things seem to happen independently, while positives require effort?

The answer here is simple: a person who creates is active and intelligent, while a person who destroys is lazy and foolish. Being lazy and unintelligent requires no effort, whereas to act and be clever, one must make an effort.

Reputation is creativity. Creativity is about what you do, what you speak, and how you appear. By taking care of our reputation, we constantly create, and the result of that creativity is the connections formed between people. Therefore, when we care about our own, our organization's, and our country's reputation, we constantly create relationships. These connections become the foundation for further creativity, bringing people closer together and empowering them to make together and collectively rejoice in the results of creativity.

My Friend Is Creating Reputation

My good friend and partner is an excellent reputation-building professional and PR consultant. However, most importantly, he is warm, open, and heartfelt. His consulting agency is among the most successful and significant in the country and the region. The agency's client list is impressive, and he is a well-known figure in his country, Estonia.

Here, I would like to tell you about my friend's hobby. Honestly, I still don't quite understand whether it's a hobby, a way of life, or a job. However, what he does is undoubtedly powerful and consistent reputation-building work. In my opinion, he has dedicated all his free time, and perhaps even money, to this activity. I'm not in the habit of prying into others' pockets, so I won't delve into the financial aspect of this matter, especially since I'm unaware of it.

However, I am well aware of the idea that my colleague calls "People's Diplomacy". I am convinced that he is passionate about this activity and idea primarily because he enjoys it, is that kind of person, and deeply needs it. Yet, simultaneously, it is a powerful, genuine, unifying, and excellent idea for building the country's reputation. Through the efforts of one individual, it creates an honest, natural, and unpretentious reputation for the country. This activity is an example of a single person, fueled by love for their country, doing what no government could do for a lot of money by hiring the most brilliant consultants. Of course, in the process, a personal reputation is also naturally being built. Let's not forget that reputation is, first and foremost, about relationships.

So, the essence of "People's Diplomacy" is quite simple – to seek things that unite nations rather than divide them and to support those aspects. My colleague is well acquainted with many entrepreneurs in his country and knows they have various interests in countries where he plans to carry out "People's Diplomacy" activities. These countries were once part of a united entity – the Soviet Union. Now they are close neighbours, but their political relations are often tense. This hampers business and people's interactions. It hampers culture as well. That's why the idea was born – to seek unifying rather than dividing elements between countries.

The first year of "People's Diplomacy" began with an event called "Tallinn Goes to Odessa". It was a week-long event where my colleague and his country's entrepreneurs and cultural figures flew to Odessa in Ukraine to bond, read works, hold exhibitions, make contacts, and have a good time. This was done informally, naturally, just as one would visit friends. Then there were "events" over the years – a big table set up on the main street of Odessa,

Odessa going to Tallinn, 1,000 Estonians travelling to St. Petersburg, a monument to the first democratic President of Russia, Boris Yeltsin, being erected in Tallinn, Tallinn travelling to Yerevan in Armenia, a literary flash mob taking place in Odessa where works by Odessa authors were read in various languages. All of this happened and is happening joyfully, playfully, and informally. The result – the best possible reputation for Estonia and my colleague in Armenia and Ukraine. I still don't understand if he's playing or consciously aiming for this. It seems to me that he is acting unconsciously, naturally. However, wherever this happens, friends emerge, stories arise, books are born, interviews occur, and connections and relationships are formed. And that is the foundation of reputation.

People remember that feeling, that joy, those meetings, glances, friendships, acquaintances. It's evident that nobody is selling anything to anyone, yet as a result of all these actions, a reputation is created, a foundation is built, a background is formed, and relationships are established, which anyone can use. Within the context of this reputation, within the backdrop of these relationships, contacts are made, contracts are signed, doors are opened, and value is generated, which would otherwise be much harder to create or might not be created.

Let's add to this idea that every individual is a media outlet today. Let's add the social media profiles of each person who participated in this event, and we'll see the tremendous power it holds, the number of contacts and relationships that arise as a result of such activity, the cultural connections that form. Ultimately, this doesn't necessarily translate into business in a straightforward manner. Yet, this reputation established by my colleague creates a marvellous foundation for future relationships, among which business relationships can be included. That's the impact of reputation.

Efficiency:

It's complicated and meaningless to quantify all the benefits of reputation because it's impossible to count the value of conversations, relationships, atmosphere, and contacts. Only episodically can certain reputation benefits be grasped. It's the same with connections.

In front of me stands a person I've met in my professional journey, selling rather complex industrial solutions that are not easily understandable to the average person. He participates in nearly all the conferences related to the systems he sells. During these events, he tries to approach as many people as possible, engage in conversations, and hand them his business card. Later, he actively calls them, arranges meetings, and he likely manages to sell something. However, I have met more than one person who doesn't like him. Why? After all, the person is trying and doing everything according to the learned rules, just as the best sales practices recommended.

Rejection happens because this persistent salesman does everything mechanically and coldly; although his smile is vast, it is artificial. To him, all the people he meets are faceless and soulless clients. People sense this, and they dislike being treated that way. Therefore, they try to avoid him and communicate only as much as necessary. He doesn't create relationships; he probably even ruins them, though sometimes, often through sheer force, he manages to make a sale.

How much he could achieve if he understood the principles of reputation is difficult to say. However, his work could become easier, and by being so active, he would eventually build an excellent reputation that would soon start working for him. Following the path he's currently on, he will likely have to keep doing the same job until he becomes exhausted.

By creating connections, we employ reputation. Over time, efforts diminish, allowing for new projects or relaxation, while regular tasks can be left to reputation.

A managed reputation will always bring benefits. In general, if a person, no matter what position they hold, at least considers how their actions appear from the perspective of society, they are already on the right track. The path is long, requiring much learning, but no matter what level is reached, it will always be higher than the one where nothing is done for reputation.

That's why I'm a prominent skeptic of various reports in the PR field. Just as improved relationships in a family don't require any reports – it's understood that based on those good relationships, the giant mountains are moved – similarly, in the case of organizations, better relationships between them, their members, and society shouldn't be artificially formalized and reported on. Usually, it's just felt that the connections are good, and strong foundations are built upon them.

I am convinced that the primary condition for reaping the benefits of a genuine reputation is understanding what reputation is. When clients comprehend the significance of reputation, they will naturally understand how to discern whether its management is in capable hands. Reputation is a personal matter, and if a client believes it's being created improperly, no matter how renowned a PR professional is, they won't be able to convince the client otherwise.

Doubts about reputational benefits will not arise, or will at least be fewer, if the client adheres to the five rules of understanding reputational benefits.

Rules for Understanding the Benefits of Reputation

First rule: (know what you want and) CHOOSE

A client should first brand in their mind the reputation tasks and expectations. They should understand why they need reputation, what kind of assistance they would require to manage it, what jobs they want to entrust, how deeply they would like to involve that assistant in their circle, and what power they could grant them. Once they have answered these questions, they can make their choice.

Second rule: (discover the connection and) GET ACQUAINTED

Once the assistant, the PR professional, is chosen, the most crucial task is discovering the mutual connection. Here, a highly significant factor is the harmony of personalities. Not every PR professional is suitable for every client, and vice versa. Sometimes the most renowned representative of our profession can annoy the client and not match their preferences, and there's not much that can be done in such cases. Our job creates relationships, but first and foremost, these relationships must form between the client and the PR person. If they don't start there, no other relationships will either. If successful, the work in the future will be very smooth. Once again, I return to the analogy of family relationships: if relationships within a family are great, they will also be great externally.

Third rule: KNOW (what you aim for and how you will evaluate it)

The client and the consultant must agree on what they both aim for. They must establish the criteria and create their own rules. I have had a client for whom nothing was more valuable than when I would call him after completing one task or another, and we would discuss all the related details. He also liked to call and talk when he believed he had valuable information for me. I hadn't written a formal report for him, yet our relationship was excellent. The most important thing was that the client was convinced that the company's reputation was appropriately managed. I receiveed appropriate compensation, and the client got the services he needed.

Returning to each of the reputational benefits discussed after each section, I want to reiterate that these agreements with the client can be pretty diverse. Answers to all public inquiries and participation in various discussions, continuous environmental monitoring, identification of potential crises, changes in the customer circle, involving employees in conversations, listening to their opinions, shifts in public opinion – all of this and many other tasks are PR tasks that can be performed in the most creative ways acceptable to the client and consultant.

Fourth rule: PLAN (and follow the course of actions)

In some cases, it's possible and even advisable to define what is being aimed for, outline a SMART[15] plan, and discuss in advance how the PR specialist's activities will be evaluated. The plan helps to keep the project on track and recall the operation's primary goal.

While I'm not a person who loves dealing with plans or reports, I have to admit that sometimes, it's not so much for the client but for oneself that this is necessary. When working, it's not hard to stray into side paths and linger in insignificant courtyards for too long. A plan helps one to remember to return to the way that leads towards the primary goal.

For every client, whether large or small, and for the entire economy, both at micro and macro levels, there are growth years and downturns. These movements are normal and inevitable; studying economics can teach much about it. During crises, of course, many think about how to save. For one of my clients, a large international corporation, there also came a time when it needed to consider whether all functions were essential and all expenses were necessary. Each functional division of the corporation was asked to identify the least essential functions they performed, in their opinion, and the costs associated with them. Which process was the least necessary in the company's PR department? Yes, you probably guessed it – report writing. It turned out that many reports, once abundantly printed and filed away, were never actually opened. This function was the first to be abandoned.

However, despite the example I just provided, I believe that accountability is necessary for PR activities. The problem here is likely that in the realm of reporting, it's easy to slide into formalities, doing things just for the sake of doing them. That's not necessary. Reports and plans should take on the most individual, unexpected forms that best suit the client's needs. In times like these, when the COVID-19 virus was just recently raging around the world and efforts were being made to limit social contact in enclosed spaces, a report could become a weekly stroll in the park for both the client and the PR specialist, a video call, short messages, or any other form that suits both parties.

A concise plan, mutual understanding, discussion of results, and informality – in my experience, these are the forms of evaluating PR work that have proven to be most effective.

Fifth rule: SHARE (with the entire organization, with all stakeholders)

The benefits should be constantly discussed with members of the representing organization or, in the case of business, with employees. Again, this should be done with as little formality as possible, more individually. However, everyone should know what reputation is, that it is constantly taken care of, and what needs to be done not to act contrary to your organization and harm it.

Reputation is built over a long period, continuously. Similarly, the understanding of its benefits doesn't come immediately. A wise leader starts thinking about reputation from the first day of their leadership because there's no better day to begin thinking about reputation than today.

1.4. Let's Think About the Terms a Bit

> A different language is a different vision of life.
>
> Federico Fellini – film director and screenwriter.

I have no desire to burden you with various terms and their definitions in this book, but I would like to draw attention to one aspect related to PR terminology. In my opinion, PR and marketing terms are significantly confused. Even though they are essentially clear to those in the field, in everyday life, few people on the street could list the key differences between PR and advertising.

This confusion starts from the beginning of modern PR, and Edward Bernays, whose book *Propaganda* (pay attention to the title!) is considered the cornerstone of PR. This confusion continues to this day when, for example, politicians, not understanding the essence of communication sciences, use terms like PR, advertising, marketing, and propaganda chaotically, substituting one for another without giving it much thought. This confusion persists when representatives of the advertising business, seeing declining sales, change not the actual practices but try to provide a fresh appeal to old, ineffective sales methods using foreign terms. Or they come up with new terms only in name, but not in essence.

In PR activities and various other contexts, it's crucial to use the appropriate terms. Otherwise, we might encounter misunderstandings, not knowing what we're talking about and speaking in vague, imprecise terms, essentially spreading confusion. Unfortunately, just like the profession itself, its terminology is often used carelessly, and this does a lot of harm to the reputation of the profession.

It's also crucial to distinguish between terms defining new phenomena and pseudo-terms, merely new names for existing phenomena. In my opinion, pseudo-terms often arise when something old is difficult to sell, there's reluctance or inability to change practices, yet there's a desire to sell it anyway.

PR and marketing create fundamentally different products: the former builds reputation, while the latter constructs image. Reputation is built by making decisions based on it, whereas image is something we buy. Reputation is a long-term product cultivated over decades, while an image might be forgotten in the following years once the advertising campaign has ended. Consider a large bakery producing various bread products: dark and white bread, baguettes, assorted rolls, cakes, and croissants. Each product has a separate image tailored to its target consumer group, involving comprehensive research. The ultimate goal is to sell as much as possible. However, each product's image, label, packaging, and distribution can change annually. After a few years, we might not even remember what the image of a particular product used to be.

In contrast, reputation isn't built for to work just for a few years. It's meant to last for a much more extended period. Relationships between the bakery and its customers, partners, and even the state are developed over significant periods, often decades.

Therefore, it's crucial to differentiate which terms belong to one activity and which belong to another.

The purpose of this section is to categorize the terms clearly and succinctly into their compartments. I've also added words to these compartments that facilitate understanding, making them easier to remember.

1.4.1. *The Duality of PR and Marketing Terminology*

> You can make more friends in two months by becoming interested in other people than you can in two years by trying to get other people interested in you.
>
> Dale Carnegie – writer and lecturer.

PR and marketing terms have an attractive characteristic – each term from one activity has its counterpart in the other activity. And even though these are two completely different practices, the words are often confused. Why does this happen?

My colleague says that PR is a strategy for shaping trust, while marketing is a strategy for shaping desire. These are two entirely different strategies. Trust is the feeling of safety and tranquillity within a community. Desire is the feeling of contentment (satisfaction, tranquillity) after acquiring something. Trust is a stable, long-term state, while desire is a stimulus. However, these two strategies share a common denominator – the interpersonal relationship between two people. In other words, trust and desire can only be realized with the participation of two individuals. In the first case, there are no products between people (although there can be, it's unnecessary), while in the second case, the product is a crucial part of the relationship between the two.

Trust and desire are confused and frequently used interchangeably, and their differences are often misunderstood. It isn't surprising if people unfamiliar with these concepts overlook the distinctions. Unfortunately, I can also confidently state that most beginners in both fields – PR and marketing – don't see these differences. What's even more curious is that I've encountered more than a few individuals working in the PR field for over a decade who, perhaps unconsciously, confuse the terms and their functions.

Defining what marketing is can be pretty straightforward. Everyone sees images, videos, advertisements, and packaging and usually understands that whoever ordered those aims for us to pay attention and purchase what's depicted in them. So, when the person responsible for marketing needs to justify their actions to the company's financial personnel, they can always present a table showcasing the quantities and estimates of the broadcasted visuals alongside increased sales figures for one product or another. It must be said that sales might sometimes decrease. Still, a severe marketing specialist will always find an explanation for why this happened: an economic crisis, a virus, shifts in consumer habits, or unfavorable weather for the season.

In other words, marketing is clear, specific, and easily measurable, and it's easy to account for the expenses incurred in implementing marketing projects.

Evaluating PR is much more complex; it's non-concrete, nearly immeasurable, and the funds allocated can be challenging to justify.

A marketing specialist can make customers happy by offering them a good discount on a product or service because they create the price of that product or service. However, a PR specialist doesn't create the price; they create value, and that's why offering discounts isn't necessary for customer satisfaction. The customer wants that specific product or service because they know people who use it, have had conversations about it, are familiar with the representatives of the product or service, and want to belong to a particular community. Price is transient, influenced by the market, weather, and seasonality, while value lives on for a long time, sometimes even longer than the business itself, as it changes or shifts its focus. The values shaped by PR activities include kindness, understanding, assistance, and friendship. A marketing specialist rarely uses these categories and often doesn't consider them part of their activities.

Trust and desire have the exact mechanism of relationship formation, which is why the words associated with them often overlap. To some individuals deeply entrenched in materialism, it might seem that fulfilled desire is equivalent to trust. "Once I acquire that luxurious car, people will trust me; I'll be reliable." However, obtaining a desired item doesn't automatically create trust. Or if it does, it's very fleeting. Fulfillment of desire doesn't generate trust; it merely temporarily compensates for its absence.

In the example just provided, the roots of confusion are evident. When we confuse trust and desire, we also confuse the other words that accompany them.

To simplify things, I've created a table where the left side contains words related to trust, and the right side contains corresponding words related to desire.

Table 1.1 Trust and desire terms.

Trust	**Desire**
I found out → I figured out → I'm at ease	I heard → I bought → I'm happy
PR	*Marketing*
This activity creates trust.	This activity creates desire.
Longevity	*Shortivity*
Trust can only be created over the long term.	After satisfying particular desires, new ones need to be created.
Reputation	*Image*
Reputation forms naturally and results from actions, communication, and display. Reputation aligns with essence, which is why it's trusted.	An image can be crafted as desired by the client, but it doesn't necessarily reflect the essence. The primary goal is to sell as quickly as possible.
Dialogues	*Monologues*
Media releases, interviews, social media posts, discussions, etc.	*Advertisement*
They are created through various bilateral means and accessible through multiple channels.	It's created through one-sided advertising methods, and there's no discussion involved here.

(*continued*)

Table 1.1 (Continued)

Style Style may not change throughout an organization's or individual's entire lifetime. Style is the expression of visual and verbal essence.	*Fashion* Fashion is created briefly, often changing yearly, and its goal is to sell as many new products as possible.
Philosophy Trust is built through thinking, analysing, accepting, and rejecting.	*Cult* Desire is dogmatic. Most often, these 'must-haves' form without much thought, influenced by advertising.
Individuality Every conversation, every person – a separate case, a different perspective, a new relationship.	*Massiveness* All marketing tools aim to reach the largest possible audience with the most common means.
Solace PR aims to balance and harmonise all parties, understanding and trust in each other.	*Provocation and obsession* The goal of marketing is continuous provocation and encouragement to purchase.
Understanding People learn more, understand threats and benefits, and make decisions based on that when they communicate and consult with each other.	*Guesswork* Without communication and by constantly observing one-sided communication, people only acquire fragmented information and make decisions based on it.
Constancy PR constantly aims for a more stable situation, a calmer environment, and a prevailing balance.	*Impatience* Marketing aims for people not to linger in a state of satisfaction for long and constantly think about new purchases.
Play & Play PR tools and channels are free: the better you "play", the better results you will achieve.	*Pay & Play* Marketing tools and channels are paid: the more money you have, the better results you will achieve.
PR (reputable) mix CREDIBILITY, VISIBILITY & NOTABILITY.	*Marketing (selling) mix* Product, price, place, & promotion.
PR "golden" age The fourth stage of PR development "Network" (from the beginning of the 21st century to the present).	*Marketing "golden" age* The third stage of PR development "Television" (17th to 20th century).
PR goal Relationships, that can be a foundation for business development, investments, attracting partners, sales, employee recruitment, expansion into foreign countries, communication with government institutions, communities, and many other activities.	*Marketing goal* Selling, the specific action, where a person purchases a product or service in exchange for their available funds.

(*continued*)

Table 1.1 (Continued)

Inevitability It is impossible to avoid reputation; it will always exist, but it can be changed. All organizations and individuals have a reputation. Not every relationship is a sale.	*Non-necessity* Marketing and the image it creates are unnecessary for many organizations; they may not have them at all. They are only necessary for organizations that sell products but not for all.
Listening *Hearing, understanding* The foundation of PR activities is to be heard establish relationships, and mutual understanding. *Maximum interest in the environment* PR goals are achieved by collecting as many opinions as possible and drawing conclusions from them.	*Speaking* *Offering, not going deep* The foundation of marketing is to offer a product as quickly as possible and close the deal. *Maximum desire to draw attention to oneself* Marketing goals are achieved by drawing as much attention to oneself as possible and making as many sales as possible.

1.4.2. *Pseudo-Terms*

> The world isn't scandalized by our freedom but by our fakeness.
>
> Tullian Tchividjian – pastor and author.

In the world we live in, everything can be divided into two parts: real things and their substitutes. We have gold and we have its substitute; we have a painting created by an artist and we have its copy; we have genuine sincere relationships and pretense; we have education and a superficial display of wisdom.

Why do substitutes arise? The answer is straightforward – genuine things are costly, and few can afford them, or they have no price, and few have the will to attain them. People often seek an easier path to possess what they cannot have quickly. Suppose there's not enough money for gold. In that case, it's easier and faster to adorn oneself with plastic, and if there's not enough will to create authentic relationships, it's easier and quicker to pretend that those relationships already exist.

A very similar phenomenon is happening with PR terms. Despite all the recent innovations in communication, PR terms have remained fundamentally unchanged since the beginning of the 20th century. Some adjustments have been made, but the essence has remained the same – the means by which relationships are constructed have remained unchanged. PR professionals were able to build dialogue before the advent of social media, and they continue to do so.

With more opportunities for communication emerging, the fundamentals of communication have not changed. On the contrary, their adaptability has dramatically increased.

The field that has undergone the most significant change and been profoundly impacted as the world has entered the "Network" stage of PR is marketing. As mentioned earlier, the strength of marketing was and still is one-way communication. However, all new communication tools are undoubtedly two-way.

For this reason, marketers have faced an existential question: whether to a) learn the art of relationships and move towards PR, b) try to somehow sustain themselves with what they have and are paid for, or . . . (c) disappear.

The first and third ways are challenging for human nature. In the first case, one must learn many new things and fundamentally change their thinking, skills, and habits. In the third case, much may be lost.

The second option is the easiest. This option often means trying to sell substitutes when selling the genuine product is no longer possible. This option creates an activity I call pseudo PR; the terms describing it are pseudo-terms.

Distinguishing between terms and pseudo-terms is relatively straightforward. When you hear a new word, you should consider whether the activity described by the new term already exists or is new. Many new terms have emerged in the PR field in recent years because new phenomena need to be explained: social media, webinars, posts, and many others. These terms are necessary because they define new phenomena that did not exist before. However, alongside genuine words, many pseudo-terms have also appeared that do not describe any new phenomenon and attempt to label an old, long-existing phenomenon with a new name.

One of my favorite examples is content marketing. We can also mention guerrilla marketing, brand journalism, and other similar pseudo-terms.

People not particularly interested in the PR market often get deceived when communicating with a "new specialist" who presents themselves as a content marketing guru. However, this is just another manipulation to label old things with new names. Global associations are created based on pseudo-terms, like the "Content Marketing Association"!

What is content marketing? Well, it's simply an attempt to blur the line between advertising and content, making promotional content appear as if it's similar to editorial content. Is it a new phenomenon? Certainly not. Essentially, it's the same old advertising, sponsored content. In short, it's a little more smoke and mirrors, more deception.

1.4.3. Coercion Terms

> In Northern Estonia, the Soviet authorities didn't have a recipe on how to fight against the popularity of Finnish TV. Audiences didn't want to watch hardcore Soviet propaganda.
>
> Jaak Kilmi – film producer.

PR can only exist in a democratic environment. Such environments can autonomously form even in less democratic countries, but PR activity is a part of a democratic society. PR requires the free dissemination of information, which is only possible in democratic societies. The further a country moves away from democracy, the weaker the PR institution becomes.

Transparency and low corruption are also necessary for PR activities because PR activity is intended for truthful and transparent communication.

However, there have been quite a few detours and barriers during the growth and development of PR. But even when left behind or bypassed, they still go by their terms, which are mistakenly used today to describe PR activities.

Propaganda

The most prominent example is the word "propaganda".

Today propaganda has a negative connotation. However, the great Edward Bernays, now called the father of PR, titled his first book *Propaganda*. He was the first to combine psychology, sociology, communication, and methods of influence. Later, especially after the Second World War, the paths of PR and propaganda diverged, and the times changed significantly. If, before the Second World War, the Goebbels-style propaganda had not yet been thoroughly tested, and we can find examples of it in the history of PR in the United States, afterwards, it became clear to democratic countries that such a communication tool was not acceptable. While it almost disappeared in democracies, it deeply rooted itself in the Soviet and other authoritarian parts of the world. Even after becoming democratic, those countries still feel the consequences of propaganda today.

Here is how propaganda is defined on Wikipedia[16]:

> Propaganda is communication that is primarily used to influence or persuade an audience to further an agenda, which may not be objective and may be selectively presenting facts to encourage a particular synthesis or perception, or using loaded language to produce an emotional rather than a rational response to the information that is being presented. Propaganda can be found in a wide variety of different contexts.

In my opinion, this definition accurately describes what propaganda is. Propaganda is manipulating opinion, not for dialogue but to impose a desired opinion or perspective.

In democratic societies, we can also observe elements of propaganda, but it thrives most where information dissemination is not free, and people cannot freely exchange opinions, information, and facts. Therefore, the most fertile ground for propaganda is in dictatorial states that restrict freedom of speech. In developed democratic states, any attempts at propaganda are quickly neutralized by alternative opinions.

Let's go back to the term itself. Calling PR activity propaganda is incorrect, just as it's incorrect to call propaganda PR. PR's goal is dialogue, while propaganda's goal is imposing a single opinion.

Black PR

Another term often associated with PR is Black PR. It's doubtful whether we can call it a term because such a thing fundamentally doesn't exist: PR is based on ethical communication. PR professionals disseminate verified information using verified and accurate numbers and facts. "Black activity" involves fabricating facts, spreading falsehoods and fake news, and manipulating public opinion. So, we cannot use the term PR in describing this activity in any color or shape.

My colleague had an excellent example – an analogy. During one of her meetings with my students, as always, she was asked: "Do you use Black PR in your work?" Her answer was somewhat unexpected but left no doubts for anyone. In response to this question, she asked my student: "Could you name the process where you pour water over yourself in the morning, and after this process, you become clean?" The student replied that he called this process a morning shower. Then my colleague asked: "Would you call it a shower, even if someone poured a bucket of mud on you while walking down the street? Do these processes have anything in common?" An interesting discussion developed. We determined that they have something in common, but only in the sense that, in both cases, something is poured onto a person. However, calling both processes a shower doesn't work. After the first process, a person feels fresh and likely has a great mood. After the second, it's the opposite.

So, there's precisely the exact relationship between PR and Black PR. In the second case, PR doesn't even come close. Yes, it's the same pouring of something, i.e. information, onto a person. However, in one case, the aim is to inform the person. In the other, it is to deceive. In one case, a positive relationship and reputation are created. In the other, relations are severed, and a negative reputation is exposed and built.

The conclusion here is as follows: although PR and Black PR specialists use the same tools and perhaps some of the same technologies, their activities are different, contradicting each other, and their objectives are radically different. The former aims to save the world by spreading the truth, while the latter, seeking narrow interests, tries to destroy it and sow hatred and lies.

PR is a term associated with freedom, while Black PR is a term associated with coercion.

1.5. His Majesty the Client

> A people that values its privileges above its principles soon loses both.
>
> Dwight D. Eisenhower – politician and soldier.

During my practice, I have had a lot of clients. I have advised people from various sectors. I must say that the majority of them were good people: many of them sought to solve problems rather than destroy or harm anyone. Many clients declared they feel good knowing that what they do benefits society.

Representatives of many professions often ask themselves – are all clients suitable clients? The answer largely depends on the profession, or more precisely, how much representatives of one or another profession identify with the client.

For example, doctors adhere to the Hippocratic Oath and don't question what to treat or what not to treat. Still, no one also thinks of calling a doctor a criminal just because they successfully perform surgery on a crime boss.

An attorney operates within a clearly defined legal framework, and their function is to perform their job so that the client is not overly punished under the applicable laws. However, no one will label an attorney a criminal, even if they defend the world's most prominent criminal.

We can see that neither a doctor nor a lawyer identifies with their client, and their reputation doesn't suffer when they choose any client.

For a PR professional, there may also be a desire to be in a doctor's or lawyer's shoes: to represent a client but not identify with them. However, unfortunately, this profession is different: it is impossible to simultaneously be the client's conscience and distance oneself from them. Therefore, the values of the client and the PR specialist must align. If it turns out that the PR specialist's client lied, or worse, that the PR specialist lied, both will suffer: their reputation will take a severe hit.

If a PR specialist starts communicating for a criminal organization, they will become a part of it themselves. If they begin working for a dictator, they will become the dictator's voice. And if they agree to work with a social democratic party but personally hold strong liberal beliefs, it will also be somewhat unusual and hardly sustainable. On the other hand, one cannot switch between being a cigarette manufacturer's PR representative one day and explaining to their child the harmful effects of smoking the next. Most likely, those who do so engage in one activity and then another end up lying in the process.

A PR specialist must be convinced that what they communicate is accurate, and they must wholeheartedly support what they are sharing. Otherwise, they will be lying. They have to choose one or the other. And there are countless moral dilemmas like this.

Assessing whether the client aligns with your cherished values is essential when starting to work. You should avoid discussing things you don't believe in or deceiving the public.

Much has been said and written about how to choose a PR agency or consultant for a client or employer. This section aims to look at this question from the other side and help PR specialists understand which clients are suitable and which are not, with whom it is worth associating their reputation and with whom it is not. Of course, there may not be an ideal client or employer, and if we seek perfection, we may end up with nothing. So, I do not suggest that if a client is not ideal according to one criterion or another, you cannot work with them. However, if a client does not meet most of the requirements, perhaps it's worth looking for something else rather than continuing an unproductive partnership.

The characteristics of an ideal client listed below can also help identify areas where the client may need to make adjustments or changes. And if both sides are willing to change, it always provides mutual benefits.

So, an ideal client is an aspirational goal, a vision, and most likely non-existent in this world. However, when you know what you're aiming for, it becomes much easier to direct your efforts precisely.

Six characteristics of an ideal client:

1. Freedom to Act

Permitting you to act freely is one of the most essential characteristics of an ideal client. The success of a PR specialist's work depends to a large extent on how much freedom they have to communicate, participate, negotiate, engage, and do so on behalf of the client.

There is no better way to make PR work inefficient than to try to interfere with the process. However, a PR specialist must also involve and invite the client's people to participate in various activities, initiating those activities.

Choosing the right PR consultant, the client must trust them and give them the freedom to operate. There should be continuous communication and exchanges of information. The client should know what is being done on behalf of the organization, but not try to control the process. Such attempts always lead to stifling initiative.

The client must understand that the PR consultant desires to spread as much information about the organization as possible to open its doors as wide as possible. This desire is not based on any egotistical trait of the PR specialist but is a natural aspiration to disseminate as much truth as possible. The more barriers we create for the public to access information, the fewer opportunities we have to steer our reputation in the desired direction.

Therefore, the client's primary interest should be in the PR specialist's active engagement, a broader network of contacts, and wider dissemination. If the client wants to see a filter instead of a PR professional, it will not lead to anything good.

That's why an **ideal client** provides the PR specialist with all possible information about the company and allows them to handle it freely.

2. Ethical Principles

Consulting someone else is only possible when you have a solid foundation beneath you. Consultation, in essence, is providing support with your knowledge. You can support someone else only when you stand firmly yourself. Otherwise, there will always be the temptation to do things the easy way, the quick way, the effortless way, the comfortable way – there will always be the temptation to yield to the client's dictates. When working, it's essential not to forget that the client is also human, with all their strengths and weaknesses, so they may often want not so much consultation as validation of their actions. And that's already a dangerous zone.

If the client asks you to use black hat techniques or manipulate the media, I do not recommend doing such work. PR specialists frequently have to decide what behavior is appropriate and what is not in a given situation.

Therefore, PR professionals must have clear ethical principles and declare them to the client immediately. The PR specialist must clearly state what they will and will not do, even if the client insists.

Every time the client's and your principles clash, you must choose your codes, or you won't be a trustworthy PR specialist. Trust in this profession is the critical value that builds relationships.

An **ideal client** values the ethical principles of the PR professional and never questions them.

3. Client's Reliability

As has become apparent in this chapter, the first and most crucial reputational factor is ACTION, meaning the client's activities, the quality of those activities, their professionalism, and the benefit of the products they produce to society. If we have a reliable client whose actions and transparency leave no doubt, we have already done half of the reputation work. All that's left is ensuring those actions continue and focusing our primary efforts on TONGUE and STYLE. If we don't have such a client, we should first work on making our client become one, identify which aspects of their activities pose reputational risks and try to eliminate those risks.

I have often pondered and tried to compromise when working with the tobacco industry. However, if you are convinced that the sole purpose of this business is to create a product that harms people, how can you engage in its PR? Yes, Edward Bernays taught women to smoke, and that campaign is considered one of the most successful in the history of our profession. But once, headaches were treated with opium, and doctors or athletes used to appear in advertisements promoting smoking. However, the world is changing, and certainly not for the worse. So why should we give a voice to those who could be called remnants of ignorance from the past?

I have the gift of quickly understanding whether a person is honest or "holds a stone in their mouth". I grasp that immediately, and when working together, I double-check it. Speech, and most importantly, actions and decisions, always confirm a person's intentions.

The client's reliability reflects on the PR specialist and vice versa. In an open democratic society, every member, first and foremost, must be trustworthy and guarantee trust in them through their reputation.

Successful reputation management is only possible when the client is trustworthy. There is no other way. We cannot communicate nonsense and expect that no one will notice it.

An **ideal client** is transparent and reliable.

4. Mutual Suitability

This one is probably one of the most subjective characteristics of an ideal client, but it is no less critical. It is impossible to ensure smooth reputation management if there is a lack of understanding between the client and the PR consultant if they do not get along on a human level. On the contrary, when the client and PR consultant understand each other almost instinctively, anticipate each other's thoughts, and trust each other, the work proceeds smoothly, even in the most challenging situations.

A PR consultant should be chosen exclusively based on trust; you need to communicate and find someone who fits best. And here, there are no objective criteria; it's more about emotions. Yes, a good consultant must be experienced and adhere to ethical principles, but these are formal criteria that can be found in many people. But what should be considered is something akin to choosing your conscience. Conversation and trust in each other are the most important factors when choosing who will help you with PR. The client and the consultant must establish an emotional connection because PR work is mainly emotional.

Before choosing a PR consultant, the client should ask themselves the fundamental question: why do they need such a person? Often, there is an expectation that the PR consultant will come from the outside and magically solve all problems. It is a mistaken way of thinking.

When choosing a PR agency or consultant, it is vital to understand one effortless thing: no one knows the client's or the organization's situation better than the client. To clarify, let's briefly shift from the corporate level to the personal level. Is there a person who knows your problems better than you do? In most cases, such a person does not exist, and if they do, you should consider whether you have entrusted too much of your life to others. You, and not someone else, know your affairs best. And if we are talking about the personal level, it would probably be difficult for you to ask another person for help solving your problems without explaining the situation to them. However, even after presenting the case, you will ultimately still be the one who knows your situation best. And in the end, you will still have to decide on how to act.

The situation is very similar to seeking a psychologist: you know your case, and you or those around you indicate that you have problems, so you turn to a psychologist. Maybe you already know them or are just choosing one now. You decide based on whether you like their personality or their methods. Perhaps you ask for recommendations. But the decision is always yours – whether it suits you or not. Then you turn to them, talk for a long time until you tell them everything you can about yourself, and then you expect to receive advice. After all, you don't expect the psychologist to do the action for you, right? The psychologist only advises, shows the way, and helps you avoid pitfalls, but the patient takes the decision and the action.

So it's very similar to an agency or consultant. The client knows their situation best and decides that they have PR-related problems. They look for a PR consultant to help solve those problems. They choose a consultant. This choice is always subjective, just like choosing a psychologist, an employee, a colleague, or a partner.

One of the biggest mistakes made when choosing is to give those you choose from tasks they should solve and select based on that. I think this should be forgotten. Choosing a PR consultant is as personal and intimate as choosing a psychologist or doctor. The PR consultant must be trusted and liked by the client. Therefore, I highly recommend talking and not choosing based on the agency's reputation, name, or similar factors because it's a lottery. If the agency has more work at that time, the client will get a junior assistant; if less, a more experienced professional. Both can be suitable for the client, or they may not be. Communication and assistance in building relationships are what the client is looking for. The paramount quality by which a consultant should be chosen is the ability to communicate directly and help the client do so.

When choosing a consultant, the client should first tell about themselves, ask to demonstrate their experience, ask about basic PR things – ethical norms, professional attitudes – and choose based on that. When they make their choice, they should spend plenty of time talking. The more attention the client pays to the consultant, the more they introduce them to their situation, and the more they can expect to receive in return. The client should remember a simple rule – the success of solving PR problems depends on two people. These people must work together, and the result will be the best. Those people are the client, who knows their case best but knows nothing about PR, and the PR professional, who knows PR well but knows nothing about the client's field. So, no miracle or magic wand will perform a miracle, only the synergy that is achieved when two professionals meet. Those who expect a miracle will be disappointed, but those who wish for advice and are prepared to find a solution will find it.

The PR professional will advise, but the client must take action. As a psychologist suggests, it shows how to help avoid pitfalls, but the patient takes the decision and action. The same goes for PR – the consultant advises and helps avoid surprises, but the client makes the final decision.

The importance of this characteristic is especially evident in crises when everyone's nerves are strained and quick decisions need to be made. If, in such situations, there is still a need to argue with each other, the effectiveness of reputation will suffer significantly. Crises act as a litmus test to show the nature of the relationship between the client and the consultant. After such situations, those relationships completely cool down or move to a higher level of trust.

An **ideal client** gets along well with and trusts their PR consultant.

5. Understanding PR

A PR professional is hired to help address reputation-related issues, but the client must understand this field. If not, they can hire a PR consultant to provide this knowledge or take an introductory PR course at a learning institution. However, situations where a client purchases PR services without a clear understanding of their purpose and later demands unusual tasks from the PR professional, which are unrelated to PR activities, should be avoided.

A PR professional is not a PR teacher; if the client requires him to teach, he should pay for this.

Today, the field of PR has changed significantly compared to what it was ten years ago. The tools, methods, and opportunities in PR evolve much faster than the thinking of PR specialists. These novelties are incredibly challenging for clients and business owners who struggle to keep up with the changing PR landscape. Often, it's difficult for them to grasp that the methods that worked a decade ago may no longer be effective today or even impossible to implement.

While clients don't need to know everything about PR in-depth, they should clearly understand what PR is and what a PR specialist can or cannot do. PR professionals must communicate openly with their clients, occasionally invite them to training sessions, and keep them updated on their expertise. However, this willingness to learn should be mutual, and the client must also be open to improving their understanding.

Engaging with your client in an informal setting and sharing real-life examples from your practice can effectively educate them about the essence of PR, demonstrate its value, and suggest relevant reading materials. However, remember that this educational effort should be reciprocal. The client should also have a genuine interest in learning and understanding PR.

It's essential to build a solid client-consultant relationship. However, remember that you are not a psychologist, and your primary role is not to address your client's psychological issues. Some clients may resist opening up and only want to hide behind you. Always remember your role as a PR specialist.

Due to the rapid changes in the PR field and technological advancements, clients may not fully comprehend the role of PR specialists and why they need them. It is a source of misunderstandings.

One common misconception is that PR is a subset of marketing, a kind of advertising. Others might think that the only function of a PR department is to deal with the media and organize events. These misconceptions can significantly limit PR professionals' work, especially those just starting out in the field.

Clients should also understand that PR consultants cannot be held responsible for the overall performance of an organization. Regardless of how valuable PR advice is, it remains advice – the decisions ultimately rest with the client, and they need to take responsibility for them.

In discussions with colleagues, agency employees, and partners, I always emphasize that we should never overstep our consultant role. We can express our opinions, but the client must decide. That decision can be good or bad, align with or diverge from our views, and have various consequences. However, it must be the client's independent choice with our guidance and, sometimes, opposition.

The worst thing one can do is to take on the client's role and try to lead. I have seen many such cases, but without exception, they led to the professional downfall of the consultant.

Additionally, it's important to remember that the ability to distance oneself from the client and their decisions is crucial for the psychological well-being of both the client and the consultant.

The **ideal client** is someone who understands what PR is and doesn't demand tasks that fall outside the scope of PR activities from the PR specialist.

6. Appreciation of Experience

One of the highest points in the career of a PR professional is reached when the routine daily work is essentially no longer performed. This situation isn't all that different from any other consultant, regardless of the field they consult in. Starting their career, the aspiring PR professional begins by assisting in event organization, then starts writing press releases, eventually acquires their client to manage projects, and ultimately reaches the point where they are compensated for their expertise.

It might seem that anyone can express that same opinion, but they will be compensated differently. Why? Because you're not paid for the opinion or thought itself. You're paid for the experience, trust, and time. The client hires you because they get a reliable and trustworthy response quickly, paying for your extensive experience, confidence in you, your reputation, and the time they can save. You once invested in it, and now you're receiving dividends.

This topic always sparked discussions between me and my students – I constantly realized that they had never considered this question.

I used to like providing them with such an example.

Imagine the situation. One day, you receive an email inquiry from a potential client. You are a consultant in one country, Lithuania, and the potential client is from Italy. They are a food industry company planning to invest in Lithuania and would like to announce their plans to the Lithuanian audience. You receive an email from the PR director of this company, whose current goal is to understand the Lithuanian media market. She wants to start with a simple service – obtaining a list of media outlets that might be interested. She asks you, "How much does a media list cost?".

The thinking of a beginner, or a less experienced, PR specialist will likely be as follows. Firstly, the result of such work will appear before their eyes – a table containing five to six media outlets, a similar number of names and surnames, a few phone numbers, and email addresses. To complete this task, they will need no more than two hours. Our young colleague will multiply those two hours by their hourly rate and provide an answer to the client.

An experienced PR specialist would think somewhat differently. Unlike their younger colleague, they would better evaluate how much experience they have accumulated working in this country, how many times they have already interacted with the individuals on the potential list, how much they know about them, and which of them are worth including in the list and which are not. The young specialist will do this mechanically by copying names from the media contacts list, while the experienced one might also refer to that list. Still, for almost every name, they will see a specific person behind it.

Anyone can do the younger colleague's work, whereas the experienced colleague's work can only be done by them because they have that expertise.

In one case, the client will receive a mechanically created list, which may not work effectively. In the other case, they will receive a list of reliable individuals, which will be composed based on experience. These two lists have different prices because, in one case, technical work is being sold, while in the other, it's the expertise.

When purchasing the second option, the client will spend more, but they will save time and receive a guaranteed quality service.

The young colleague is likely to overlook another aspect as well. Without experience, they won't appreciate the potential that their more experienced colleague has accumulated. They probably won't even consider the value of simply living in the country where they are asked to provide the service. What seems obvious to us may appear very complex and incomprehensible to someone from a different market.

When evaluating the price of a service, one should look at it not so much from their perspective but from the client's standpoint. What you can do quickly and without much thought, your client can also do it themselves. However, it would take them much longer, and they might still have doubts. You should ask yourself not how much time it would take but how much time it would save the client. They would probably waste a lot more time. If it's the same client from abroad, they would first need to find out which media outlets exist in our market, understand which ones are the most important and most suitable for their topic, and then determine which journalists are most familiar with the subject matter. Ultimately, everything would culminate in the fact that the work would need to be done in Lithuanian. They would spend more than just one day to complete this task, and the result might not be better than what they would get from you.

So, we are not selling the time it takes us to do a particular job but the time we invest to acquire the knowledge we have. If time were measured not in hours but in tangible objects, let's say gold nuggets, then our experience would be our accumulated gold nuggets. When consulting, we are selling those gold nuggets to the client. Since time is measured not in gold nuggets but in hours, we are selling the hours we spent over a certain period acquiring experience to the client.

When it comes to such intangible things as PR services, it can indeed be difficult to imagine that experience. However, I believe every PR professional can tangibly feel that they possess it.

For those who have a hard time imagining it, I joke about a dentist and his client who, after half an hour of work, is unpleasantly surprised to receive a €200 bill and complains to the dentist about such an expensive hourly rate. The dentist responds very simply: 'I could have worked for half a day, but I don't think that would have been any better for you.'

So, the client pays because the dentist is there, and they don't have to do it themselves. The client pays for the dentist's investment in education and their reputation, which guarantees they have already extracted hundreds of such teeth.

The **ideal client** understands why paying more for experience is necessary and confidently invests in hours of expertise.

Notes

1 Chartered Institute of Public Relations. https://www.cipr.co.uk/CIPR/About_Us/About_PR (accessed on 21-02-2024).
2 Public Relations Society of America. https://www.prsa.org/about/all-about-pr (accessed on 21-02-2024).
3 Bernays, E. (1923). *Crystallizing public opinion*. New York: Boni and Liveright.
4 Bernays, E. (1928). *Propaganda*. New York: Horace Liveright.
5 Number of monthly active users of January 2024. https://www.statista.com/statistics/272014/global-social-networks-ranked-by-number-of-users/ (accessed on 21-02-2024).
6 Bernays, E. (1928). *Propaganda*. New York: Horace Liveright.
7 *The Bible*, John 8:32.
8 Tannen, D. (1990). *You just don't understand*. New York: Ballantine Books.
9 Bain, N. (2013). Reputation and the board. Guidance for PR consultants and board. CIPR. https://issuu.com/cipr_uk_members/docs/reputation_and_the_board_report (accessed on 21-02-2024).
10 Smith, P.R. and Taylor, J. (2004). *Marketing communications*. London: Kogan Page.
11 Video summary of world PR forum 2014. https://www.youtube.com/watch?v=sLakRXvjZQE.
12 Demonstrating the value of public relations. CIPR, January 2013. https://issuu.com/cipr_uk_members/docs/demonstrating_the_value_of_pr (accessed on 21-02-2024).
13 Demonstrating the value of public relations. CIPR, January 2013. https://issuu.com/cipr_uk_members/docs/demonstrating_the_value_of_pr (accessed on 21-02-2024).
14 Carnegie, D. (1936). *How to win friends and influence people*. New York: Simon and Schuster.
15 The term was first proposed by George T. Doran in the November 1981 issue of *Management Review*. He suggested that goals should be SMART (specific, measurable, assignable, realistic, and time-related).
16 Wikipedia. https://en.wikipedia.org/wiki/Propaganda (accessed on 21-02-2024).

2 Transformation

> I started using the internet in 1999. That was pretty late. But as soon as I did I just stopped watching TV. The idea of sitting down and waiting for a TV show at a certain time, I couldn't do this anymore. The internet is a better form of entertainment to me.
>
> Tom Anderson – founder of Myspace.

Time magazine has been selecting its Person of the Year every year since 1927. Each year, except for 2006, it was a person or people. In 2006, the Person of the Year was also a person, but a different kind. In 2006, *Time* named "You" as the Person of the Year, or as they explained it, every person became the Person of the Year. The magazine's cover featured a computer, and below it was the inscription: "Yes, you. You control the Information Age. Welcome to your world."

The editorial decision was quite logical. The editors wanted to clearly and unambiguously convey that we had entered a new era. In this era, the monologue had turned into interactive dialogue because social media, which had become prevalent, would be nothing without a diverse range of people and their interactions. The foundation of social media is continuous dialogues, and it could also be called an endless multilogue.

Today, we all live in the "Network" stage of public relations and are diving deeper into it. The main attribute of this stage is undoubtedly the internet. And even though we already have much of what perhaps only the most terrific dreamers could have imagined 20–30 years ago, we are probably still in the very early stages of this phase.

The previous "Television" stage began in the early 17th century with the emergence of the first newspaper and ended in the late 20th century, with the advent of the internet. The "Television" stage lasted for 400 years. Assuming that the "Network" stage will not be shorter and will end in about the year 2400, we have only progressed about 5% into it so far. However, it could last longer, so we may have moved even less in this grand timeline.

Predicting what awaits us at the end of this stage is probably as uncertain as what people living in the 17th century could have foreseen about the end

DOI: 10.4324/9781003466802-3

of the 20th century. Considering that many of the most significant innovations reached us only in the second half of the previous century, we know little about what the next 400 years may bring. However, I do not doubt that if humanity still exists at that time, we will be faced with a breathtaking pace of development and associated innovations.

Today, we are at the beginning of the "Network" stage, and it is most exciting and meaningful to think about how to live in the here and now, perhaps even a few years ahead. Communication-related questions are of utmost importance for someone interested in public communication: how to communicate effectively today and tomorrow, what principles to apply, and how to help build reputations for individuals who see meaning in it.

In my opinion, the best approach is to assess what has changed and what has not, draw conclusions from it, and construct effective communication models for the near future.

Evidently, there has been a transformation in the field of public communication, and for some, it's even considered a revolution. I think of myself as among those who see it as such. If it had been a simple transformation based on evolution, we wouldn't have the "everything old is bad, everything new is good" effect. However, in this transformation, we do have that effect. The new generation categorically rejects the one-sided communication tools of the "Television" stage – newspapers and television – and replaces them with "Network" stage tools based on social media.

I encountered the term "revolution" in this sense for the first time when I read Erik Qualman's book *Socialnomics*. That's when I thought: "Wow!" Before that, I had been looking at processes in the field of public communication quite narrowly and thinking in traditional categories. *Socialnomics* may not have told me anything radically new, but it neatly organized everything. I had felt it, but Qualman articulated what was buzzing inside.

"Nothing exists until it's on television," said representatives of the Baby Boomers and Gen X generations.

"Nothing exists until it's on social media," say Millennials and Zoomers.

Not only have the stages of PR changed but also the importance of the principles of these stages has shifted. From Chapter 1, let's remember that the paramount nature of communication in the "Television" stage was global one-way communication, and it ended when the main drawback of this stage – one-sidedness – was eliminated. It ended when the "Network" stage began, where the leading nature of communication is global two-way communication.

In the realm of one-way communication, the marketing jungle thrived and it was advertising, advertising, advertising. It was an excellent form of one-way communication until effective two-way communication emerged. PR lived in the "Television" stage, where marketing reigned supreme. However, in the "Network" stage, the dominance shifts towards PR based on two-way communication. Reputation begins to play a crucial role in being heard, selling, or acting. PR plays a significant role in building that reputation.

For the first time in human history, dialogue must be everywhere, even in autocratic structures like companies. And it's essential to recognize that companies didn't naturally start changing independently; the evolving world is compelling them to do so. Being autocratic is no longer sustainable.

One-way communication or traditional marketing is dying. All the foundations of communication are changing because, in the new era, every individual can disseminate information at any moment. The primary task of any PR specialist today is to provide information not to the traditional media, as it used to be, but to active individuals who will then spread it further.

Yesterday's communication was like playing darts – we tried to hit the target as accurately as possible. Today's communication is like tennis, where playing the game without the involvement of the other side is impossible.

My colleague said that yesterday, it was about aiming and persuading, but today, it's about involving people in activities to gain their preference and loyalty to your organization or products. I would also add that this involvement needs to be continuous. As soon as we finish the game, someone else may start, and we might have to wait for our potential customer or partner to return to the game table.

Let's recall the terms "Desire" and "Trust" from Chapter 1. Desire arises when a seller strikes a chord with us and ignites a longing. It hits us, and we must either seek a remedy or remain wounded. On the other hand, trust isn't something that someone shoots into us; it's something we build through playing, learning, and needing a partner we trust. This partner has a reputation and is ready at any moment to help us solve one of life's tasks.

Therefore, several changes occurred with the transition from the "Television" stage to the "Network" stage of public relations. It replaced one era with another, shifting from the first era dominated by marketing and mass media, often called the "Marketing Era", to the second era where PR and social media reign, which we call the "PR Era".

Figure 2.1 The transformation of communication from playing darts to playing tennis. Figure by the author.

2.1. Two Eras

Regard your good name as the richest jewel you can possibly be possessed of.
Socrates – Greek philosopher.

My partners from Germany, Scholz & Friends, created an excellent animated short film that tells in three-and-a-half minutes what happened when the "PR era" replaced the "Marketing era". You can watch the movie yourselves[1], but the main idea of the movie was that during the Marketing era, life was much easier because we had only a few brand names, the choice was easy, customers trusted individual recommendations, and they were loyal.

Information overload, the internet, convergence, and information society moved us to the PR era, and here, life is much more complex because we have many brand names, the choice is difficult, social media dominates, customers are hard to reach, and dialogue is crucial.

The 20th century, especially its second half, is often called the golden age of advertising, as this was when advertising reached its peak. The world was recovering from two world wars, and much of humanity began to live a peaceful life filled with various goods. Countless products that replaced each other were created, leading to an abundance of goods and the opportunity to sell everything that was produced. As a result, marketing thrived, an activity whose primary goal was selling a product or service. Advertising was a part of marketing, and its creators became almost like gods.

In their book *The fall of advertising and the rise of PR*[2], Ries and Ries effectively articulated what happens to various aspects of life when they lose their original function. Adding a bit more, I'll remind you of this concept.

In my opinion, when they lose their primary functions, various objects or fields disappear as unnecessary or evolve into something more significant than when they served their original purposes. Examples of vanished phenomena can include the telegraph and fax machines, typesetting in printing presses, dirigibles, bartering with furs, and other things that are now only familiar to us throughout history.

As Ries and Ries note, transformed phenomena can become art, sports, or collections. For example, painting, initially meant for depicting reality, evolved into a form of visual art with the advent of photography. Horses, once primarily used for transportation, became part of equestrian sports with the arrival of automobiles. Similarly, originally designed to reproduce sound, vinyl records became collectable as more advanced audio playback devices emerged.

Alongside this process, there's another one happening as well. Phenomena that have lost their primary functions tend to become significantly more valuable. Compare the prices of Vincent van Gogh's paintings when he created them to what they are today. Or consider the cost of racehorses today compared to when horses were primarily used for transportation.

The same has happened with advertising. As Ries and Ries assert, the primary function of advertising was to inform and, through information, to sell.

However, today, "high advertising" no longer sells; it has become more about image. There are festivals where the best advertisements are celebrated, yet many of the advertisements showcased there are not used in practice. They are excellent standalone works of art, and their creators deserve recognition for their creativity, sharpness, and originality. They are genuinely creators and artists. Doesn't this resemble the loss of primary functions in other phenomena? Advertising has turned into art and has become significantly more valuable, while that which has not transformed continues to serve its narrow informational function. The internet is full of advertising artisans who, for a small sum, can craft excellent advertising plans that, through information, will sell.

As consumers became saturated with advertising and it lost its primary function towards the end of the "Marketing Era", the "PR Era" emerged. It was a natural succession, and as I mentioned earlier, a global phenomenon, not exclusive to our field.

In the "Marketing Era", one-way communication advertising solutions were excellent, and I wouldn't hesitate to refer to this era as the "Information Scarcity Era" as well. Advertising had its golden age in this era of one-way communication channels like newspapers, radio, and television.

Society continued to evolve, and the internet emerged. Even the early internet (by which I mean the internet before the advent of social media) represented a significant step toward more active information exchange among people. Traditional media outlets began to lose their monopoly on information dissemination shortly after the internet's arrival because opportunities to directly and rapidly access experts started to emerge. Of course, these were isolated cases in the initial stages, but we see today almost a free market of information exchange. It's as if someone removed the cap from the information bottle, and information began to flow freely.

What happened? Well, what happened is that advertising became just one of the countless ways to make recommendations about what, when, and where to buy. And it's not even the most reliable because many people realise it's not about what they want, but rather what the advertiser wants.

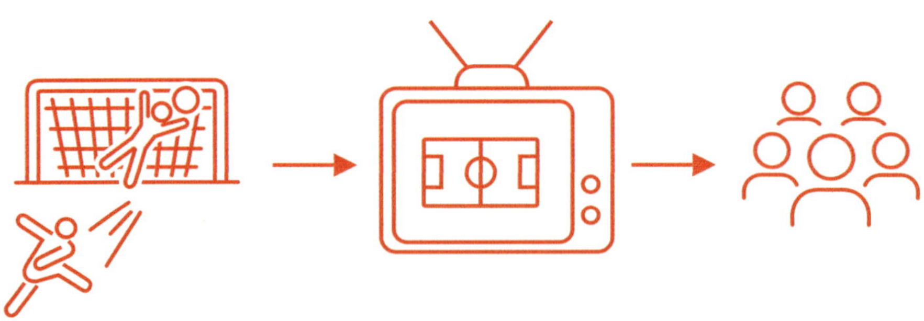

Figure 2.2 Global communication during the "Marketing Era".
Figure by the author.

The primary criterion for selection has become not a one-time flashy advertisement that maintains certain niche positions but trust. The most crucial factor is not the communication itself but the object being communicated. If, in the past, good advertising could cover up less favorable product qualities, today, it is almost impossible to do so. If a product or service is of low quality, good advertising can even harm it because it will be immediately ridiculed on social media.

Our understanding of reality during the "Marketing Era" could have been considered, to some extent, as the perception of reality conveyed and presented to us by the media. Events not covered by the media were often treated as if they had not occurred. Social media has significantly changed this dynamic.

The term PR (public relations) in contemporary society has transformed into PR (people relations). This transformation means we shift from an organization's relationship with the public to intercommunication among societal groups. Every individual's opinion becomes crucial, as there is no longer an intermediary – the media – and everyone can break down issues and create. The era of social media has arrived.

Social media isn't something entirely new that fell from the sky; it's a logical stage in human development. Human beings have always sought to communicate, convey and receive information, be understood, and understand others. All historical means of communication, from cave drawings to writing, books, newspapers, telegraphs, radios, movies, computers, the internet, and, now, social media affirm this. Social media is a natural and logical continuation of the human desire to communicate freely and conveniently.

Yes, social media has brought a lot of information noise, but its most significant achievement is the creation of a direct expressway from information sender to receiver. Today, only social media, as a platform for immediate information exchange, can accurately tell us what people are reading and are genuinely interested in. In the past, this task was performed by editorial teams, and it must be admitted that they did it at least somewhat self-interestedly. They provided readers with content that brought the highest circulation and the most advertising orders, not necessarily the content they needed most. Traditional media outlets accustomed readers to what was trendy, creating demand for certain types of information, which they later satisfied by delivering content through media channels.

Social media is nothing extraordinary. The world has reached a state where resource sharing is natural, profitable, and resource-efficient. Previously underutilized resources have now started working. Social media is the same phenomenon in public relations as it is in accommodation (Airbnb), automobiles (Bolt), capital (Kickstarter), knowledge (Wikipedia), design (Fab), management (Holacracy), and many other areas. Social media employs anyone who wants to share knowledge, write, film, draw, and create. In the past, such people were either very isolated personalities or often wasted their talent. It turns out that many people are multifaceted. The corporate world's gray and dull financier is a good swimmer, maybe even an expert in swimming in exotic countries. CEOs of other companies are interested in tulips and participate in the most famous exhibitions in their free time. Moreover, both individuals are excellent writers, have a unique sense of humor. We only discovered this when social media appeared – it employed the untapped resources of financiers and CEOs, and we received unique content that only they could provide us with.

Social media has significantly disrupted the foundations of marketing and journalism. No, the media itself did not disappear, but it had to shift and welcome new players onto the stage of public relations specialists. It turns out that the definition of a journalist is no longer so clear, and neither is that of the media. Is a famous individual with a follower count exceeding a media outlet's circulation a journalist? Or perhaps a politician? Or a baker?

The most significant advantage of social media, which unites everyone, is that people learn about all these things directly from each other. There is no longer an intermediary controlling the content of information. Perhaps social media, like everything else in the world, is not perfect and ideal, but it is the most democratic form of communication humanity has had to date.

Winston Churchill once said: "It has been said that democracy is the worst form of government except all the others that have been tried." I believe that if the charismatic leader of Great Britain had lived in our times, he might have expressed a similar sentiment about social media. It may be flawed, the poorest

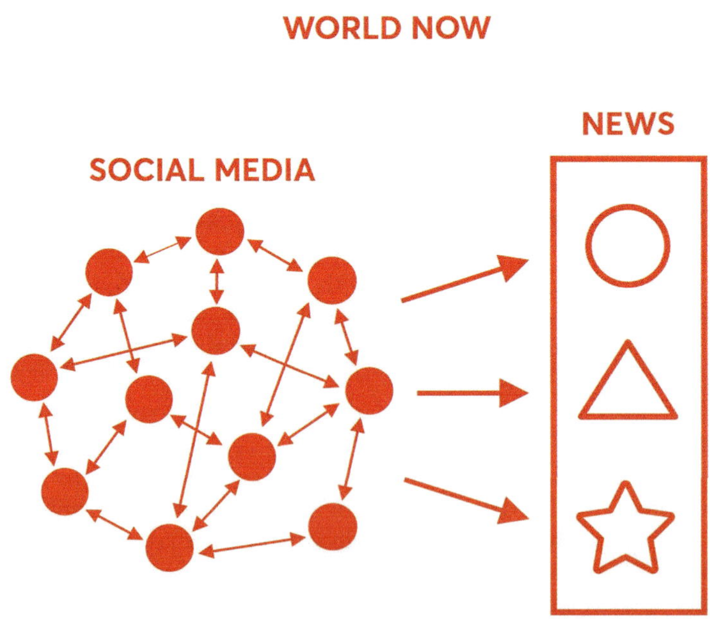

Figure 2.3 Global communication during the "PR Era".
Figure by the author.

form of communication with a lot of noise and clutter, but humanity has not seen anything better yet. No previous generation has experienced such a free flow of information as we have today.

I remember when I was very young, just past primary school age, and decided to publish a newspaper, on my own at first and then with friends. I still have copies of those newspapers – black and white, written in pencil with printed letters. My children, from time to time, enjoy looking at those archives. As they look at them, they skeptically ask me if I wrote those texts in pencil, and I proudly confirm it.

When we made such a newspaper, we had to find a way to make copies. I would turn to my father, and after much persuasion, he would bring home 20–30 copies of those "treasures" in the evening. Because there was a magical copying machine at his workplace, and he was on good terms with the machine's keeper (by the way, there was one). It was a great joy back then to distribute those copies; not everyone who wanted them could get one. There were various conflicts over this. This distribution happened in the 1980s, "just" about 30–35 years ago, and it seemed incredible. I also remember when, in those same primary school classes, my classmates and I sometimes speculated that there would probably be video phones in the future. I can't imagine who came up with that term. Still, I suspect it had to do with those illegal cassette tapes that circulated from hand to hand so you could watch *Rocky* or *Rambo.* which had been copied a hundred times onto cassettes, sometimes recorded illegally in movie theaters, and dubbed by specific Russian actors who spoke in a way that made it seem like their noses were plugged with laundry pins.

Today, any student can create, let's say, 100 "newspapers" on various topics, and they can be read in any corner of the world. This change is hard to grasp intellectually but entirely natural – both then and now, we wanted the same thing: to disseminate and receive knowledge.

Before social media existed, the world of public relations was relatively straightforward. If you needed to spread a message, there was an information sender, media outlets, and tools to reach the information receiver (or audience). You had to know how to write a compelling press release and how to send it correctly. If everything went well, your message would appear in the media.

With the emergence of social media, the clear distinction between the information sender, the media outlet, and the information receiver has blurred. However, while some fear it's an uncontrollable flood, that's not entirely true – social media also operates with precise logic, principles, and rules. They may be more complex and intricate, but they exist. Moreover, they are much more natural than the "Marketing Era" rules because they develop among people directly interacting with each other rather than being artificially created by media editorial boards. A public relations specialist must understand this logic and follow it. If the communicated object is reliable, social media is the perfect space for communication.

Social media has also revealed two fascinating and unexpected phenomena.

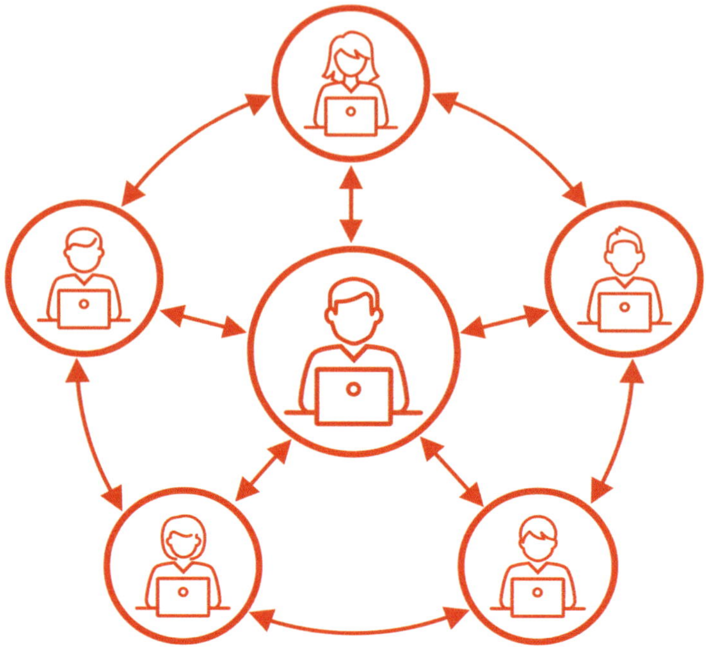

Figure 2.4 The information dissemination possibilities for every child.
Figure by the author.

The **first** one is that it turns out that in any society, a large number of people want to spread knowledge. People write, film, post, and discuss phenomena because they enjoy it. Of course, much of this information may be of little value and only satisfies the self-expression needs of those who create it. However, there is also a part that does it consistently and provides valuable information to society. The most exciting thing is that social media has revealed many people for whom writing is not a direct source of income, and they do it not because they want to earn money. People enjoy the opportunity to share information and feel important because of it. For some, it's purely about self-expression; for others, it's about establishing expertise. And for still others, it's about being a leader in a specific group of people, and so on. There can be countless reasons why people write, and we have a large portion of society for whom sharing information is a natural need.

The **second** unexpected phenomenon is that through social media, often without even realizing it, people's personalities are revealed. While we often say that people on social media are not the same as they are in real life, on the other hand, social media very clearly shows who they would like to be in real life.

One of my colleagues had an interesting perspective on what happens in the virtual world. She argued that the virtual world reflects the real world, and there is nothing new in it. Every phenomenon in the virtual world has its counterpart in the real world.

People often suppress traits they don't want to show to others, but on the other hand, they very clearly present the qualities or values they wish to promote. This presentation is revealed through their vocabulary, photos, statements, and comments. People often don't even realize the strong impact that simple expressions like "Great!" under a photograph can have on their reputation. Here, exclamation marks, capitalization, apparent typos, and many other details play a role.

We can also consider the comments from different generations and how they may not understand what is acceptable. For instance, my parents' generation views social media as a platform where you can somehow vent your complaints. Social media says a lot about a person, even if they are not very active on it or only share a minimal amount of content. It may not necessarily be an objective portrayal, but it's the image a person wants to create about themselves, whether successful or not. Not everyone understands what kind of image they're making in the eyes of others. Without communication skills, someone might think sharing certain information will create a specific embodiment, but that's not always true. Sometimes, it disappoints them, while other times, they do it quite successfully.

Let's get acquainted with the six main shortcomings of the "Marketing Era" that social media, which emerged in the "PR Era," addressed.

2.1.1. Marketing Era; or Six Weaknesses of Mass Media

> No one wakes up excited to see more advertising, no one goes to sleep thinking about the ads they'll see tomorrow.
>
> Jan Koum – entrepreneur and computer programmer.

The "Marketing Era" gave us mass media. With the advancement of technology, people learned to convey one message to hundreds, later to thousands, and eventually to billions. In the 20th century, we realized that we could control the masses, spread information, and so on through the media. Although mass media grew to unprecedented proportions, it still had several significant shortcomings.

The first drawback: costliness

In the "Marketing Era" you needed to have money to start even with the most minor mass media channel. The editorial team, office space, journalists, paper, and many other expenses are why mass media is costly. Unlike the amount required to start a media outlet online, offline world media outlets seem like large and expensive fortresses, even if we're talking about small print publications.

In the "Marketing Era," the main principle of knowledge dissemination could be described as "Pay & Play". I don't know the origin of this term, and

I can't remember where I first heard it. This principle means that to spread your message, you had to think first about the amount of money you would need to pay to mass media for advertising placement.

The high cost of information dissemination was also influenced by massive resource wastage. Let's consider just the amount of paper needed to print one day's newspaper circulation! These vast quantities and sums gradually sank into the waters of history. While the forecasts provided by the Future Exploration Network[3] about the disappearance of newspapers are not entirely precise, it is evident that newspapers as a mass media form will soon vanish, and their costliness and inefficient resource usage will be one of the main reasons for this.

The second drawback: impersonality

Impersonality, or the inability to personalize information, is the inability of mass media to combine transmitting one piece of information to thousands with the reverse – delivering a thousand pieces of information to one individual. Everyone received the same or very weakly personalized news through specialized mass media. However, compared to the power of social media to personalize communication, where ten people living in the same house can have their own personalized media outlet and constantly receive news relevant only to that group, the level of personalization in offline mass media was practically non-existent.

The third drawback: globality and locality

Mass media can only exist when the news it broadcasts attracts a large audience.

I believe that every public relations specialist who worked in the "Marketing Era" encountered situations where the biggest obstacle to spreading news was often mass media.

This obstacle would happen because the information was relevant to too small of a readership. I vividly remember the beginning of my career in public relations when the refusal of the country's only business newspaper to publish my client's news felt like a death sentence for the information itself. Not because the news was uninteresting (although that sometimes happened) but because the newspaper was too small, and the news was interesting to too few people.

Paradoxically, while being global on a regional scale, mass media is local globally because it only exists where it is read or accessible.

The distribution of newspapers from one country to another is limited due to the localization of their topics, language, and logistics. Therefore, envisioning a single newspaper published in two or more countries is impossible, even theoretically.

Even classic mass media giants like the *Financial Times*, *USA Today*, or the *Guardian*, while theoretically available worldwide and covering global topics,

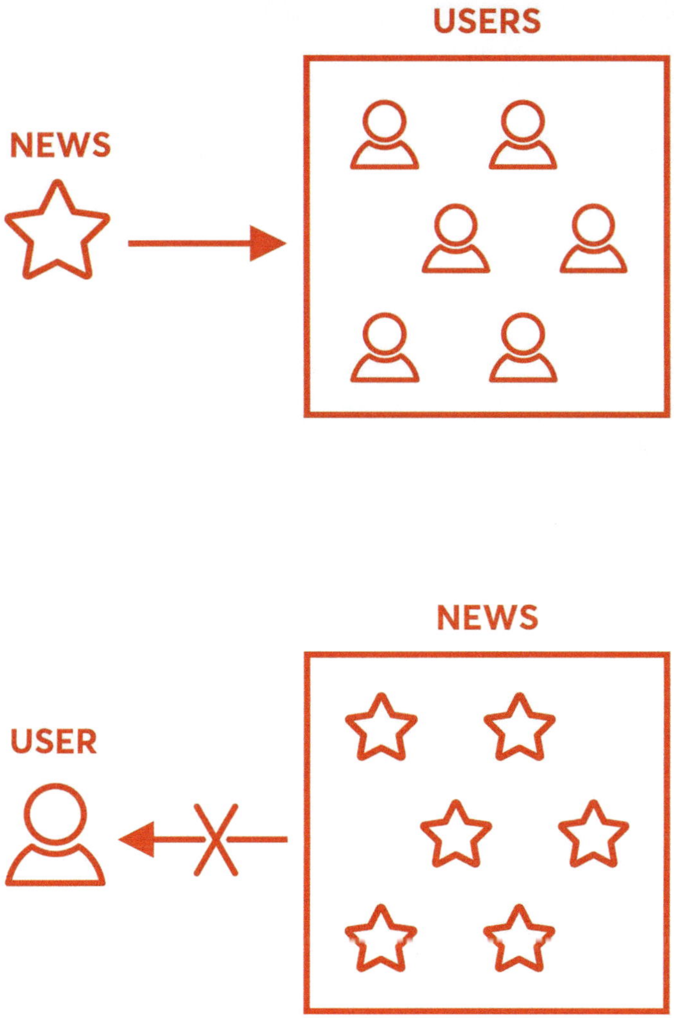

Figure 2.5 Traditional mass media cannot personalize news.

Figure by the author.

in practice, especially in smaller countries, the number of readers could be quite limited.

The fourth drawback: deception

The traditional mass media consumer couldn't and can't know what's on the other side of the media they consume. It's one thing if that consumer is in Scandinavia, where one might not doubt the transparency of traditional mass media. However, many interests could be hidden if the consumer is in another country, which is not so high in transparency indexes.

In the early 1990s, just after my country had regained independence, institutional trust in the media was at its peak. I remember vividly that the most trusted institutions at the top of trust ratings were the church, the mass media, and firefighters.

Why? Well, it's because people who had escaped the communist regime believed everything would become like in the West after shaking off authoritarian rule, maybe not in a year, but certainly in five. They thought the media would be free, independent, and perform the function it did so well in Scandinavian countries. Unfortunately, that's not how it turned out. The beauty of those first days quickly descended into hell, and a lengthy recovery period followed, during which the media had to regain its trust.

Why did this happen? It happened because the owners of free and independent media, seeing the power they had accumulated in their hands, began to abuse that power. They started selling content to those who needed it, only "forgetting" to inform the readers about it.

The fifth drawback: lack of cooperation

Mass media had minimal means to interact with their consumers. This situation happened more due to technical limitations than a lack of willingness to collaborate. Technically, reaching a reader, viewer, or listener was quite challenging, so there wasn't much effort put into gathering their opinions on the content being created. The approach often led to a very aggregated understanding – if they buy and subscribe, that's good enough.

It should be mentioned that traditional mass media did attempt to communicate with their customers. There were efforts to create radio shows with live call-ins, television programs with voting options, and newspaper readers were invited to write letters. Although mass media consumers were somewhat willing to engage in these interactions, it only underscored this drawback rather than negating it.

The monopoly on news creation remained in the hands of the editorial offices, and the desire of mass media consumers to be heard was greatly limited by technical capabilities.

The sixth drawback: a strange marriage

Here I mean the marriage between mass media and advertising. Mass media and advertising have as much in common as shoes and bananas. In other words, they have nothing in common: we need shoes when we want to go somewhere and bananas when we want to eat.

Similarly, mass media and advertising have nothing in common with each other. The function of mass media is to inform, while advertising's purpose is to sell. The only commonality is that to sell, you also need to inform. It seems that this is where the beginnings of this marriage emerged.

The consequence of this marriage is that if we want to read about what our country's parliament decided yesterday, we must almost forcibly read about how excellent the new razors, which we don't need, are.

Why was it so? It's because mass media merchants traded on our attention. We gave it to them for free, and they turned it into a valuable commodity.

English brewer and Conservative politician Richard Moss once said: "The greatest gift you can give another is the purity of your attention." Although Moss lived in the 19th century, he already understood the greatest gift one person can give to another. Since that time, the price of attention has increased significantly. The more information we have, the more valuable attention becomes.

The situation could be portrayed in quite an absurd manner, as if a shoe merchant struck a deal with a banana merchant, and together with the bananas, they offered us a pair of shoes that we didn't need at all.

During the heyday of newspapers, we paid a bit for the shoes, i.e., the work of journalists, by buying newspapers, but we were told that newspapers were so cheap because they contained advertisements. In other words, advertising was presented to the reader as an add-on that they shouldn't worry about because its function was merely to reduce the cost of the newspaper.

In contrast, with advertisers, newspaper advertising managers spoke in a very different tone. They presented circulation figures, i.e., the number of newspaper readers, as a value to advertisers. They sold this value to advertisers as the probability that a newspaper reader interested in current affairs would also pay attention to the advertised new razors. And advertisers were willing to pay substantial sums for this. For what? For our attention. This deal meant that our attention was sold for large sums without asking us if we wanted it.

Of course, there's no criminality involved here – if you don't want it, don't buy the newspaper and find news elsewhere. Unfortunately, during the "Marketing Era," few other sources were available.

Let's leave this situation to history. Someday, I believe it will be recognized as a great deception of thought, but many barbarian things happened a few hundred years ago.

With the advent of the internet, we were led to believe that we could get shoes (the work of journalists) for free, and that advertising was there to make it possible. However, this is just another illusion. We pay for journalists' work with our attention or time, which has become increasingly valuable.

Therefore, it's only a matter of time before the marriage between advertising and mass media ends in divorce. This process is already underway. More and more media outlets offer paid content, meaning we pay for the work of journalists directly; in return, we get articles without advertising. We become interested in advertising when we need something or, in other words, we buy shoes when we need to go somewhere and bananas when we want to eat.

2.1.2. PR Era; or Six Strengths of Social Media

> Social media is reducing social barriers. It connects people on the strength of human values, not identities.
>
> Narendra Modi – politician.

We have discussed the drawbacks of the "Marketing Era", which were essentially unsolvable due to insufficient technology. The internet and the advent of social media eliminated all these shortcomings. While, like all new phenomena, they brought along both good and bad aspects, from the perspective of public relations professionals, they were the missing puzzle piece needed to make the whole river of information flow smoothly.

Let's review the advantages of social media.

The first advantage: affordability

Social media is cheap. Starting your own media outlet in the "PR Era" is inexpensive, or more precisely, doesn't cost anything. The developed internet infrastructure allows anyone to become a means of public communication. The number of friends or followers on social media is the circulation of your media outlet. And numerous examples show that many "editorial teams" on social media become much more popular than traditional media outlets.

The main principle of knowledge dissemination in the "Marketing Era", "Pay & Play", is giving way to a new concept, "Play & Play". This principle means that to spread your message today, you no longer need to worry about where to get money. Today, you can start sharing it. The success of your message will depend solely on you and how relevant it is, as well as how effectively you can attract your readers.

What's also interesting is that, along with this shift in principles, another fascinating trend has emerged – some people are interested in writing, and not for the sake of making money. They are willing to perform some of the same tasks that journalists used to do, but they do it faster, more in-depth, more interestingly, and so on. They do it because they receive compensation in various non-monetary forms: popularity, expertise, job satisfaction, attention, a desire to help society, and many other incentives.

The cost has disappeared; being on social media doesn't cost anything, and competition with traditional media has increased. This competition is a very positive trend: content has become more diverse and exciting, and numerous media groups, pages, and events have emerged that cater to tiny groups of people with specific interests. Today, every rural community, class, gardening or homeowner's association, workplace, or group of people with common interests can have their own media outlet and effectively disseminate news that is important specifically to them. Often, this news is the most crucial for them.

Meanwhile, traditional media that can compete are discovering new ways to present information from different angles.

The second advantage: personalization

Social media excels at personalizing news and addresses one of the main shortcomings of traditional media – the inability to curate a set of important information for an individual. In practice, this means that we can receive only the news that is most relevant to us.

Indeed, in the age of non-personalized media that many of us lived in for many years, we often lacked the skills to manage our information flow. However, it's only a matter of time before those skills emerge.

During a morning walk with my daughter, I heard her say that she had cleaned up her YouTube channel subscriptions the previous week, reducing the number from 200 to just 30. Her reasoning for doing so seemed quite logical: "I used to subscribe to some channels just because they were created by people I know, but now I've realized that the sheer volume of content was drowning out the news and topics I'm truly interested in." So, with a few clicks, she took action, removing some channels from her media landscape while making others more accessible. She quickly and effortlessly personalized her media stream. Let's imagine this action in the context of the "Marketing Era".

I believe that a significant portion of the population has not fully developed the ability to personalize information. However, the emerging Gen Z generation has grown up with it and sees it as a natural phenomenon.

Paradoxically, this advantage of social media is often the feature for which social media is frequently criticized. Critics argue that personalization means an inevitable isolation in "echo chambers" or "information bubbles", where society estranges itself because each group or bubble receives support for their most distorted ideas. While I can understand this point of view, I don't see how it is exclusive to social media. The drawbacks presented by these critics seem very similar to those faced by any technological diversity invented in any era. People smashed looms because they "stole" their jobs, and there were fears of the end of the world with the advent of electricity. As I've heard, the mobile phone that preceded social media was blamed for the loss of privacy.

However, blaming innovations instead of acknowledging the inability to change oneself and make the most of all the beautiful opportunities brought by the latest human inventions is as old as the hills.

Indeed, tools like the printing press, electricity, the internet, the telephone, and social media are remarkable and sometimes seem like unbelievable human inventions. And we, each of us, are entirely free to decide whether to use them.

So, staying within "bubbles" is a personal choice. People have chosen, are choosing, and will continue to choose. Opting to isolate oneself within one's chosen circle is much better than living within the mass media circle against one's will. The vast mass media circle hasn't disappeared; it can still be chosen, but now there are many new circles to choose from or not to choose. Everyone can choose to be in one process or not, consume what the masses do, or focus only on what matters to a small group of like-minded individuals.

Figure 2.6 Perhaps it's time to work on addressing your negative character traits? Nobody reads my blog.

Artwork by Christiann MacAuley.

Today, we can access personalized news, which is a significant advancement in terms of the information society and the dissemination of free information.

The third advantage: globality and locality

In the "Marketing Era", I mentioned globality as a drawback, but this drawback turns into an advantage in the "PR Era". Social media allows the existence of the smallest audiences of information consumers, starting from as few as three people. With three family members, I can create a highly effective and cost-free media channel for my family in just a few seconds. I can also easily keep it private from prying eyes. Without social media, such channels would not have been possible or would have required inordinate efforts.

What's more, my tiny family media channel can also be entirely global, meaning my family members can live on different continents and still have access to the latest and most relevant information.

In other words, there are no media outlets that are too small in social media, but at the same time, there are no geographical limitations. News doesn't lose its importance because it's relevant to a small circle or because its recipients are far apart.

While during the heyday of the mass media, there were attempts to have small local media outlets (for example, large companies publishing internal newsletters, community newspapers, or other tangible media), the contemporary popularity of internal company groups, intranets, and similar communication means for small groups of people unquestionably demonstrates what was missing until now.

Social media has addressed another drawback of traditional media – it has provided the opportunity to have one's own media outlet with any number of users.

The fourth advantage: openness

Here, we encounter yet another paradox. In the "Marketing Era", and often even after it, there were attempts to claim that the only professional media was the traditional media. Of course, these claims were made by conventional media representatives, clearly trying to defend their stronghold.

A myth was created, suggesting that editorial boards were the professional filters that sifted through insignificant information and left what truly mattered. At the same time, it was argued that social media was an unfiltered stream of information where anyone could create any profile and disseminate information.

However, completely different trends have emerged, with social media becoming a part of our lives. It turned out that while you can create anything about anything, such "projects" have a very short lifespan and don't gain much support. To create something more long-lasting, you must do it openly and adhere to your established rules. As soon as you start breaking those rules, readers notice it, and they turn away from you and choose something else. In other words, for every participant in social media, the most important thing becomes what is the core element of the "PR Era" – reputation. In social media, the relationship between the information disseminator and its recipient is empathetic – it directly affects the growth or decline of the audience. Due to the high volume of individuals involved in information exchange, deception becomes either impossible or is quickly exposed, damaging a reputation that took a long time to build.

Let's take any politician as an example and compare the information from that politician's social media account with the knowledge from traditional media. Which data is more reliable?

While this may not be immediately obvious, a politician's direct thoughts on social media often appear more reliable simply because it is their unfiltered opinion. I will only hear it in traditional media after it has been interpreted by the specific media outlet's editor or journalist. It's OK if they do it objectively, but what if that media outlet is one of those that trades in trust but hides paid content from readers?

To choose which politician to vote for, I first look at the politician's social media profile because here, I get what that politician wants to convey. Then, I can read other opinions, assess them, and draw conclusions.

The fifth advantage: collaboration

Collaboration is one of the four legs on the social media table[4]. It's also another transformation of a drawback of traditional media into an advantage of social media.

Information exchange is the fuel that drives the engine of social media. People and organizations exchange their available information and create various types of content, striving to present it as clearly and attractively as possible.

Just think about the opportunities it has opened up for corporate communication! In the "Marketing Era", a company's know-how often remained confined within the company's offices or production facilities. Getting acquainted with it, at best, was possible through visits or learning a few things from the company's employees. Moreover, this knowledge was often deliberately hidden and claimed to be a commercial secret of one organization or another.

Today, everything has been turned upside down: value is created not by how much you hide but by how openly and creatively you can explain how you solve various challenges.

Collaboration is the foundation of social media, not an additional function, as it was in the case of traditional media.

Imagine that you are a public relations specialist for a sewing company. What kind of news could you create about the company in the "Marketing Era" if we don't focus on those "pushed" for advertising purposes? There weren't much: you could occasionally expect interviews with the company's executives, a few press releases about achievements, some about new collections, perhaps more exciting employees, and a few other things. However, the news arsenal was minimal because traditional media could only take as much as they could or wanted to.

But was that everything you wanted to say about the company? No! Your company would have accumulated a vast amount of fascinating and unique information about choosing the right costume, what materials are suitable for what, why one model is discontinued and another is produced, and many other things. However, in the "Marketing Era", the opportunities to disseminate this information were limited or costly.

Today, social media allows you to disseminate all your information. While it doesn't guarantee quality, it opens up unlimited possibilities. Your relationship with your information consumers ensures quality, i.e., if you can deliver what they expect from you – you can do it anytime without any restrictions. You can collaborate directly with your audience:

- Answer questions.
- Provide requested material.
- Address complaints.
- Share market innovations from other countries.
- Engage information consumers in dialogue, or
- In short, you have unlimited collaboration opportunities.

The sixth advantage: partnership

The strange marriage of the "Marketing Era" is being replaced by partnership in the "PR Era". In today's world of social media, we see various examples of information and advertising partnerships: from complete divorces, where data is created without any connection to advertising (Wikipedia, paid media outlets), to internet portals that still operate on an advertising basis, where information creation is still funded by advertising revenue.

That's how it should be. I believe that in the future, we will see various other types of partnerships, and that's very good. I will discuss this in more detail in Chapter 5. I wouldn't say that the marriage of advertising and information will completely disappear, but advertising will no longer have a dominant role in information creation.

Social media has shown us many more types of partnerships than the traditional marriage of information and advertising. It has already colored the world and will continue to paint it with various shades of information.

Of course, every era has its advantages and disadvantages. There are likely areas where the "Marketing Era" had advantages over the "PR Era". However, my goal was to highlight the essential drawbacks of the "Marketing Era" that prevented the world from moving toward a free flow of information and how the "PR Era", with social media at the forefront, addressed those shortcomings.

2.2. Three Main Reasons for the Communications Revolution

> Life is a song – sing it. Life is a game – play it. Life is a challenge – meet it. Life is a dream – realize it. Life is a sacrifice – offer it. Life is love – enjoy it.
>
> Sai Baba – spiritual master and fakir.

Having discussed the main drawbacks and advantages of both eras, it's worth briefly reviewing why one replaced the other.

When changes occur in any field, it's always essential to determine how much of those changes are natural and long-anticipated, meaning irreversible, and how much are new fashions or trends, i.e., temporary things. With the same perspective, it's essential to look at the changes that have occurred or are taking place in communication.

In the world of technology, different innovations spread at different speeds. Data from various sources may vary slightly, but the essence remains. According to established tradition, a technology is considered widespread when at least 50 million users use it worldwide. It took 62 years for automobiles to reach this number. While cars can be viewed as a communication platform to some extent, let's move on to some things closer to what we are discussing. Wired telephones reached this number in over 50 years, electricity in 46, television in 22, computers in 14, mobile phones in 12, the internet in 7, Facebook in 4, and WeChat in 1 year. Pokemon Go reached this number in . . . 19 days!

Why is the popularity of social networks so rapid? Of course, technology and the services' immaterial nature play significant roles here. Previously, to get people to purchase cars or to introduce electricity or phones (even mobile ones), a lot of investment was required beforehand – into roads, transmission lines, and signal transmission towers. For social networks, the infrastructure, for the most part, was already in place, and it was just a matter of using it. Infrastructure is critical. However, a social network with millions of users also requires substantial investments – in servers, personnel, and offices. And most importantly, if these services were not needed, users would probably not rush to use them, even if everything worked flawlessly.

Without dismissing the importance of infrastructure, the main reasons for this boom were different.

So why did social media become so popular worldwide so quickly? Was it because having your accounts and sharing information became trendy, or did social media provide people with new technologies and opportunities? My answer is unequivocal – people have been eagerly awaiting the day when they would have the communication opportunities that social media provides today.

As mentioned when describing the differences between the two eras, new things establish themselves when their appearance changes the primary functions in place until then. For example, the role of art before the invention of the camera was obvious – to represent as accurately as possible what the artist saw. The artist was essentially a craftsman with an apparent task – to reflect reality as accurately as possible, sometimes even by using strong exaggeration. Those artists who could do this well received good pay for their work. However, recognized masters like Van Gogh were poor because no one understood their art. They were believed to be dilettantes and incapable of doing their job well. But as soon as photography emerged, art became art. Photography took over its primary function, i.e., depicting reality, and artists began to be evaluated by other criteria. Today, an artist who can accurately display what they see is considered inexperienced and the creator of kitsch.

Van Gogh's paintings have indeed come to be appreciated for their use of color and shadows, their uniqueness, and many other criteria that have nothing to do with depicting reality. Even more interesting is that when art lost its primary function, its value rose. People started searching for unique originals; today, they are willing to spend millions to acquire them.

Indeed, there are many examples of this phenomenon. Horses and automobiles, honor guards and security companies, horses and farming, vintage cars and aeroplanes – all of these are characterized by two things: the loss of the primary function of the old phenomenon, the better fulfilment of the role by the new phenomenon, and the increased value of the old item.

However, what about communication? Similar processes are constantly occurring in communication. We can start with how we used to communicate long ago, but primitive cave drawings today are considered valuable, rare, and objects protected by states or even international organizations. In ancient times, their function was purely practical – conveying news and recording information. Then came writing and books. Today, bibliophiles are willing to pay exorbitant amounts for the first books when their primary function was straightforward – conveying news and recording information.

Indeed, evolution and technological progress have brought about significant changes in communication: the wired telephone, mobile phones, text messaging, and ultimately – social networks.

In the 1980s, people used to speculate whether it would be possible to communicate with each other without collecting phone numbers and without being tethered to a cord. Today, these questions are no longer relevant. Today, you can communicate in the forest, in the countryside, by the lake – the world has become accessible anywhere. Moreover, this communication is practically free compared to the costs of international calls in the 1980s.

Each new means of communication has taken over the functions of the old ones and supplemented them. Like traditional media, social media can spread information to a large audience. Often, this audience significantly exceeds the audience of traditional media outlets.

Social media has provided each of its users with the opportunity to:

- Construct their personalized news feed based on their needs.
- Become a media outlet themselves.
- Participate and collaborate in creating content.

These opportunities are a significant leap forward indeed. In the virtual social space, many people can simultaneously share information and opinions, comment, and react. All of this happens in real time. To put it in perspective, think about when you had to wait until the next day to get news from a newspaper. Social media's instant and interactive nature has transformed how we communicate and access information.

I believe there are three main reasons for the change of eras. I have named these reasons with the words that most closely relate to them: DREAM, INFERIORITY, and OPPORTUNITY.

2.2.1. Dream

> We need men who can dream of things that never were.
>
> John F. Kennedy – politician.

Dreams come in two types: some come true, and others do not. However, most likely, to have at least one dream come true, you also need to have 99 which will not be destined to happen. This principle applies to other areas:

- If we want to have a top-level basketball team, thousands of children must play sports.
- If we're going to have a unicorn, we must have thousands of start-ups.
- If we want to receive one Nobel Prize, we must have thousands of creative scientists.

And while not all dreaming people are creators, all creators are dreamers. And dreaming begins when something is lacking. Human dreams are always about what one does not have.

I would divide the dream of direct communication into three parts:

- Reaching large groups without intermediaries.
- Being the face of an organization.
- Being more significant than large organizations.

Until the advent of social media, many people dreamed of **communicating directly without intermediaries with large groups of people**. I am sure that many of these dreamers were communication specialists because they were significantly frustrated with the dictation of intermediaries, i.e., mass media.

It turns out that many other people had this dream as well. With the advent of social media, it became evident that many people had a strong desire to express their thoughts but had kept that desire locked away because there were no means to realize it. Well, perhaps not entirely "no" means, but those opportunities were minimal: communicating during lunch breaks with colleagues or at a party with friends certainly did not provide the kind of audience social networks offer today.

The desire of the person who wanted to communicate was not satisfied with one-way mass media and those breaks and parties.

Similarly, public relations professionals were not satisfied with the limited opportunities offered by traditional mass media: press releases, press conferences, interviews, and other such public relations classics.

Traditional public relations were highly dependent on the media. If the media did not pick up the sender's message, it essentially determined that the news would go unheard. Although there were opportunities to communicate directly with the public or specific groups during the era of traditional communication, those opportunities were minimal, and the reach was often quite symbolic.

There were extensive guides on how to appeal to mass media: writing a press release that would suit mass media, organizing a press conference to attract mass media, and preparing material that mass media would "buy". Nobody worried about the information recipient – mass media's primary goal. Of course, mass media claimed that they only published or broadcast what was attractive to their audience, but that wasn't true because there weren't the technical means for it.

I'm not saying that the skills to capture the interest of mass media are worthless these days, far from it. However, the significance of mass media itself has dramatically diminished.

During the Marketing Era I knew of two groups of dreamers: the larger one, i.e., people who wanted to communicate widely, and the smaller one, i.e., public relations specialists who lacked the tools to disseminate their information.

This dream can be called a dream of dialogue or many dialogues simultaneously – a multilogue.

Public relations are an ongoing dialogue and public relations specialists have always been skilled at three things – communicating, organizing, and writing. Today, conversations can and do take place in small groups, involving people of various professions and backgrounds, and each person is both media and consumer. The number of friends and followers each person has on social media is undoubtedly their media outlet's circulation. People were dissatisfied with the lack of communication and dreamed of times when there would be no shortage, and those times have now arrived.

Do you remember that world without the internet? The one with newspapers, television, and landline phones? The one where, after calling on that landline phone and not hearing a voice on the other end, we decided that the person wasn't at home?

In that world, people could only dream about calling three people at the same time, seeing them, or writing a message that a hundred people would read. It was simply impossible.

However, impossibility in no way means a lack of desire. On the contrary, the more a person naturally feels the desire for something but also feels that they cannot attain it for some reason, the stronger that desire grows.

We can say that in the era dominated by the traditional media, the "Marketing Era", whether consciously or unconsciously, people ardently desired to communicate without limits, without intermediaries, without geographical boundaries, and without the influence of the media.

Today, public knowledge is formed through various channels and in multiple directions. If we imagine all the world's information as an ocean, that ocean has many rivers flowing into it, forming seas within it. The currents of these rivers vary in strength: some create new tides in the water, while others have a lesser impact but still contribute to their waters. Information also enters the ocean as rain: sometimes heavy, sometimes very fine. The raindrops are each of our contributions to the sea of information. The organization Future Exploration Network[5] visualized this nicely and described it in the section The Future of Media.

In the past, our imagined ocean was more like a sea, with one large tributary – the vast river of traditional media – and many very tiny streams.

Of course, like a natural ocean, the ocean of information evaporates; that is, water flows into and evaporates from it. In the form of information vapor, each of us takes our portion. Some people overindulge and suffer from an excessive amount of informational water.

In the past, the sea also used to evaporate. Still, the evaporating water had a significantly lower concentration then because the sea received information water from a much smaller number of tributaries.

The second part of the dream of direct communication – the dream of **being the face of the organization** – also came true in abundance. In the "Marketing Era", in public relations theory, it was customary to divide all public relations into two parts – internal and external. Internal relations were those intended for the organization's employees, while external relations aimed at various audiences – mass media, communities, politicians, partners, and investors.

We continue to work successfully with external and internal audiences, but all public relations specialists have long changed their attitude towards them. While in the past, these audiences were the ultimate goal of the messages conveyed, today, all of these (both internal and external) audiences

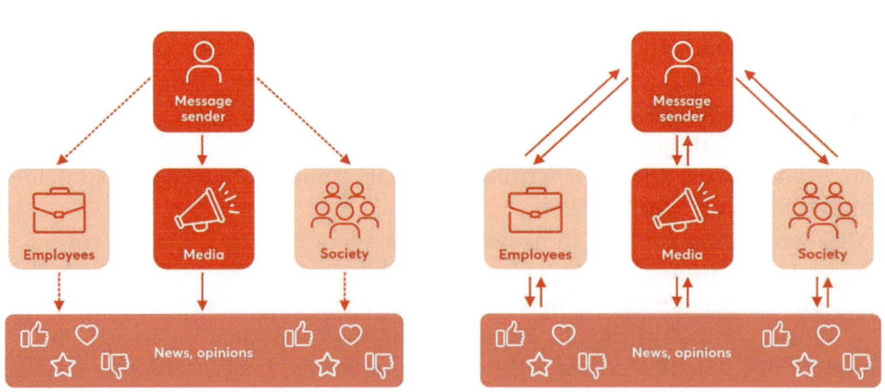

Figure 2.7 Today, knowledge and opinions are formed through various channels and directions.

Figure by the author.

must be seen not only as the goal but also as a means of further message dissemination.

Formerly internal audiences have become particularly important today.

Today, public relations professionals in organizations have a much broader range of mass media tools than in the "Marketing Era". One of these media tools is employees with significant social media followings. In other words, public relations specialists in organizations today must not only think about reaching traditional media or other external audiences but also be able to prepare exciting content for their employees and encourage them to share it.

Here, we can also remember simple tricks like employee awards, participation in various activities, as well as more complex ones, such as proposals for employees to share company news and presentations, speaking on behalf of the company, participating in discussions, etc.

Some employees today want and can represent organizations, so it would be strange to limit, ignore, or underutilize their willingness to build the organization's reputation.

The third part of the dream of direct communication – is the **opportunity for every person to be more important than any organization, no matter how large**.

The practice of social media has shown that individuals can be much more significant in shaping public opinion than organizations of any size.

At the time of writing this book, NATO's Twitter account had more than 700,000 followers, and its leader, Jens Stoltenberg, had more than 500,000; the World Health Organization had 9.2 million followers, and its leader, Tedros Adhanom Ghebreyesus, had 1.4 million followers; The White House had 5 million followers, and US President Joe Biden had 29.7 million followers.

While not always the case, the popularity of individuals can often surpass that of organizations, and the opportunity for one person to have audiences numbering in the hundreds of thousands or even millions is evident. A famous, important, influential person can have direct contact with their audience completely unrestricted by either the organization they represent or, even more so, the media. This situation is entirely different than during the "Marketing Era".

While many organizations have their Facebook and Twitter accounts, unfortunately, not many effectively utilize these channels, often unsure what to do online. The first step to ensure social networks work effectively is to ensure a continuous flow of information rather than sporadically posting occasional updates. Additionally, swift responses are crucial – news should be fresh, and reader queries should be addressed promptly. Some organizations find it challenging to do this because each message has to go through a lengthy approval process, often causing them to become outdated by the time they reach the audience.

Indeed, this opens up an entirely new space and new functions that public relations specialists must implement. They should be granted more authority to communicate directly, with top-level management coordinating only the essential messages. The importance of trust in the public relations professional and reputation significantly increases in this context.

Before the era of social media, a person could be their source of information for themselves, their close ones, friends, and colleagues. However, an intermediary – the media, sometimes called the "fourth estate" – was required to speak to millions. But with the advent of social media, every individual became a potential media outlet.

In the PR era, many dreams of the "Marketing Era" have become a reality.

2.2.2. Inferiority

> Wherever an inferiority complex exists, there is a good reason for it.
>
> Carl Jung – psychiatrist and psychoanalyst.

In the "Marketing Era", we all lived in conditions of communication inadequacy. This inadequacy meant that we either accumulated or received much information but lacked the means to disseminate it. Social media has practically allowed us to spread information without significant restrictions.

Once again, communication inadequacy can be divided into three parts:

- Information restriction.
- Social schizophrenia.
- Mass media business peculiarities.

Many people believe that the role of a public relations specialist is to conceal information, but I say the opposite. My experience tells me that 95% of the information a client possesses is what they could and would like to make public. Still, there are too few channels, or those channels have limited reach, allowing only a portion of the information to be disseminated. The remaining 5% is confidential company information that the company could release but is restricted by confidentiality commitments.

Let's imagine a funnel at the bottom with a small hole. All our information is the funnel's content, and the possibilities to disseminate it are like the small hole at the bottom of the funnel. It could be said that the hole was the mass media, which only let out a tiny portion of the information – sometimes, the information was consumed very slowly, and sometimes, it was poured out because it went wrong. On the other hand, I don't want to blame the media here – it spreads as much information as possible. A more appropriate name for the small hole would probably be **technological underdevelopment, which limited information**.

With the emergence of new forms of social media, societal awareness has increased. People seemed eager to solve various issues in various fields: politics, economics, education, community life – you name it. This eagerness has

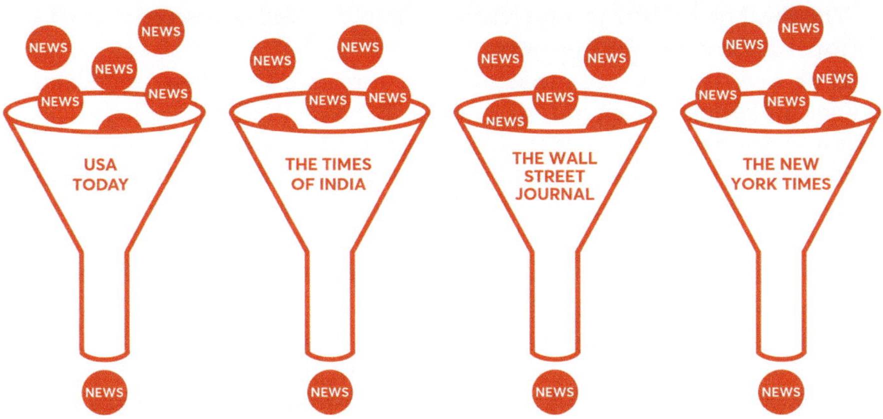

Figure 2.8 Communication inadequacy caused by technological underdevelopment.
Figure by the author.

always been a hallmark of democratic systems, but the deluge of information brought about by social media fundamentally changed the landscape.

The second part of incomplete information is **social schizophrenia**. This phenomenon is described in the book *Socialnomics*[6] by Eric Qualman. Due to social schizophrenia, during the "Marketing Era", we only knew a small part of the information about most acquaintances. For example, a company's financial specialist was known to his colleagues at work only by what he wanted to reveal there. However, he became a completely different person once he left the company's office. Returning home, he became a father, about whose work life his family may have had only limited knowledge. In another part of his life, he lived as someone meeting friends for basketball games and cheerfully raising glasses of beer for his favorite team's victory. All this was contained within one person who changed depending on the time and place.

It's possible that even today, our financial specialist lives like that and perhaps fears social media. Still, statistics say that in 2022 out of 333 million US residents, 302 million, or 91%, used social media today. In China, just over 1 billion out of 1.4 billion, or 72%, used social media; in Brazil, 166 million out of 204 million, or 81%, used social media; and in the UK, the number was 62 million out of 68 million, or 91%.[7]

So, it's more likely that our financial specialist is on social media than not. It means we know at least a bit more about him than we did during the "Marketing Era". Perhaps he's an active scuba diver on vacation, and we find out from his Facebook profile. Or maybe he gives excellent presentations and shares them on his LinkedIn profile. While he may not fully reveal himself to us even today, we see him as a more well-rounded and human individual than ever before.

For many people, social schizophrenia wasn't very acceptable, and many tried to avoid it. The inability to be fully visible in society significantly impacted people's communication shortcomings.

The third part of the incompleteness complex is the **characteristics of traditional mass media in business**.

If we look at traditional media, we'll see it relies on a peculiar foundation – trading in people's attention. The reader is given the illusion that they are getting the content cheaply or for free. However, this is not the case – the individual is treated as a commodity, and their attention is traded. If we delve deeper into this phenomenon, we realize that it's a quite significant and widespread deception. When people notice advertisements, they are giving away a portion of their attention and mental resources. It can also be said that they surrender some of their leisure or work time.

Various research findings differ, but today, most scientists agree that the eight-hour workday is not based on a person's ability to work productively for that many hours per day but on factory workers' shift patterns. In the late-18th century, factories required employees to work 10–16 hours daily. Later, the eight-hour workday was fought for and established, but this calculation still doesn't have much in common with modern office work. It simply transfers hours from the factory to the office setting.

Researchers still don't have a unanimous opinion on how productive a person is in the office daily, but most tend to lean towards . . . three hours! Even if it's four or five hours, there are still at least another three or four hours during which a person does something in the office. So, what do they do there? We all know the answers: they talk with colleagues about non-work matters, look for other jobs, smoke, talk on the phone with their significant other or children, make and drink coffee or tea, write messages, and prepare food and snacks. However, a significant portion of this time is dedicated to consuming media. Today, this portion is shared by traditional and social media, but before the advent of social media, it was all traditional media.

Returning to the fact that the traditional media business relies on trading in people's attention, and the majority of the time not spent on work-related tasks is dedicated to consuming media, we can understand that this is an excellent example of the utilization of the incompleteness complex. A person, obligated to be in the office according to their employment contract but having nothing to do there, is essentially held in a mild form of captivity. To compensate for their incompleteness at the office, they resort to various substitutes for passing the time. The most popular of these is the media.

We should not forget another characteristic of the mass media business that has different implications depending on the country. This characteristic is the trade in trust. While this trade was almost non-existent in some countries, such as Scandinavia, in many Eastern European countries, for example, this type of trade was deeply rooted.

Today, many young people are distancing themselves from traditional media. Social media allows them to see the content they want to see and participate in discussions they want to engage in. Even if they are still confined to offices, their media consumption habits are much more meaningful because they consume identical content and participate in its creation.

Indeed, suppose we add to this shift the trend of not being tethered to a physical workplace and working from anywhere. In that case, we will achieve complete liberation from the communicative incompleteness complex. Future generations will work as much as they need to and consume media only when they want and to the degree they want.

Today, the caps on the bottleneck are no longer there, and all that pent-up flow has poured into the public domain. Of course, this is not solely a positive process, as because everyone has access to the means of information dissemination, they are used by both those who know how to use them and those who do not.

At one point, with the rapid rise of social media, I had a hobby of observing how former authorities seemed to "degrade". There are many examples where even former professional journalists, who used to work solely under editorial filters, struggle to manage their information flow when they enter the public domain. Instead of utilizing their skills to produce quality content, they become individuals with extreme views.

One particularly memorable example is the former chief editor of a central news agency, who used to be a significant authority in the era of traditional marketing. Unable or unwilling to understand the power and purpose of social media, they began to speak openly and unprofessionally on social networks. This lack of understanding eventually cost them their job.

Managing information is as crucial as driving a car, preparing meals, or handling one's finances. Sometimes, you hear about cases where people win a million in the lottery who had previously struggled to make ends meet. Not only do they not improve their lives, but with a crash, they plunge into deep debt after squandering the million they received. Ultimately, it's not the amount of money but the ability to manage it that determines everything.

Communication works in a very similar way – successful communication is determined not by the quantity of communication tools, or the money spent on communication, but by the professionalism of the communicator.

A social media profile is not a mirror of a person's face; it's a mirror of their ability to communicate and of the substance they have to communicate.

2.2.3. Opportunity

> Any human anywhere will blossom in a hundred unexpected talents and capacities simply by being given the opportunity to do so.
>
> Doris Lessing – novelist.

In the Marketing Era, not everyone had the technical means to disseminate information. However, in our current era, particularly in democratic countries, technological advancements have empowered individuals to spread information instantly. This shift in communication has unlocked boundless opportunities for professionals in the field.

This transformed landscape is akin to the vast array of channels in Brian Solis's Conversation Prism, illustrating the many options available for communication and engagement. Yet, this portrayal merely scratches the surface of what lies ahead. We stand at the threshold of a new era in public relations, characterized by an intricate web of connections and interactions.

The first version of Conversation Prism, with the central slogan "The Art of Listening, Learning, and Sharing"[8], aptly encapsulates the essence of contemporary communication dynamics. Within this realm are professionals, artisans, amateurs, creators of trivial content, and even revered figures. Like traditional art forms, social media artistry encompasses trends, geographical nuances, and influential personalities. In essence, it embodies all the hallmarks of a proper art form.

Today, various devices that are always with us allow us to respond to a conversation, comment on news, and express our emotions at any time. It's not even necessary for the conversation partner to be nearby. If you suddenly become a witness to an event, all you need to do is turn on your camera and start streaming. If the event proves to be interesting enough, you may have hundreds or even thousands of viewers. People find it very important to see how everything unfolds: unedited footage travels directly from witnesses' phones to the screens of millions of viewers. Therefore, quality is no longer critical here – speed and being on the scene is crucial. These events can be local and significant to a large group of people. People not only want to film or photograph but also share their opinions, talk about their activities, and, in this way, seek recognition from the public.

In 2014, Aerosmith visited Lithuania. The visit wasn't short, so Steven Tyler and Co. had time to walk around the old town, meet with the country's president, and sing along with their fans, who greeted them with violins and rocked out to "Crazy".

Steven Tyler wrote two Facebook posts about this stroll.

The first was about the fans they met: "I KNEW WE WROTE THAT SONG FOR A REASON. DRAGGIN THEM ON STAGE FOR SURE!! #VILNIUS #LITHUANIA."

The second one was about meeting the President of Lithuania: "AN HONOR TO MEET SUCH A POWERFUL FORCE OF LOVE, UNDERSTANDING & POLITICS Dalia Grybauskaitė SHE IS A GIFT TO LITHUANIA."

Even though such words certainly warmed my Lithuanian heart, here I would like to draw attention to a slightly different important aspect for us public relations specialists.

More than 30,000 of his readers supported the first post, and the second one had more than 24,000! These numbers represent the people who liked or reacted to the posts, and I won't venture to guess how many read them. Steven Tyler himself has more than 2 million followers on his Facebook account. Over 1.1 million viewers viewed the video on his YouTube channel!

Would such a situation have been possible 20 years ago? No. Would such a situation have been possible with traditional media? Most likely not, as they weren't around when Steven Tyler sang with his fans. The media was not invited to the meeting with the president either. But even if the Lithuanian media had covered these events, it's doubtful that anyone abroad would have paid attention to it.

In this case, Steven Tyler's posts were of immense importance in communication, both to his fans and to the Lithuanian president – they significantly contributed to the reputation of those young women and the president herself. And the most important thing is that it happened without any help from traditional media. It was an excellent example of public relations that occurred without traditional media and was far more effective than it might have been with their assistance.

Is Steven Tyler's account a media outlet? Undoubtedly. Is Steven Tyler a journalist? As far as I know, he is not, but unquestionably, he is an opinion leader and significantly influences the people who follow him.

This example summarizes all three reasons for the communications revolution:

- Traditional media were not needed to ensure visibility.
- The information was interesting to Steven Tyler's fans and therefore garnered such interest.
- Technology allowed this news to spread worldwide within minutes.

This small example reveals the tremendous opportunities social media has opened up for people: the ability to communicate directly, provide unfiltered and uninterpreted information, share content, and react. And let's not forget the possibilities to track the popularity and reach of your news, engage in two-way communication, and measure the effectiveness of your activities! If you can gather a dedicated audience and consistently deliver high-quality information, having your own media outlet is relatively straightforward.

I often used to ask my students whom they trust more – a political blog or traditional media. I tend to trust blogs much more because there's an obvious criterion here – either I trust the person writing it, or I don't. The choice is very clear-cut – if they deceive me even once, I won't trust them anymore and won't read their content. Meanwhile, finding out who is directly or indirectly behind paid articles appearing in various media outlets is difficult or even impossible. It's like a smokescreen where it's hard to see whose interests the information serves.

The logical transition from one era to another occurred due to the natural human desire and need to communicate with many people freely. One-way communication was not very human. In the past, it was possible to deliver one message to thousands, but it was impossible to convey a thousand messages to one person. The size of the group ceased to be necessary, and accessible two-way communication emerged, replacing monologue with dialogue.

Today, the public relations profession is more necessary than ever because, for all these reasons, reputation has become highly valuable. The significance of reputation will only continue to grow in the future.

2.3. What Is Changing and What Stays Stable Forever?

> The three main elements of public relations are practically as old as society: informing people, persuading people, or integrating people with people. Of course, the means and methods of accomplishing these ends have changed as society has changed.
>
> Edward Louis Bernays – pioneer in the field of public relations and propaganda.

I'm a big admirer of all the new inventions of humanity. I believe that humans exist to learn more, discover new things, travel, fly, dive into the depths of oceans and the Earth, and explore the universe. No invention is made immediately and without mistakes. On the contrary, many inventions result from countless errors. Until humans understood that there was enough sunshine to satisfy all of today's electricity needs, they had to dig deep into the Earth, burn enormous amounts of fossils, and heavily pollute the environment.

On the one hand, these are mistakes, but on the other hand, in this journey of mistakes, we discover amazing things and create technologies that now send us images from Mars. It's fantastic, and I believe that during my lifetime, I will witness many things that our ancestors born in the early-20th century couldn't even dream of. I am convinced that today, humanity and the world are living in the most beautiful times, and the future will be even more beautiful.

However, alongside the admiration for what has been achieved and how technology has changed, there is always a feeling that something remains unchanged, just as it was. Recently, I discovered handwritten memoirs by my grandfather from the mid-20th century. They are about his childhood, adolescence, and youth. It is exciting to read them today, at the end of the first quarter of the 21st century. However, the most important thing is that while reading them, I was accompanied by a strong feeling – how similarly he and I think, reason, express feelings, and assess the events happening around us. He was born in 1901 and is long gone, and I am 76 years younger and in the middle of my life. It doesn't matter that he had the chance to ride in horse-drawn carriages, while I can fly in aeroplanes today, observe images from Mars, or communicate with anyone on this Earth without regard to distance.

I feel that while modes of transportation and communication have changed beyond recognition, our need and desire to travel or say something to someone in another city remain the same. I feel that no matter how many years back in time we travel, we will always discover the same human desires, needs, and aspirations.

So what changes and what does not? The answer, I believe, is obvious: **technology changes**, but **humanity remains the same** – in its desire to love and be loved, to explore and strive for the unattainable. Each technology is invented to facilitate the pursuit of what does not change.

2.3.1. Ever-Changing Technologies

> The advance of technology is based on making it fit in so that you don't really even notice it, so it's part of everyday life.
>
> Bill Gates – business magnate, software developer, investor, author, and philanthropist.

Technology provides humans with tools that possess three characteristics that are constantly changing and allow us to achieve more extraordinary dreams. Here's a brief overview of each of these characteristics.

Speed

While I often hear from Gen Z that the internet lags, freezes, or barely moves today, I understand that we have come a long way compared to the speed at which information was transmitted, even at the end of the 20th century. Today, we can communicate in real time and see the interlocutor from anywhere in the world where there is an internet connection. We can transmit information to any corner of the world in an instant. Not to mention that we can already receive images from Mars. On the other hand, internet connectivity is not yet available everywhere on Earth, and it takes a day or so to receive images from Mars. So speed will continue to change, i.e., increase.

Accessibility

Recently, I took my child to the doctor, and while I was waiting in the car, I chatted with colleagues from two other countries for half an hour. While driving, I had a great conversation with my son and discussed what had happened in his life the day before. Then, we visited my mom, wished her a happy birthday, and had a slice of cake each. After half an hour, my son and I attended two different activities: he was in class with 25 classmates, and I was in a work meeting with colleagues from ten countries. Afterwards, we could spend another hour chatting with my mom. Isn't that amazing? No, it's the reality we live in. We can be reached anywhere and anytime if we need to, or we can turn everything off and enjoy a book or our favorite music. It's when we want, not when we can.

On the other hand, sometimes we are temporarily unreachable – when travelling by train, the connection may drop, and there is no signal on a ship or plane. The last time I was mushroom picking during one of my client's international conferences with a hundred participants, I noticed places in the forest without signal. And, of course, those spots had the most beautiful mushrooms! So accessibility will continue to change, i.e., increase.

Platforms

And finally, today, we have the most excellent platforms that cater to our various needs, the most significant being communication – being part of social interaction. Today, without thinking, we exchange images, texts, and comments; we laugh simultaneously in different parts of the world, listen to music, and conveniently store information. Recently, while looking for family photos, I came across my late grandmother's notebook, where she had neatly written down phone numbers alphabetically. How ancient it seemed! I had one like it back in my childhood. Today, we share numbers, store long texts and images, and work together on a single text or visual content.

On the other hand, we do everything on flat screens, looking at a small computer screen, without feeling like we're sitting together at a table. But it's only a matter of time. So, platforms will continue to change, i.e., they will become more convenient and realistic.

The changing technologies have opened up vast opportunities for public relations professionals, but this is just the beginning.

2.3.2. Never-Changing Man

> When people appear to be something else than good and decent, it is only because they are reacting to stress, pain, or the deprivation of basic human needs such as security, love, and self-esteem.
>
> Abraham Maslow – psychologist.

Fundamentally, a person never really changes. And I certainly won't come up with anything more innovative in this area than one of the world's most renowned psychologists, Abraham Maslow, who created the brilliant Maslow's Hierarchy of Needs.

I am writing this book while the world is under the cloud of the COVID-19 pandemic – countries are closing their borders and restricting social activities. In some countries, even going out on the streets is forbidden. What is the first thought that comes to a person, even from the freest and wealthiest country in the world? Of course – what will I eat? When a person has to eat and calms down about it, the second questions arise – will I have money, a job, or not get sick? And then, a person rises to the third level, which is the need for friendship, family, and communication. On the fourth level, respect, status, recognition, and freedom are required; on the fifth level, one wants to achieve what others have not.

Maslow's pyramid is universal, even for someone we no longer remember, even those who lived millions of years ago when there were no modern means of communication.

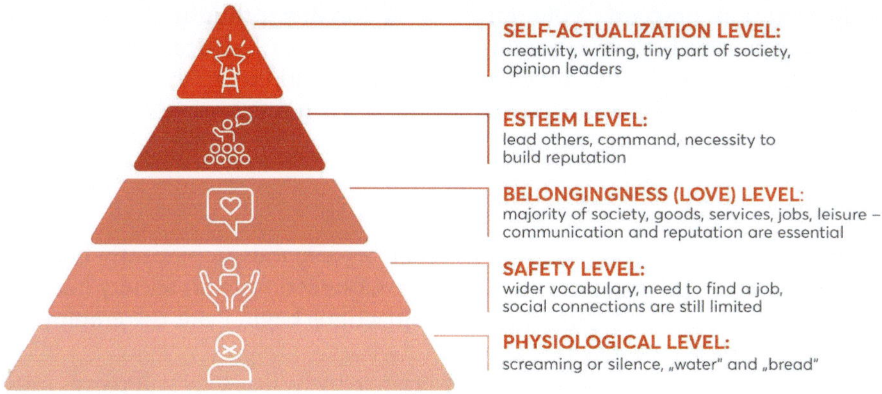

Figure 2.9 Maslow's Hierarchy of Needs in communication.

Figure by the author.

However, I want to draw attention to one aspect that is especially important for us specialists in communication with the public. Each level of it, even the lowest one, has its communication, language, humor, and jargon. Perhaps primitive man, to obtain food, communicated by scaring or even killing another, but it could have been different – perhaps communication helped them share the mammoth they killed one day and the next day, another.

Public relations professionals must constantly sense which level of Maslow's hierarchy they and the person they are communicating with are at. If communication shifts from self-actualization level to physiological, such communication can bring more harm than good.

Every public relations specialist must be at the same or higher level on Maslow's hierarchy compared to the audience they are communicating with. If a public relations specialist is at a higher level than the audience, they must always lower themselves to the level of the audience before communicating. The ability to descend to a lower level on Maslow's hierarchy is one of the critical qualities of a public relations professional.

I will briefly overview how public relations look at each of the five levels of Maslow's hierarchy, which are the following: two foundational levels – physiological and safety, two psychological levels – belongingness (love) and esteem, and a final self-actualization level.

Physiological level

The first basic level has minimal connections with society. The vocabulary is usually limited to only those words needed to satisfy physiological needs, i.e., to obtain water, food, warmth, and rest. Sometimes, if a person is caught in a drug addiction, there may also be a need to get a drink, indulge, or otherwise obtain a dose.

If a person descends voluntarily or is forcibly brought down to the physiological level, their communication at all ages has been and remains the same. Primitive man, driven by instinct, would either shout or remain silent when necessary, and a captive would learn the first words of a foreign language – "water" and "bread".

Safety level

At the second basic level, a person's vocabulary expands significantly because one of the main things here is to find a job. Connections with society become relevant because active reputation-building actions begin from the employer's and employee's perspectives.

Often at this level, employers think very narrowly, i.e., they will pay as little as possible, and if you don't like it, there's always someone else waiting. However, such thinking is only suitable if you plan to stay at the same level for a long time. This thinking is typical of countries where dictatorship prevails for a long time; they stagnate, and no one, at least shortly, plans to change.

However, if one finds themselves at the security level for a short period, it is usually the result of some crisis. In the future, it is planned that a more significant part of society will move up to a higher level. Disregarding employees is a very short-term strategy.

I vividly remember when new shopping centres emerged in my country, and the nation was climbing out of the post-Soviet pit. There was high unemployment, and employers had an abundance of potential workers. However, different employers behaved differently in that situation, which later had varying effects on their reputations. When the situation changed, and there began to be a shortage of workers, those who had developed a bad reputation during the previous period had to pay or put in much more effort than those with a different reputation.

It can be said that at this level, social connections are still quite limited, but neglecting them here is a mistake.

Belongingness (Love) level

The first psychological level for social activities is significant. The majority of society spends most of their lives at this level. People with food, a job, a family, and friends often do not strive for much more.

People actively make choices at this level – goods, services, jobs, and leisure places, so communication and reputation are essential here.

In today's interconnected society, people at the third level of Maslow's hierarchy are often the most active participants in various discussions, commentators, and disseminators of information.

Esteem level

People at the second psychological level seek to lead others, command people, and be leaders. Here, discussions often revolve around creating new businesses, constructing new objects, conquering new mountains, elections, and projects. This level has many specific tasks but not much creativity.

The role of communication with society is twofold here: on the one hand, it's often necessary to reach leaders, which is not as easy as reaching people at lower levels, and on the other hand, the leaders themselves must manage their relationships with society, build their reputation, and be leaders.

Self-actualization level

This relates to only a tiny part of society. Discussions about ideas, creativity, and writing dominate at this level. These people represent the intellectual potential of any society – scientists, artists, writers. Each one is often a unique and highly individual personality.

This level is not the most active in terms of communication with society. On the other hand, representatives at this level are often opinion leaders and can significantly influence others.

In summary, this section highlights the idea that as time passes, technology constantly changes, but human needs remain the same. Regardless of the era in which a person lives, their needs have been and will be the same, and if they were to change, they would likely no longer be human.

Edward Bernays was correct, and the quote you saw at the beginning of this section rings true: three things never change – informing people, persuading people, and involving people in various activities others perform.

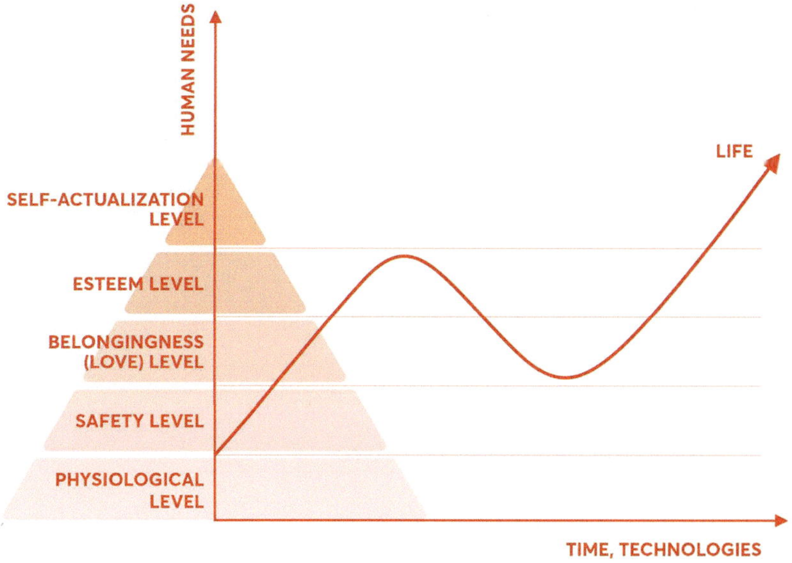

Figure 2.10 The relationship between Maslow's Hierarchy of Needs and technology. Figure by the author.

From a public relations professional's perspective, each of these aspects means that there will always be a need for:

- Delivering news (informing people).
- The ability to tell those news stories effectively (persuading people).
- Building relationships among people (engaging people in various activities others perform).

In their quest for security, people used to inform each other by sharing information on stone walls, using smoke signals, messengers, letters, newspapers, radio, television, and writing on electronic walls. The need for communication neither increased nor decreased – people wanted to know as much as possible in the past, and people want to know as much as possible now. A significant message captures attention, just like a good speech, a good book, a good headline, a good novel, a good article – all of this was relevant in the past and remains so now.

And we have the changing element – technology. Technology in communication is constantly evolving and, one could say, constantly advancing to a more perfect state. What is a perfect communication technology in communication? It's straightforward – the one that allows reaching the most significant number of people as quickly, smoothly, and cost-effectively as possible, with a personal touch.

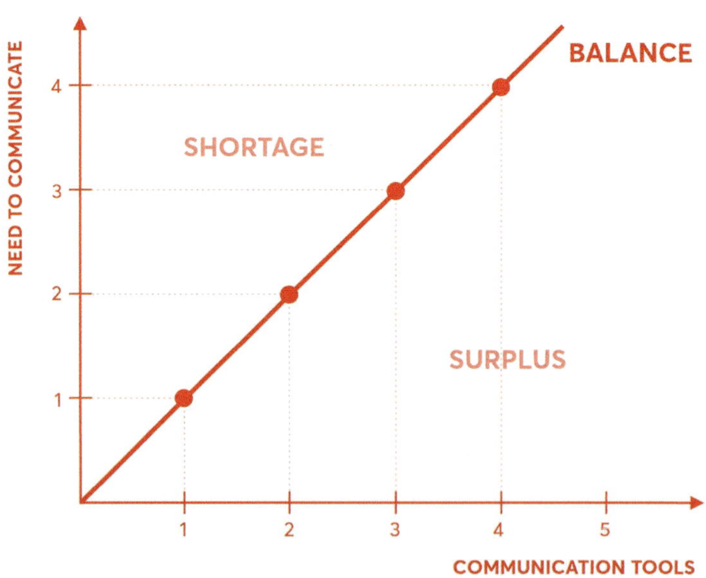

Figure 2.11 Communication balance.

Figure by the author.

Today, many countries live in conditions of communication surplus, meaning they have more communication tools than the need to communicate. This surplus is neither inherently good nor bad, but communication surplus and deficit have pros and cons.

Being in an information surplus is a new state because, before the "Network" communication stage with society, we had never experienced this state. Mass media did not provide sufficient communication tools, while social media significantly exceeded the needs.

Communication is one of the fundamental values of humanity, and it is not without reason that we are called social animals. It is vitally important for us to exchange information and believe in what we learn – that's how we feel secure. Throughout history, contact and trust have always been highly valued. We must trust each other and expand our communication network – the broader and more robust it is, the easier we can shape our future. The younger generations are very open and honest, so they will value quality communication even more and will be even more resistant to broken trust. That's why it's likely that the media, as the primary source of information, will not disappear – people will always need quality content. It can only be created by highly skilled professionals. Of course, considering the activity of the new Generation Z and their desire to be part of the information, the status of a journalist may also evolve beyond the traditional boundaries. So, we live in exciting times where everything seems to be changing, but values remain; we need to remember them.

I once read a communication magazine, and I honestly don't remember which one or whose idea I'll quote here, but I admit I didn't come up with it myself. However, it seemed to me that it was very accurately formulated. So, in that magazine, experienced communication specialists were asked about the most common mistakes made by novice communication specialists, in their opinion. One thought was formulated as advice to a novice communicator: don't hide behind an email. Go straight to the target!

I believe that the younger generation suffers from chronic texting syndrome. This syndrome may be an unnamed condition, or perhaps it has already been

Table 2.1 Shortage and surplus of communication tools.

	Shortage	*Surplus*
+	Easily controllable information, minimal information noise, and chaos, public information is usually reliable.	A multitude of means to share information, news reaches instantly, and skills in filtering information are developing.
-	Much of the media is in the hands of the government; there is a lack of means for people to communicate with each other, and many rumors are difficult to verify.	Fake news, information noise, chaos, it takes quite a bit of knowledge to understand which information is reliable and which is not.

thoroughly researched, where a person shifts all their communication to text, avoiding speech – phone calls, face-to-face conversations – but eagerly writes emails and messages.

Writing is not inherently harmful – I do it daily, and modern technologies are well-suited for texting. However, there's a difference between writing to someone you know well and receiving a message from the internet (the online equivalent of a stranger). Texting facilitates accessibility speed and allows you to accomplish much more than constantly making phone calls or meeting in person. However, it can also work the other way around. Texting should not replace but rather complement and expand communication. This principle applies to all technologies. Technologies will never be a threat if we approach them openly and understand their purpose and potential opportunities.

However, technologies can become a threat if we don't know how to use them and try to replace real life with a virtual one. A simple example illustrates this. Take the social network Facebook and your profile on it. It's beautiful to have a circle of friends and share thoughts, experiences, joys, and concerns with them. But it works best when our profile is an extension of our authentic self, and the people around it are real acquaintances we've interacted with. If we only seek friends within Facebook itself, we risk becoming isolated individuals in the online world.

Virtual life should follow real life, not the other way around. This direction is significant for a public relations specialist. A public relations specialist should first be able to engage in real-life interactions, initiate conversations, communicate, feel, and listen to what is left unsaid. Constantly honing these skills is crucial. Only then should one master all possible communication tools. Suppose a public relations specialist excels in using electronic tools but cannot speak in person, at least for now. In that case, such a person has no chance of becoming a professional in public relations. Personal relations will remain faithful because all technologies will evolve to allow us to express our thoughts and feelings better, and other aspects challenging to convey through text. Emojis will significantly improve, and their current form will appear somewhat amusing. Therefore, a communicator's most essential skill is communicating and building emotionally driven relationships. Only emotionally driven relationships can be effective, whether aided by technology or not.

So, the main mistake of this age is hiding behind technology. And I specifically say "this age", not the new generation, because both older and younger generations successfully hide behind technology. Older individuals often do so as they learn to master new technologies, while younger ones have been doing it from the beginning of their lives. Therefore, don't hide behind technology; view technology as an extension of yourself, not a replacement.

Very often, when I ask colleagues to do something or get in touch with someone after a few days, I receive a response like, "Yes, I sent them a message."

There's nothing wrong with the actual writing of an email. We live in the 21st century and have many communication tools that previous generations did not. Today, we can find someone on the other side of the world in a matter of minutes and converse with them while looking them in the eye through a computer screen. There's a strong desire to see and know that there's a natural person on the other end. Once you know the person is natural, you can communicate without constantly looking them in the eye.

In short, effective communication occurs when we first establish a connection with a person, and then, to expedite the process, we use all available communication tools.

And here, the most crucial aspect is relationships. If we can establish a relationship through electronic means, and I believe more and more people will be able to do this – that's great. Whether the relationship is initiated through electronic means or not, what matters is that it's established. Writing electronic messages is not yet the establishment of a relationship. Something more is needed. And that "more" is the essence of our profession.

When someone writes an electronic message to someone they haven't met or interacted with before, they generally don't know how or are afraid to communicate. What's the best way to hide in communication? Writing an electronic message! An electronic message will never shout back, won't forward your message, and won't give a negative response. After sending it, you can wait and see what happens – they might respond, and then you can figure out why they didn't respond. But will this help establish a relationship, and is it effective? Certainly not. When you call with an important question or make an arrangement to talk about something, you receive an instant response, and you don't have to ponder for long – you know how to proceed. But you might wait a long time when you write an electronic message. My observations in recent years indicate that only a significantly few communicators recognize this. A significant portion succumbs to the tendency to prefer writing over direct communication.

Avoiding communication, especially in crises or conflicts, can be harmful. Instead of meeting and talking with someone you find unpleasant, it's much more convenient to write them a letter and wait for their response. But I emphasize that it's more convenient, not more effective. After writing, you may wait for weeks or even months, or you may not receive a response at all, and in the meantime, you may make incorrect decisions. Meanwhile, if you meet or call, you can start addressing the problem in the first few minutes of the conversation.

Firstly, you can discover why your counterpart is dissatisfied with you and why they are angry. Or maybe it's the other way around? You can also find that out immediately, because your interlocutor will have no other way out, and only a few will be able to say nothing in response to a straightforward question. Secondly, let's view the conversation partner not as a threat to ourselves but as someone whose involvement is necessary to resolve the issue.

The problem will undoubtedly begin to be addressed.

2.4. From Hierarchical to Picnical

> If you want to hire great people and have them stay, you have to be run by ideas, not hierarchy. The best ideas have to win.
>
> Steve Jobs – business magnate, industrial designer, investor, and media proprietor.

We became accustomed to hierarchical communication for many years of public relations during the "Television" stage. At that stage, there was no other choice. Various other hierarchical structures, such as corporate management, national governance, and the education system, significantly influenced hierarchical communication: somewhere at the top, a message was conceived and transmitted downward.

Theories were developed – one organization, one voice. In organizations, it was not allowed to speak in public until it was coordinated with the organization's public relations department, and the latter had to coordinate everything with the management.

Mass media, organizations, and individuals – all had accepted these rules of the game and lived in a straightforward world. However, that world disappeared, along with the entire "Marketing era", and today, we live in a completely different set of rules – in many cases, the 'one voice' policy has disappeared. Even the leaders and employees of the largest corporations are visible in the sea of information, often independently commenting on what is happening within their organization, their country, and the world. The coordination of what to say still exists, but organizations, to engage in dialogue, must change and are changing.

Returning to the three characteristics of technological tools I discussed in the "What is Changing and What Stays Stable Forever?" section – speed, accessibility, and platforms – anyone wanting to communicate today must adapt their processes to these three attributes. An organization wishing to be visible on social media can no longer take a week to coordinate text, let alone responses to an ongoing discussion – social media demands an immediate response, at the latest, within a few hours. Therefore, the speed of the organization's communication processes must be changed. The same organization can no longer be accessible only during working hours, as a discussion can arise on a Sunday morning. The communication opportunity will be lost if the response only arrives on Monday. Therefore, the approach to the availability of the organization's employees must be changed.

And, of course, the organization must be where its audience is, so it must constantly monitor various platforms where essential people gather and have its content. Therefore, the approach to communication platforms must be changed, trends must be followed, and content should be disseminated not where it is customary but where the action is happening.

All of these changes represent a new approach to public relations and the role of a public relations specialist because it is on their shoulders that the management and smooth operation of all these processes lie. The functions of a public relations specialist in the "Network" stage have greatly expanded. If in the "Television" stage, one needed to know media representatives, be able to write press releases, organize interviews and events, prepare materials, and perform other classic public relations tasks without much concern for precise and predictable audiences, today, perhaps the most crucial task of a public relations specialist is to navigate well among the audiences, groups, and discussions that are happening by the thousands on social media.

In short, if in the past the most critical task of a public relations specialist was to create content and neatly deliver that content hierarchically to stakeholders, today, content creation is still necessary. Still, that content can change based on speed, accessibility, and platforms. It can be shortened, lengthened, respond to questions, send queries back, and engage in conversations. It's also important to understand that there are no longer clear and strictly defined stakeholders. Take, for example, the media. Many people and groups are spreading and sharing news, interacting with each other, and constantly changing.

I have named this new communication reality "picnic-style communication", because it reminds me of a large picnic in a park where many tables are set up on the grass, around which different groups gather. These groups of people around the picnic table represent the new, constantly changing, emerging, and disappearing stakeholders. The most essential skill for a modern public relations professional is to know all the picnic tables in the park well and be able to engage in those conversations when necessary. I will discuss this concept in more detail in Chapter 3

As I mentioned earlier, the transition from hierarchical to picnic-style communication has led to the disappearance of clearly defined stakeholders and the boundaries between them. This disappearance occurred because every individual now has access to technologies that allow them to become media outlets. Essentially, everyone has become a media channel today. Employees, partners, government institutions, customers, competitors, investors, and all other stakeholders are no longer just recipients of information – they can all disseminate information on a large scale.

Therefore, a public relations specialist's activities are fundamentally changing. If, in the past, content was created to reach stakeholders, today, one must think about how those stakeholders will further disseminate that content. Today, it is necessary to constantly think about providing stakeholders with content and encouraging them to share it.

Most organizations should take a fresh look at their stakeholders and identify the type of content they have been receiving so far and how suitable it might be for the communication picnic in the park. For example, if a company has been organizing outings for its employees in nature, has it been considered how the employees might share that experience externally? Perhaps there is a need to assist and encourage employees to share that content. Is it worth hiring a photographer to capture moments at the event and send all the photos to each employee through social media, encouraging them to share? Is it worth helping each employee compile content from those photos?

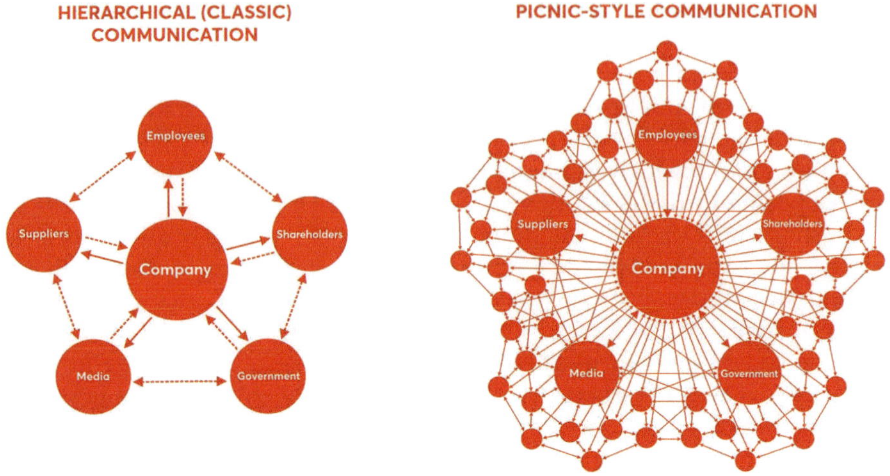

Figure 2.12 Hierarchical (classic) and picnic-style forms of communication organization. Figure by the author.

The example mentioned above is one of many: there are many stakeholders and even more ways to provide them with content that naturally enhances an organization's reputation.

Essentially, today, it's worth looking at anyone associated with an organization as a potential media outlet because today, every person, equipped with simple and readily available communication tools, has the potential to become a media channel. Furthermore, each person armed with technology today is significant for building the reputation of any organization.

Notes

1 Scholz & Friends. "Dramatic shift in marketing reality" (aka "A short history of marketing"). https://vimeo.com/2897291 (accessed on 21-02-2024).
2 Ries, A. and Ries, L. (2004). *The fall of advertising and the rise of PR*. New York: HarperBusiness.
3 Newspaper extinction timeline. https://futureexploration.net/future-of-media (accessed on 21-02-2024).
4 Safko, L. and Brake, D.K. (2009). *The social media bible: tactics, tools, and strategies for business success.* New Jersey: John Wiley & Sons.
5 https://futureexploration.net/future-of-media (accessed on 21-02-2024).
6 Qualman, E. (2012). *Socialnomics: how social media transforms the way we live and do business.* New Jersey: John Wiley & Sons.
7 The data is prepared according to statistics: https://www.statista.com/statistics/278341/number-of-social-network-users-in-selected-countries/; https://www.statista.com/statistics/263762/total-population-of-the-united-states/; https://www.statista.com/statistics/263765/total-population-of-china/; https://www.statista.com/statistics/263763/total-population-of-brazil/; https://www.statista.com/statistics/263754/total-population-of-the-united-kingdom/ *- estimated population data (accessed on 21-02-2024).
8 https://briansolis.com/2008/08/introducing-conversation-prism.html (accessed on 21-02-2024).

3 Social Picnic

Imagine a picnic.

I'll admit – I'm a big fan of John Lennon's work. And not just his work: his struggles, life journey, growth, and search for meaning resonate with me. Often, it feels like I understand this person very well, and if I had had the opportunity to meet him in life and talk to him, the first thing I would have said would be: "You are not the only one." Unfortunately, at least in this lifetime, that's not possible.

I know that "Imagine" was written in a completely different world than the one we live in now, and perhaps John was thinking about entirely different things than I am now. However, that's the beauty of art – each person can see what is visible to them. A creator may have one idea, but after passing the work of art through their personal and societal context, the receiver can have many new, different, supplementary, and ultimately illuminating thoughts about that work.

For me, "Imagine" today sounds like a clear anthem for the Picnic Society and the "Network" stage of public relations.

Let's pause for a moment and consider this song. Like any work of art, this song should not be taken literally.

"Imagine there's no heaven . . . No hell below us." John Lennon was neither a communist nor a fervent opponent of religion. However, he understood that religions contained dogma, uncertainty, and complexes. All this was created for a person in the dark, not seeking truth but content with simple answers. John suggested imagining what the world would be like without religions. In his time, especially during his childhood, this seemed almost utopian. In today's advanced information society, all religions are fading away fast, in a way none of their direct opponents were able to achieve. They are disappearing naturally, and "above us, only sky". If it's not happening today, it will happen tomorrow, but it's clear that in the future, religions will be like artefacts in museums today – we will go, look, and marvel at how people used to live in the past. This process will happen because of the unification brought about by limitless human communication, which will dissolve any remnants of religions.

DOI: 10.4324/9781003466802-4

"Imagine all the people . . . Livin' for today." The future is advancing at a cosmic pace, and I believe that space, in the literal sense of the word, awaits humanity. Today, it's possible to create only "for today" because predicting what will be "tomorrow" is impossible. The sharing generation, for whom material goods are only as valuable as they need them, has already grown up. Today, they don't cherish things for the future because they feel that in the future, things will be different. This generation thinks of the future as an entirely unexplored state and lives for "Today", trying to do everything "Today".

And finally: "Imagine there's no countries." I can hear the drums of nationalists ready to pounce on me, but the future clearly says one thing – the world will be one. One doesn't mean that we won't have bad people, killers, and dictators in the future, and that we won't need to defend against them. That would indeed be a utopia. However, rational people and nations will think about common interests. More precisely, they are already thinking about it. Projects like the European Union, NATO, the Euro, Bitcoin, the United Nations, billionaires' involvement in solving problems in developing countries, the internet (both the conventional one today and the one accessible through a swarm of satellites in the future), addressing climate issues collectively, Mars colonization, immunization – these are not projects of one or a few countries; these are global projects where political borders are irrelevant. Of course, we will continue to defend ourselves against those who attack, are aggressive, and want to halt progress. Still, all these projects will increasingly dissolve political boundaries because they require not countries but a global community of forward-thinking individuals. So, "no countries" in this context means not so much the physical disappearance of countries themselves but participation in joint projects and unrestricted communication among nations.

In our eyes, a globally interconnected society is forming, where various relationships are constantly forming based on interest groups. Due to technological advancement, physical borders between states become less significant as virtual boundaries of interest groups come to the forefront.

I want to emphasize that I am exclusively talking about states that operate based on progress without touching on states that are ruled by dictatorships and where progress is impossible. As long as North Korea remains as it is, the only effective way to distance oneself from it will be a physical border. So, while I am a dreamer, I am by no means naive and do not believe that we will bring order to the world by releasing white doves over a dictator's nuclear weapons.

However, leaving the underdeveloped countries (which include many dictatorships, even the most modern ones like the UAE, which may shine with novelty but can only consume rather than create) to develop and rejoice when they succeed either on their own or with the help of other countries, I am talking about those countries that lead in the world. Progress is always associated with leaders, not the other way around. Leading can only be achieved through creation, which can only happen in free countries.

In the preceding sections, I showed how public relations began and was transformed. Today, we are living at the very beginning of the "Network" stage of public relations, and it's time to describe how PR activities and the roles and responsibilities of a PR specialist should look like.

As I mentioned in the Introduction, I had the opportunity to visit a PR agency in Helsinki and hear the word "picnic" from a colleague. She said that everything that's happening now is a big picnic. Imagine your social media account as a picnic blanket – you spread it out, start laying out the food, friends gather, and conversations begin. Now, imagine that there are many such picnic blankets around – you can approach each one, share your thoughts, move to another, come back, and continue this constantly.

The idea brewing in my mind for a long time eventually crystallized into the concept behind this book. I thought the word "picnic" was a perfect fit for describing an individual social media account and characterizing the emerging interconnected global community. Having only one picnic in our backyard corresponds to a social media account in relationships. If the yard is not enclosed, the picnic is private, but it is not difficult to gain access to it. Such yards align with our private social media accounts, which are private but do not have significant restrictions on reading or commenting on them. If the yard is closed, with a fence and gates, the picnic is incredibly private,

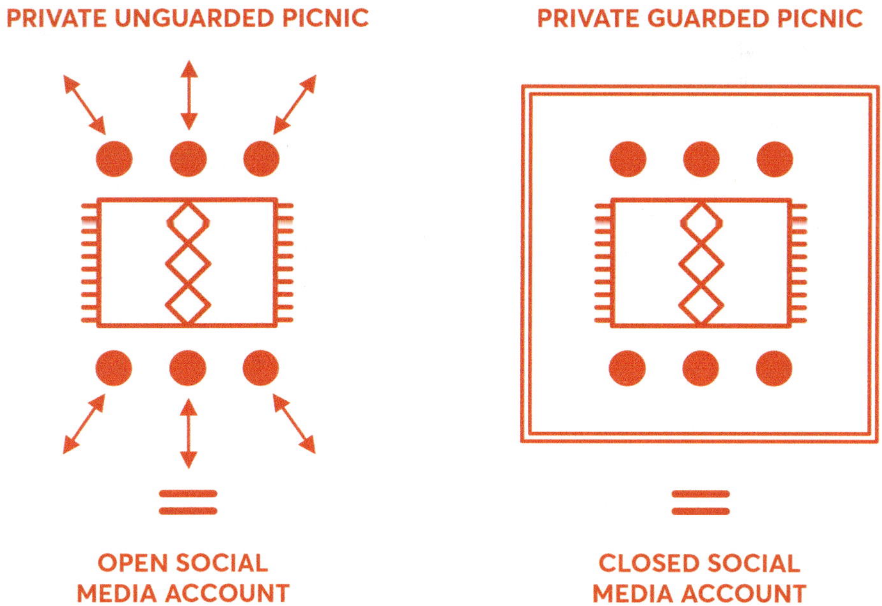

Figure 3.1 Social media account in a material world.

Figure by the author.

and only guests can enter. Such yards correspond to closed social media accounts or groups where communication occurs while safeguarding against prying eyes.

I will continue to refer to the picnic in one yard or the relationships developing in one social media account as "Plaids".

The "**Plaid**" is the smallest unit of contemporary communication; an interest group, or a social media account where communication occurs on topics relevant to that group.

If we were to transfer "Plaid" to a park and imagine a picnic at the level of a town, city, country, or even internationally, we would have a phenomenon that I will refer to as the "Social Picnic".

The "**Social Picnic**" is a contemporary communication model that connects a large number of "Plaids". Members of Plaids communicate with each other on various topics within their Plaids or interact with other Plaids, but all Social Picnic participants share one or several common interests. It is easiest to imagine a Social Picnic within one country. Still, they can be smaller (e.g., universities, schools, professional groups) or more significant (e.g., corporations, space, climate change) Social Picnics.

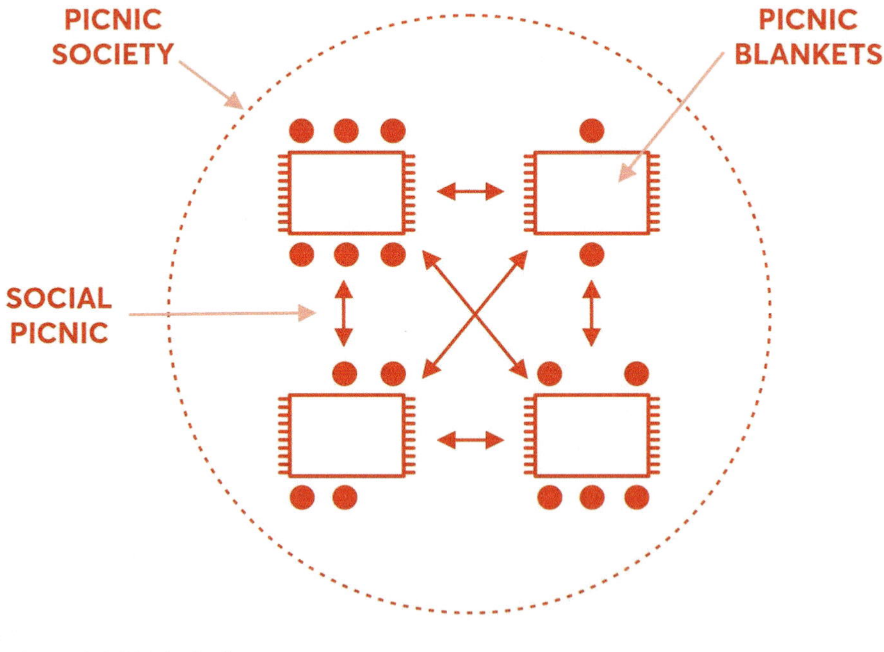

Figure 3.2 Picnic Society structure.

Figure by the author.

I have named the worldwide community connected by communication-enabling technologies, consisting of many Social Picnics, the "Picnic Society".

The "**Picnic Society**" is an advanced and technologically-connected global community in which every member can belong to an unlimited number of Plaids and freely communicate with any other member who wishes to. The Picnic Society's slogan is: "The World Is a Picnic."

"Picnic Society" is a much broader term than the theme of this book. This book focuses only on that part of the Picnic Society that I have called the "Social Picnic", which describes the relationships between Plaids. I leave the remaining parts to be examined by specialists in other fields, such as sociologists, psychologists, political analysts, and others.

The primary enabling factor of the Picnic Society is unrestricted and continuously evolving communication. How these relationships are formed – spontaneously or strategically – largely depends on who creates them. Most relationships are formed spontaneously, just like in any society that has existed before, including the Picnic Society.

However, there has always been a need, and as time goes on, this need will become even more pronounced, to build relationships strategically by planning and aiming for specific goals. The growth of this need is directly related to the development and integration of the Picnic Society itself. As the number of people joining and their involvement in a broader range of activities increases, so does the need to have the skills to communicate with increasingly diverse interest groups, influence them, and convey their knowledge.

If the world continues to move in the same direction, the demand for PR specialists will proliferate. In the multifaceted relationships of the Picnic Society, PR specialists are the people who can help establish relationships for those Picnic Society members who, for various reasons, cannot do so themselves.

As with any society, the Picnic Society includes people adept at building relationships and those who need assistance. The need for help can stem from various reasons, but fundamentally, the old and wise outsourcing principle applies here – do well what you excel at and leave everything else to those who excel in it the best.

In previous stages of PR development and up to the present day, the relationships between members of society were best understood and managed by PR professionals, or in other words, relationship experts who could lead, advise, help understand, and consistently build reputation. These professionals and their skills have not disappeared; what has changed is that their portfolios now include more tools. PR professionals are well-versed in various Social Picnics, Plaids, the conversations around them, the connections between Plaids, styles, languages, and many other aspects.

In the space of the Social Picnic, modern relationships are formed and implemented. These are not new relationships that somehow significantly differ from past relationships. Modern relationships are the same old relationships but with more significant opportunities for dissemination in a more competitive environment. They have with new tools, but are still fundamentally based on an age-old foundation – trust.

Human beings are inherently social. People feel good when they are among others. They want to be recognized and valued. The primary aim of a social person is unrestricted communication – communicating whenever they want, with whomever they want, and about whatever they want. We have come a long way towards achieving that goal.

The idea of the Social Picnic model has been brewing in my mind for quite some time. I have read books, observed my surroundings, interacted with colleagues, implemented various PR projects, and actively monitored, analyzed, and experimented with social media. The Social Picnic is a model of how communication should ideally be in the future. Real life may introduce corrections, but the trend will likely remain the same.

The Picnic Society is the global community that lives according to new written and unwritten rules, norms, etiquettes, and sometimes even laws, all created by the emergence of new technologies that have transported us into the "Network" era. While many of these things quickly became a part of everyday life for most people, due to the countless emerging and disappearing Social Picnics and an enormous number of communication channels, knowing how to behave everywhere has become impossible. In other words, it has become clear that we can now behave as never before, precisely according to our norms, principles, and beliefs – there is a place for all of them in the Picnic Society today.

Let's have a picnic!

3.1. Concept

> You bring your own weather to the picnic.
>
> Harlan Coben – writer.

Imagine a picnic. You have just arrived at the park with your family. It's warm, with occasional gentle breezes, and there's a fantastic atmosphere all around – lots of people, laughter, the sounds of children playing. You can hear live music from a recently constructed stage somewhere in the distance. As you walk across the meadow, you must be careful because there are plenty of picnic baskets, spread-out blankets, a few folks playing badminton, and children kicking a soccer ball. Feeling a bit hesitant, you stand there, thinking, "This is the space where everyone will spend this Saturday."

You spread out your picnic blanket, set up your basket, unload it, and the kids start running around, playing with other children. Soon, familiar faces gather around your blanket. The children's friendships lead to parent-to-parent introductions. Eventually, the territory marked by your blanket becomes a bustling hub of discussions and good vibes, where continuous communication occurs. This territory is now our familiar Plaid, the smallest unit of contemporary communication.

If we were to look at the picnic from a bird's-eye view, it would appear as a map of various colorful blankets scattered across the green landscape. People would seem like ants moving around the blankets: some lazily lounging near one blanket, while others move from one blanket to another. This picture is the Social Picnic, a contemporary communication model that connects a large number of Plaids. This is the picture you can see on the cover of this book.

When I first saw the aerial photograph by Jason Hawkes, I immediately thought that it was a perfect visualization of my concept for the contemporary communication model, the Social Picnic. I reached out to Jason and acquired the photograph, believing it would make an excellent cover for my book: those tiny figures around the blankets against the backdrop of the green meadow perfectly portrayed what had been nothing but an image in my mind for years.

It's time to discuss all the elements of this model.

No picnic, including the Social Picnic, would be complete without these elements: Sun, Meadow, Plaid, Sharer, and Food. Additionally, two more elements might not be necessary but are essential for a more substantial picnic – a Vase and Concert.

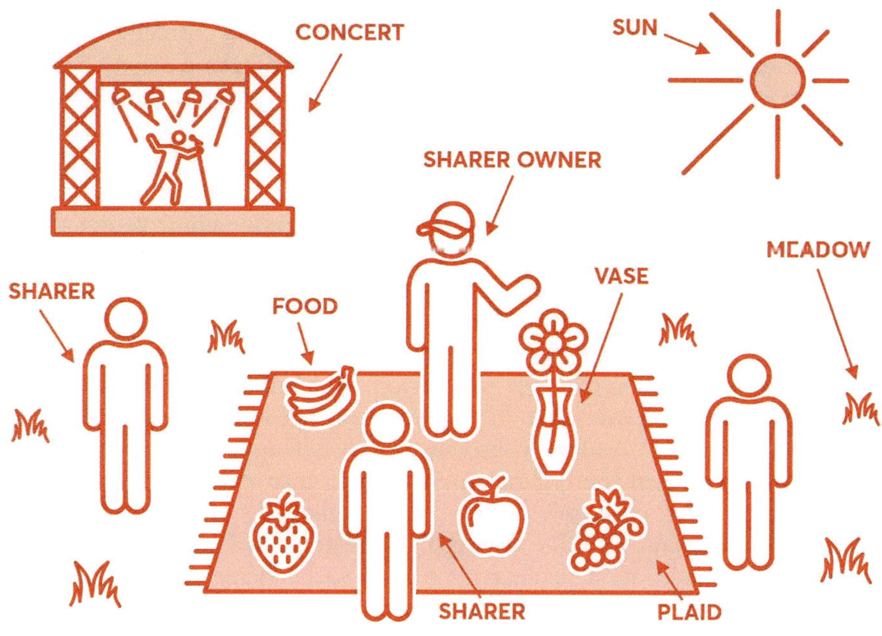

Figure 3.3 Five essential and two optional elements of the Social Picnic.

Figure by the author.

3.1.1. Sun

Let us make hay while the sun shines.

Miguel de Cervantes – writer.

Any picnic taking place under the open sky can easily be spoiled if it suddenly starts to rain. Although it may seem like a simple factor, the sun is the foundation of a picnic. Without the sun and good weather, there is no enjoyable picnic.

In the Social Picnic model, "Sun" represents well-functioning communication channels. The Social Picnic won't occur if the internet, Facebook, or Teams aren't working. Today, a Social Picnic cannot be fully realized without technology, even when people meet in person and internet connectivity is not required for communication. It's challenging to imagine such a meeting without presentations, films, or music playing. Of course, there may still be Plaids that interact regardless, but technology remains the foundation of the Social Picnic.

Social media enables real-time broadcasting. Just 15 years ago, this was unimaginable. There's no need for a physical journalist to be present; a much wider audience can be invited to such broadcasts than just journalists. Anyone can watch them directly in bed or on a beach by the sea. These incredible opportunities allow us to accomplish more, save time, and work much more efficiently. On the other hand, these possibilities can only be utilized when the "Sun" is shining, meaning when technology is functioning correctly.

However, not every picnic in nature has the luxury of taking place when the conditions are best, i.e., when the sun is shining the brightest. Some picnics can be adjusted based on the weather, while others must occur at a fixed time. Similarly, in the Social Picnic model, it's essential to ensure that technology functions as efficiently as possible. Fast internet, the ability to have backup internet options, connected cameras, sound, microphone control, and other technological aspects should be on every PR professional's radar when organizing any Social Picnic. Even the best speakers or the most engaging content will become ineffective if not visible and accessible.

It's crucial not to forget another rule: to be prepared for unforeseen circumstances. We must remember that, no matter how much effort we put into it, no picnic will ever have perfect weather. It's almost entirely beyond our control. We can't control when rain clouds will obscure the sun, just as we can't control when the organizers of a conference venue decide to make long-awaited updates precisely during your meeting. It's not worth trying to avoid these situations; we must be prepared for them. If umbrellas, raincoats, or tents can partially save a picnic in the park, a Social Picnic will most likely be saved by being prepared for cases where technology might fail. For example, a recorded broadcast can save a live stream; an alternative internet connection can overcome network issues; a battery can compensate for a power outage, and so on.

The "Sun" element of Social Picnic represents high-quality and well-functioning information technologies.

3.1.2. Meadow

Many eyes go through the meadow, but few see the flowers in it.

Ralph Waldo Emerson – essayist, lecturer, philosopher, abolitionist, and poet.

Every picnic takes place somewhere and needs to have a foundation. Most often, that foundation is a meadow. In the Social Picnic model, the Meadow serves as the basis on which the picnic occurs and the space defining the specific boundaries of the picnic. These boundaries can be geographical or delineated based on areas of interest.

The global Picnic Society comprises many Social Picnics, and each Social Picnic has its Meadow, meaning each Social Picnic has its boundaries and a set of topics that interest the Sharers of that particular picnic.

Social Picnics take place everywhere today, and the boundaries of each Social Picnic are not clearly defined. However, most Social Picnics resemble a political world map and are organized based on countries or languages. The language barrier is significant and the primary obstacle to engaging in a specific country's Social Picnic. It is a big mistake to assume that the world is becoming English-speaking. In countries, there are Social Picnics rooted in the local mentality and language. To understand and, most importantly, feel these picnics, you need to speak the country's language and understand its subtleties, and in this sphere, local PR professionals play a crucial role.

Meadows can be permanent, but they can also be temporary.

Permanent Meadows are typically established on a geographical or thematic basis. These are often ongoing Social Picnics within each country, which do not have a clear beginning or end; they continue indefinitely. For example, it could be ongoing communication within a country on political topics or more minor communities of gardeners, sports enthusiasts, grill enthusiasts, and other Social Picnics.

Permanent Meadows can also develop without regard to geographical boundaries. For example, these could be people interested in Mars missions, global politics enthusiasts, car enthusiasts, and so on.

The *Temporary* Meadows formation is based on specific events. While writing this book in Riga, the World Ice Hockey Championship is taking place, and around it, an Ice Hockey Fans' Meadow has formed.

Sometimes, a large part of the world's Social Picnics converge, focusing on a particular global theme, and most often, it is a crisis. Events such as natural disasters, acts of terrorism, wars, pandemics, or US presidential elections temporarily unite them, erasing the boundaries between local Social Picnics.

However, the picnics return to their local frames and Meadows and interact with each other only through individual picnic participants.

The "Meadow" is the element of a Social Picnic that represents the boundaries of the Social Picnic, separating one picnic from another.

3.1.3. Plaid

> Whenever this moment comes up, always bet on the community, because that's the difference between long-term thinking and short-term thinking.
>
> Matt Mullenweg – CEO WordPress.

As mentioned, the "Plaid" is the smallest unit of modern communication. On the other hand, it is also the most crucial component, without which neither the Social Picnic nor the Picnic Society is possible. In contemporary communication, Plaid is like a cell in a living organism. Without cells, there is no organism.

The essence of the classical stakeholders map is to have an object at the center with specific stakeholders around it, each having a clear one-sided or mutual interest in the object. The Social Picnic map looks a bit different. There is no central object, and there are no specific groups around the center. All groups, all Plaids, are highly-diversified, changing, and interconnected with each other in various ways.

In picnics that take place in nature, a Plaid represents an individual family, a group of friends, like-minded individuals, or a larger or smaller community.

In the Social Picnic model, it is also a community united by one or several themes and interests. Becoming a member of a Plaid is done in a completely informal manner – simply by being interested in a particular theme or sharing the same interests. Of course, within the Picnic Society, you can also find very formal communities where membership might involve taking oaths, but most Plaids are informal.

If in a park picnic, a Plaid community typically gathers up to a few dozen participants, in the Social Picnic model, a Plaid community can have several thousand or even tens of thousands of Sharers (participants).

Community relations have always been a part of PR. I would say it is the purest form of PR because any intermediaries are eliminated here: information is transmitted directly from the sender to the community members. Because today we live in a Picnic Society, surrounded by communities of various sizes and natures, I believe that community relations is the PR sphere that must be developed the most.

The classic PR theory clearly distinguishes between internal and external interest groups. Evidently, these boundaries are fading, and they may practically cease to exist in the future because almost every organization's members can be members of different Plaid communities. They can receive and disseminate information and have the necessary tools for it. PR specialists need to constantly consider employees or any other organizational insiders as an important, or perhaps even the most important, target audience. In this picnic, traditional media is just one large Plaid.

Remarks at the World Public Relations Forum in Madrid in 2014 indicated a future where distinguishing between employees and customers would be challenging. It was emphasized that employee communication was crucial in achieving company objectives, particularly in terms of technologically-empowered individuals.

While members of an organization's Plaid community, employees are also members of various other Plaid communities. For example, Ben, from the Red Shoes organization, is not only a member of that organization's Plaid community but also a member of his son's school's Plaid community, a member of a fishing club's Plaid community, a member of his family's Plaid community, and likely a member of many other Plaid communities.

Everything seems as before, but living in the Picnic Society, there is one essential difference – all Plaid communities are tightly interconnected and empowered by technology to spread knowledge here and now.

So, there is no longer a significant difference between employees, journalists, decision-makers, or even customers in Plaid communities – and in the future there may be no difference. All these communities are equally important and interconnected. The Social Picnic has practically erased the boundaries between the sender and receiver of information – they have become very similar and have similar tools in their technological toolbox.

The distinction between internal and external stakeholders no longer makes sense – essentially, internal and external stakeholders need the same content, just presented differently. Today, it is already difficult to determine who is an internal and who is an external stakeholder.

Today, any stakeholder group is no longer just a target and ultimate information recipient. Today, any stakeholder group serves as an intermediary

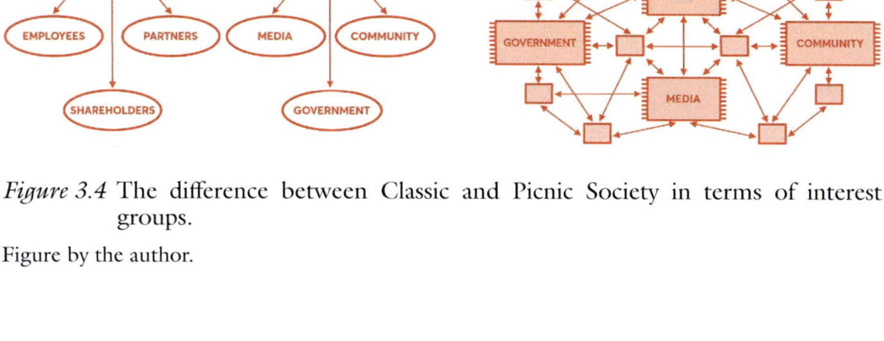

Figure 3.4 The difference between Classic and Picnic Society in terms of interest groups.

Figure by the author.

information station, i.e., a Picnic Plaid, where information is received, understood, transformed, and further directed to the respective Picnic Sharers within the Plaid.

In this situation, imagine you are a PR specialist for a car dealership, and you've invited a famous athlete, a recent Olympic medalist who is also a customer of your dealership, as a guest. This athlete has agreed to take photos with people in the dealership. Your colleagues and customers all want to have photos taken with the star. In your opinion, who is more important? The classic theory would say customers. However, I believe that customers and employees are equally important in this situation – they will all share those photos through their Plaid social media networks.

Not long ago, one of the main tasks of a PR specialist responsible for client relations with the media was to write a press release or prepare other text that could pique the media's interest. Today, it becomes significantly more important to create information that – once armed with technology – Picnic Sharers will share within their Plaid, understand correctly, and spread further as they move to other Plaids. Often, interested Plaid communities disseminate the message much more effectively than the media.

Customers, employees, partners, and suppliers are all separate Picnics within one Social Picnic. We must view each of these Picnics as a separate media outlet. Let's say that one-in-three members of the Picnics has an account on one or another social network, which means they have their readers. It also means that each Picnic is a media outlet. One may have a hundred readers, another a thousand, and some even have several thousand or even millions.

Of course, traditional media hasn't disappeared, and there's still a need for press releases. However, the circle of information recipients has significantly expanded, and most importantly, the possibilities for these recipients to further disseminate the information have expanded as well. Social Picnic media, or traditional media, are just one of the Plaids. Not the smallest, but in many cases, not the most important.

The number of groups of people that PR specialists could consider as media outlets in the broader, or if you will, in the new sense, has significantly increased. The demand for content and its variations has also grown.

Not only have more groups emerged but also new ways to understand what is relevant to those groups. While in the past, finding out what interests a journalist could often be done almost exclusively through personal communication, today such information can often be obtained from social networks.

By following discussions on social networks, you can actively participate, provide your available information, answer questions, and direct readers' attention in the desired direction. You can suggest topics to both journalists' Plaids and any other Plaids.

Don't forget about closed, limited-membership groups on social networks. These groups can consist of professionals in various fields or people interested in specific topics, community members, or even leaders of those communities.

Imagine that you represent a company that is located near a primarily residential neighborhood. Naturally, the company and the residents of the neighborhood will have common interests: they will share the use of roads, perhaps noise or other pollution may spread from your premises, maybe the residents of that neighborhood will work in your company, and their children will attend a nearby kindergarten, which will require support.

Community members are already members of more than one Plaid here. The residential neighborhood has as many as three closed Plaids where various topics are discussed. Make sure to join those Plaids if you are allowed to do so.

However, no matter how many Plaids have been created, create one where you will be the host. Invite PR specialists from nearby companies and community leaders, a small number of people, but most importantly, they should be genuine and active members of that community. Promise them that in this Plaid, you will publish all relevant information about planned noise, changes, initiatives, news, photos, and events – everything necessary for the common well-being of your company and the residents. And, of course, keep this promise.

Being in such a Plaid doesn't oblige you to anything, but it becomes a convenient tool in a PR specialist's arsenal. As a PR specialist for your company, you gain a channel to convey information directly to those people for whom it is relevant, and they receive reliable information from you that they can share with their community members. This exchange strengthens both their and your authority.

We can create such Plaids with anyone: community members, experts, media representatives, and government institutions. The most important thing is that everyone involved should benefit from the information.

Your Plaid (group, profile, or page) is your controlled territory within the Social Picnic. Here, the action takes place according to your rules and belongs to you and your friends, colleagues, partners, and clients. In it, everyone openly and transparently shares information.

Plaids can take many forms. They are no longer the old, precisely-defined stakeholder groups; they are new, colorful, informal, diverse, constantly emerging, and often disappearing groups of people. Their number is large, just like at a picnic in the park.

An example provided in Chapter 1 was about a hotel and toothpaste. In that case, we understood that tourism information center employees were one of the Plaids who were both the target audience and the media. We understood what it meant if news about that unfortunate toothpaste incident started to be discussed among the Plaid members, who were essentially the driving force of the entire tourism sector.

Since Warren Buffett wrote in his letter to Berkshire Hathaway executives in 2014 that it took just five minutes to destroy a reputation, some time has passed. During that time, the Social Picnic has strengthened and matured, and the timeframe for the destruction of reputation has shortened. It's possible

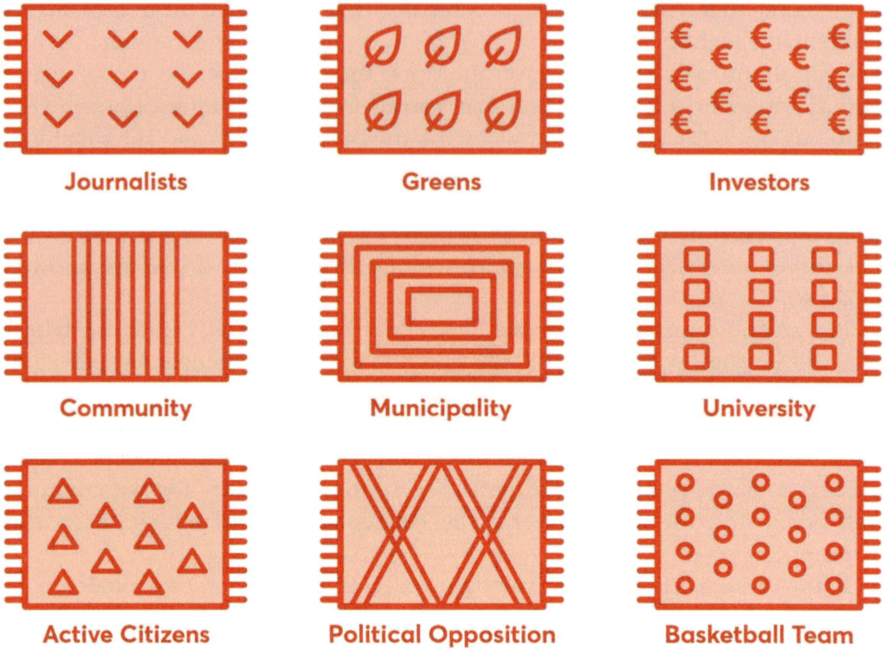

Figure 3.5 The diversity of Plaids.

Figure by the author.

that today, damaging a reputation may only require one social media post, and sometimes it doesn't take more than a minute to write it.

The Plaid is a fundamental element of the Social Picnic, a community formed around one or several interests. This community is closely connected with other communities through information technology.

3.1.4. Sharer

> A dream you dream alone is only a dream. A dream you dream together is reality.
>
> John Lennon – singer, songwriter, and peace activist.

I have chosen to describe a person participating in Social Picnic with the word "Sharer", which, in my opinion, most accurately describes the two main functions performed by all Social Picnic Sharers: participation (as a shareholder) and sharing (as a sharer). The first function – participation and having a share of information – is essential for the Social Picnic to take place; the second – sharing – is a very quickly occurring foundation of social networks.

As soon as we enter the park, we become picnic participants, and as soon as we go online, we become Social Picnic Sharers. Even if we don't have a social media account, we are still Social Picnic Sharers who don't have their Plaid but still walk around the picnic and observe and listen to what's happening. When a picnic Sharer lays out a blanket, i.e., creates an account on social media, they become a Sharer with their Plaid.

Social Picnic Sharers seek companions, invite friends to their Plaids, engage in discussions, move from one Plaid to another, and stop where they find interesting topics. Some Plaids are similar, while others have nothing in common.

A Social Picnic Sharer, I believe, is almost everyone reading this book, and around them, there are hundreds or even thousands of other Social Picnic Sharers. Each Sharer is free to decide whether to participate in the Social Picnic, and they depend entirely on their Plaid friends. Every step a Sharer takes on social media is constantly observed and evaluated. Each of their steps contributes to their reputation.

Some Sharers understand the reputation they are building, but the majority do not. Some are cautious and behave discreetly, while others are like open books, sharing everything they have. It's just like in real life. The only difference is that every action is much more visible in the Social Picnic and almost always receives reactions.

It's fascinating to observe how people of different generations use social media. Older individuals often struggle to grasp the abundance of emojis and tend to use more capital letters and exclamation marks. Meanwhile, younger people use numerous abbreviations that can convey different meanings. Older individuals' texts may seem outdated, with significant differences in their sense of humor and many other subtle nuances.

Texts and images speak about complexes, obsessions, wisdom, and the pursuit of exhibitionism, reveal artistic souls, break down the old, and create new authorities.

The personalities of Social Picnic Sharers are revealed both when they actively participate in it and even when they don't. I believe that each person's or organization's Plaid is an excellent field of study for any psychologist. I will leave that to them. However, what interests me the most are the patterns and deliberate efforts in building a reputation within the Social Picnic.

The Social Picnic Sharer is never alone. There is always at least one, and in many cases, dozens of other Social Picnic Sharers with whom they interact, forming relationships among them. These relationships are of particular interest to PR professionals.

The relationships among Social Picnic Sharers ultimately determine everything: where they choose to go on vacation and even what laws may be passed. Knowing the relationships between certain Sharers allows you to know whom to approach at a given time to resolve a particular issue. This has always been the case, with the only difference being that today, the necessary Social Picnic Sharer is much more "connected". In the past, to reach someone further away from you, you needed to know another person who could help you do so. Today, the required individual is often connected to many Social Picnic Sharers, so there are many more opportunities for such connections.

Let's say you need a Social Picnic Sharer, a government official in one of the ministries. In the time before the internet, there would be several ways to approach this official directly:

- Scheduling a visit.
- Attending an event where they will be present.
- Attempting to establish a personal connection.

Today, with a quick online search, we can find many Social Picnics which that government official frequents or engages with. Unless they are remarkably discreet about it, we can discover that the official enjoys fishing, has children, is an active member of a suburban community, frequently reads a specific portal, and is interested in science fiction literature, for instance. So, we have an abundance of Social Picnics to explore, and by visiting them, we can quickly get acquainted with the official. Once we've made a connection, we can invite them to our Social Picnic and draw their attention to our question or issue without making any extraordinary efforts.

Or another example. You need to reach one of the journalists working on a popular news portal. Today, she is not just a journalist whose name you would see alongside an article. Today, she is not just a journalist from the portal but an individual representing an organization, a media outlet, and an active personality with a strong presence on social media, involved in various activities, just like everyone else, actively expressing her opinion and commenting.

The journalist writes articles and builds her personal reputation, which allows her to be more highly regarded and earn a higher income now or in the future. The journalist personally cultivates her circle of Social Picnic Sharers, which changes independently of the organization she represents. Shortly, everyone will directly receive compensation for their created content (discussed in Chapter 5), and having a substantial circle of Sharers will guarantee success.

A journalist's reputation largely depends on how many essential individuals they can interview and the data they can obtain. This dependence provides PR specialists with various new opportunities. A journalist will always take pride in securing an interview with a well-known, influential person. PR specialists can capture these moments and share them with the journalist, who, in turn, will share them with their audiences through social media.

When looking at clients before the arrival of the Social Picnic, we used to feel longing when we couldn't reach them, anxiety when our competitors reached them more effectively, and fear of losing them. However, today, we must increasingly remember that the client has become a Sharer and is not only the target but also the means to reach other clients. Today, constructing information solely for traditional media is no longer sufficient; we must also construct it for clients in such a way that they want to spread it further, i.e., they want to publish that information in their own media outlets, on their social media accounts, on their blogs, on their YouTube channels, in their groups.

If you are a sports club owner, what information could you create for your clients? What do people like to share the most on social media? Of course, photos and videos. What's the hardest thing to do while working out, especially at a sports club? Take photos, of course! So, let's try to provide the new journalists with their photos! Hire a photographer who can walk around the club and offer to photograph people exercising, and then send them their photos. You'll see that you won't need to create content yourself – clients will gladly do it for you! Take a simple step – take and send the photos – and clients and social media will do the rest. If these photos are professionally done, clients will not only share them on the Social Picnic, praising your club, but also consider it a valuable added benefit. Furthermore, keep an eye on what happens to clients' photos, participate in discussions, provide clients with the information they want, and let them feel like sports professionals who can share information with their Plaid friends.

By providing and creating content tailored to each audience, we will help build the reputation of every Social Picnic Sharer because they will have unique information to share with fellow enthusiasts. This way, our content will spread even further without our direct efforts. People will share our content because they will feel unique and knowledgeable about having it.

This applies to every Social Picnic Sharer, and even if a Sharer is not a very active social media user, plenty of people in their circle constantly involve them in one way or another. Many people fear the loss of privacy and the associated threats this poses, but I believe those threats are much smaller than the benefits. Because Sharers participate in various Social Picnics, society becomes more transparent, open, straightforward, and unrestricted. And if you desire to hide somewhere, disconnect, disappear, or take a break, those options haven't disappeared – you need to turn off your mobile phone and not appear on social media. If you can't do that, it's a psychological issue, not a technological one. It should be addressed.

Every Sharer can easily control which Social Picnic participants they want to be a part of, which Meadows interest them, and which ones they want to ignore: visit some Social Picnics while ignoring others, turn off one Meadow and join others. Everyone who engages with any social media channel today automatically becomes a participant in one Social Picnic or another, even if they remain passive observers, never comment, and don't contribute.

In the Social Picnic, the Sharer is a person who directly or indirectly participates in the Social Picnic, is connected with others, and is easily accessible to other picnic Sharers through technology.

3.1.5. Food

> Food for the body is not enough. There must be food for the soul.
>
> Dorothy Day – journalist, social activist, and anarchist.

If a picnic occurs in the park, food will always be on the picnic blanket. However, the food is not there because we are eager to eat or because our goal in going on a picnic was to have a good meal. Our goal is to socialize and enjoy our time, and our food serves as an addition, enhancing conversations and providing comfort. So, when we gather around the picnic blanket in the park, we eat in two ways – spiritually and emotionally (food for the soul) and directly (food for the body).

The Social Picnic element "Food" is also twofold – it consists of conversations and data.

The most significant part of Food in the Social Picnic context is the conversations, texts, and comments, the continuous communication, operating non-stop 24 hours a day, 7 days a week, 365 days a year due to technological advancements. Like the Social Picnic itself, these conversations take place constantly; food here doesn't have working or resting hours, but it does have trends and fashions.

Almost as important is the data, which is the content that supports, enhances, and diversifies communication. Content is often presented in facts, numbers, research, presentations, infographics, and various other formats, providing a foundation for communication.

The ongoing Social Picnic has fundamentally changed the work of a PR specialist. In the past, when we didn't have all the technologies we know today, textbooks used to say that a PR specialist must be prepared to react immediately, and if the media asks a question, they should be able to answer it no later than within two hours. However, that sounds quite old-fashioned today. The Social Picnic demands lightning-fast reactions and constant preparedness, and sometimes, not responding within the first five minutes can mean a missed opportunity that's impossible to catch up with.

Being prepared to react in no way means reacting every time, but observation and a constant state of readiness are the daily bread of a modern PR specialist.

At the picnic in the park, you can imagine the PR specialist as someone who is either constantly by their picnic blanket and ready to treat everyone who comes to that blanket or as someone who constantly walks around the park with their basket and is ready to sit down at any time at the picnic where a meaningful conversation is taking place. And not just sit down but also treat the picnic members to the contents of their basket.

If we return to the concept of Social Picnic, the PR specialist is constantly by their Plaid or Plaids and is ready to provide information (the treat) at any time to anyone who approaches that Plaid. Similarly, they continuously browse through the Social Picnic. When they find the right Plaids, they sit down (start a discussion with the Plaid members) or even share a treat from their basket (provide knowledge and information).

The Social Picnic element Food is the conversations and data that Sharers constantly share.

3.1.6. Vase

> A flowerless room is a soulless room, to my way of thinking; but even a solitary little vase of a living flower may redeem it.
>
> Vita Sackville-West – author and garden designer.

The term "Vase (with a Flower)" just mentioned refers to the visual aspect of each Plaid, which includes elements like logos, colors, images, visual materials, and other visual components. In contemporary terms, this is often referred to as branding, and it's a crucial part of an organization's identity. However, in the context of the Social Picnic, various Plaids can participate, and they may not necessarily be corporate entities or even formal organizations; they can be informal groups or even one-time gatherings.

Many books have been written about branding, and I certainly won't say anything new on this topic. Branding is essential for the identity of any organization.

However, many Plaids in the Picnic Society are not mature organizations, and lack the Vase element. This scarcity is especially characteristic of spontaneously formed communities that do not think strategically, aim for a specific goal, have a solid emotional disposition, and often believe that "all these refinements" are unnecessary. However, over time, even such communities often pay attention to how they appear visually, and then – they create one type of "Vase" or another on their Plaid.

In my practice, I have had such an example. A city community actively fought against their city's persistent, annoying odors, such as sewage, burning, and the like. It was a just and necessary fight for a clean environment and a quality life. I do not want to focus on the fight, which has not yet ended, so I will name that city Smelltown. I am interested in the exceptional reputation of this activity. So, several Smelltown residents created a group on one of the social networks and named it South Smelltown Stinks. It was a spontaneously conceived name, born in great anger. And this name has lived for several years. More and more people joined the group, and today, the group unites more than 7,000 community members. It so happened that the platform, South Smelltown Stinks, became the leading group of that community, where broader issues are addressed, and sometimes even non-issues. This group sometimes organizes children's Christmas celebrations or neighborhood cleaning events. Don't you think the name South Smelltown Stinks might have become somewhat peculiar and perhaps even alienating? It's odd to suggest a child go to a Christmas celebration organized by the South Smelltown Stinks group, and sharing pictures from that event is quite strange.

This example illustrates how, spontaneously, a Plaid was laid down. But, later, Plaids demand a Vase; Plaids need to be redecorated, new colors appear, the style is slightly tidied up, and owners start to think more broadly.

Therefore, South Smelltown Stinks changed, and started to raise the odor issues on a separate website, which they named www.smelltownsmell.xx, and renamed the overall group Clean South Smelltown. So, in this group, Plaid gave way to Vase, and positive visual communication emerged, which is the essence of Vase. Interestingly, many people, including the Sharers, are visually sensitive beings. Although they often indulge in negative images, they want a haven where they can see the positive in the long run. Long-term negativity begins to irritate and is usually turned away from. An explanation as to why this happens lies again in psychology, which I will not delve into, leaving it to the professionals. Here, I have provided only a subjective observation from my practice.

The Social Picnic element Vase is a positive and visual Plaid identity.

3.1.7. ***Concert***

> Live concerts were to train the ears and to introduce, constantly, new musical ideas to the audience so the next time they showed up or the next record they would be ready and receptive.
>
> Gail Zappa – wife of musician and composer Frank Zappa and trustee of the Zappa Family Trust.

Like Vase, "Concert" is a frequent but non-essential Social Picnic element. A Concert is an event temporarily attracting the attention of one or several Social Picnic Sharers.

At the picnic in the park, there is often a stage, and when a speaker steps onto it, or music unexpectedly takes over, everyone at least momentarily falls silent, and all attention shifts to the stage.

Thus, in the Social Picnic, when something that interests the majority occurs, a Concert takes place. The Concert becomes a theme that connects the individual Plaids. In other words, a significant number of the Plaids, previously constituted by different sets of themes, converge for a specific time, and the Concert theme prevails among them.

In the Picnic Society, both collectively and in each Social Picnic individually, communication is decentralized; no one has a monopoly on topics, and diversity of opinions prevails. However, everyone's attention for a certain period is monopolized during the Concert.

If the Social Picnic represents a country, the Concert could be considered the country's primary elections. The Concert could also be military aggression, a major natural disaster, national holidays, cultural and sports achievements, pandemics, and various other similar events that attract the attention of all residents of that country.

In some cases, Social Picnics and the Concerts within them can be significant and global without geographical boundaries. The COVID-19 pandemic, the Olympic Games, climate change, and space flights are the kinds of Social

Picnics that can be called global, and the Concerts within them capture the attention of the entire world.

Of course, Social Picnics and Concerts can also be very small, limited to a small community of sometimes just a few dozen people.

Concerts not only happen, but during them, new ideas are often raised, which previously circulated only around or among certain Plaids. During Concerts, these ideas are made public, spread to a large circle of Sharers, and receive positive or negative evaluations. After disseminating these ideas, new Plaids often emerge that either support or oppose them.

The Social Picnic element Concert is a theme that temporarily becomes the central focus among Social Picnic Sharers.

Summary

Today's ideal PR professional knows everything that happens in the Social Picnic, perhaps even in more than one. They are familiar with all the Plaids, know the participants of each theme, know when the Sun shines, and what Concerts are planned. The ideal PR professional is aware of all the ongoing processes within the Social Picnic and can utilize these processes to achieve their goals. Of course, ideal phenomena do not exist in the world, but it is there to serve as an aspiration for us.

The PR professional is an expert in one or several Social Picnics, whom one can turn to when wanting to make an appearance in one or another Social Picnic to pursue their goals within it.

Table 3.1 Social Picnic elements.

Element	*Explanation*
Sun	High-quality and well-functioning information technologies.
Meadow	The boundaries of the Social Picnic that separate one picnic from another.
Plaids	A community united by one or several interests; this community is closely linked with other communities through the use of information technology.
Sharer	An individual directly or indirectly participating in the Social Picnic, connected to others and easily accessible to other picnic Sharers through technology.
Food	Conversations and data that Sharers constantly share.
Vase	Positive and visual Plaid identity.
Concert	The theme that temporarily becomes the main focus among Social Picnic Sharers.

3.2. Four Pillars: ConCrEtE formula

> Success is neither magical nor mysterious. Success is the natural consequence of consistently applying the basic fundamentals.
>
> Jim Rohn – entrepreneur, author, and motivational speaker.

Lon Safko and David K. Brake, in their 2009 book *The social media bible: tactics, tools, and strategies for business success*, effectively formulated the critical elements of a successful Social Picnic (four pillars): communication, collaboration, education, and entertainment. I thank them for this brilliant and straightforward summary of complex matters.

I have named this formula ConCrEtE for the Social Picnic. If we think broadly, these four pillars are the foundation of the Social Picnic and any other long-term relationships.

My colleague constantly compares PR to romantic relationships. He says that a family is not a campfire made to warm one up for just an evening, but a hearth that, when constantly fueled, can burn brightly for a while and then smoulder but never go out.

What, then, is this fueling in the context of PR? What are those logs? The answer is quite simple – ConCrEtE. To have a successful family, we must constantly do four main things: communicate with each other (communication), help each other (collaboration), teach, complement, and improve each other (education), and enjoy, relax, play, and rejoice with each other (entertainment).

PR professionals create or help create relationships not within families but in other areas. Families are a field for psychologists. The field of PR professionals is the relationships between different groups of society. However, the same rules have been applied in both spheres for a long time.

If you occasionally still read print newspapers or used to do so in the past, you would quickly notice that they also clearly expressed the ConCrEtE formula. Even the most severe traditional media outlets were composed of four parts: communication (news), collaboration (interviews), education (summaries of information necessary for a new activity), and entertainment (horoscopes, anecdotes, and comics).

How is a media portal structured? Precisely the same way!

How should the work in a Social Picnic be constructed? The answer is obvious: by using the ConCrEtE formula. If a Sharer visits your Plaid, you want them to leave inspired, fascinated, and wanting to come back, so they must receive four things: learn news (communication), get information that they could use further (collaboration), learn new things (education), and have a bit of fun (entertainment).

The ConCrEtE formula is a universal basis for any relationship, a set of what people expect from each other.

3.2.1. Communication

> Words are wonderful form of communication, but they will never replace kisses and punches.
>
> Ashleigh Brilliant – author and cartoonist.

It would probably be naive to expect to describe what communication is in this small section. Large books have been written on this subject, and it is taught in various universities worldwide. All of this is true, and the relevance of communication has not disappeared. I highly recommend delving deeper into this field than what is presented in these pages.

Here, I narrow down the concept of communication and try to summarize very briefly what is most relevant when dealing with communication during a Social Picnic. Once again, the image of a picnic in nature has greatly helped me here.

Communication through style

You come to the park and see an extensive array of blankets. What will catch your eye first? Where will you want to go first? Will you go to where someone sits gloomily on a faded blanket, and there is nothing else except the person sitting there? Perhaps. However, the vast majority will be drawn to where the blanket is vibrant, where many people walk around it, laughing and talking, where freshly baked buns are offered to newcomers, where someone quickly strikes up a conversation, makes a joke, and involves you in the action.

So, the blanket in the park must be visual, lively, inviting, and fragrant, or, in short, stylish.

The same happens with the Plaid present at the Social Picnic. The Plaid must have its style; it must be appropriately designed, with style-appropriate action taking place. When you visit, click, react, or comment, a particular form of response, encouragement, and attention must be drawn to it. So, the presence of a specific style, visual appeal, and form is one of the necessary conditions for the Plaid to be popular, desirable, and attractive.

Style, of course, is a subtle matter and highly dependent on the audience. What one person finds beautiful may not necessarily be beautiful to another. However, this is a matter of sensing your audience. It may be that the style is created to attract some and push away others. However, it must exist. Every professional PR specialist should remember to take care of the style first.

A sustainable style cannot be created without establishing a hygienic environment. We might have the most beautiful blanket in the park, but if it emanates a foul smell or the nicely displayed wine has gone sour, the style won't last long: uncleanliness will overshadow beauty.

This exact process is also happening with communication hygiene. Not uncommon are examples where excellent branding work is overshadowed by communicative uncleanliness. Communication hygiene encompasses not only visual and visible elements that branding takes care of but also those that we may not immediately notice: grammatical errors, email addresses, the ability to access a particular service, responses to calls and chats. Often, we see large corporations whose English appears excellent and are covered by the global media. Still, if we were to try to find out something about them, for example, in Bulgarian, which is supposedly available on their website, we would see poorly translated texts, non-functional navigation, and impossible-to-find contacts. However, visually, everything seems in order, according to the brand book.

These mistakes often happen with artists and designers. For several years, I have been observing the activities of a famous clothing designer in my country. This artist creates attention-grabbing presentations for the elite, stage designs for popular operas, and is visible and well-known. However, despite all of his merits, he is constantly followed by an almost invisible loop of communication anti-hygiene:

- His social media posts are a total of grammar mistakes and clumsiness.
- Messages about unpaid debts constantly appear.
- His interviews in the media reflect a lack of sophistication.

He fails to create a coherent and sustainable style; his brand has many visitors, but often they leave it, and sometimes they stay away altogether because they have experienced a lack of communication hygiene with him.

Style doesn't mean everything must be polished, smooth, and impeccable. Not at all. Style can be messy, but it must be clearly understood and anticipated in advance; it must be intentional. Suppose a letter is skipped due to carelessness in a word. In that case, if there are missing punctuation marks in a sentence, these will be mistakes demonstrating a lack of sophistication and appearing unstylish and off-putting. If the same letter is omitted consistently in the same word, having a particular concept behind it, perhaps after explaining why it is done so, the same mistake can become an element of style.

Communication through topics

By appearance, one may be attracted, but it's through intellect that one is won over. That's what people say in my country. Style invites you to the Plaid, but whether or not you turn away from it is determined not only by communication hygiene. Rather, the themes discussed are one of the most crucial factors that eventually make one Plaid more popular than another.

Themes were the factor that unified or divided people during the "Television" phase. People chose their friends, went to parties, and made or broke relationships based on themes. People bought newspapers and magazines and participated in various group activities based on themes.

The same thing happens around the Plaid; nothing has changed fundamentally, it is only that people's hobbies have become more public. There is often talk about how society has become divided, enclosed within its bubbles and circles, thanks to social media. However, social media is as much to blame here as a mirror is to blame for reflecting an image. Social media did not create but highlighted and publicized the thematic division within society. What used to remain within the confines of one's kitchen or living room is publicly visible. Often, one thematic group cannot believe that there are other groups whose topics are uninteresting, and vice versa.

This book is being written during the COVID-19 pandemic, and the world is divided into two opposing camps on one particular issue: vaccine advocates and anti-vaxxers. Such a division may seem like a new and contemporary phenomenon to some. However, to think so would be a significant mistake. Resistance to vaccines has existed since the end of the 18th century, when the British physician Edward Jenner tested the first smallpox vaccines. But today, we see it more. We see more information from those who create vaccines and try to convince people to get vaccinated, and from those who oppose vaccines. Many Plaids are visible to everyone, but the opposing camp's Plaids are only visited to mock or express indignation.

So themes unite or push away, but only those who are for something or against something. It is difficult or even impossible to expect to create a Plaid that would attract everyone because the choice of themes is inevitable.

Therefore, when creating a Plaid, it is worth carefully considering the spectrum of themes to be discussed. People who visit certain Plaids also get used to the spectrum of themes there. Therefore, every attempt to involve them in considering new themes risks losing some participants altogether. Unless it is a Plaid dedicated to the generation of new themes and new themes are part of everyday life.

Communication through tone

Although the tone is undoubtedly a part of the style, it is worth mentioning separately. Interestingly, many people react not to what is said but how it is said. Some can understand a sentence in one tone as humorous, while others may perceive it as an insult.

This happens because the ears of the message sender and receiver are different. That is why people often do not understand each other. The difference in the ears is caused by education, empathy, age, location, and many other factors. That is why message conversion, transformation, and interpretation are needed. And this is the essence of the work of the PR professional: we **take** the message from the sender after first getting a deep understanding of it, reshape it without changing the essence, just making it suitable for the receiver, i.e., **pack** it, and **deliver** it to the receiver in a form they can receive it.

At the Social Picnic, we can constantly observe phenomena where those Sharers who like one kind of Plaid speak about other Plaids as offensive, arrogant, unaccepting, or mocking. Meanwhile, participants of the latter Plaids look down on the former, disdain their lack of sophistication, and laugh at their mediocrity. These are all mismatches between the sender and receiver of the news.

The hosts of every successful Plaid either understand the importance of tone themselves or seek the help of a PR professional. Maintaining and adjusting the tone of the Plaid is a subtle and delicate factor. Still, this very factor often determines the final decision of how often and whether Sharers will visit our Plaid at all.

Communication through empathy

Every person seeks to be understood. The same applies to any Sharer who dedicates their time to one Plaid or another. Usually, when they come to the Plaid, they not only listen but, if they are bold, they express their opinion right away, and if they are more timid, they do so when the right moment arises. It is crucial how that opinion is reacted to, or whether it is reacted to at all. Therefore, for the Plaid owner aiming to have a growing circle of Plaid Sharers, it is essential to closely monitor new Sharers arriving at the Plaid and react to their actions – actively engage with the active ones and encourage the more timid ones to express their opinions.

Many conversations are killed because one person is too shy and another person is too confident. And it is also true that showing yourself confidently in public does not necessarily mean you are clever, but just loud. A PR professional is someone who should first listen and only speak second; you should know that listening only to those who are loud is a smooth way to the wrong decision. So listen and try to speak with those who are shy. They also have a lot to say, and you need to find a way to have a conversation with them.

Communication through novelties

And finally, and deliberately left for the end of this subsection, comes news. Communication without news is impossible; people get tired without receiving news, and the same information becomes dull, which is a direct path to disappointed Plaid visitors.

Every Plaid must provide news, regardless of the prevailing themes. If it's a community Plaid, we must report on new events happening within that community. If it's a Plaid for a newly constructed factory, we must report on the stages of construction and the results achieved. If it's a Plaid for humor, we must link our topics to current events. If it's an astronomy Plaid, we must provide news from space.

A Plaid without news is moving towards contraction or extinction. In growing, thriving Plaids, news must be continuous. Sharers must be the first to receive the latest information directly and feel privileged, i.e., know that they are exclusive members of the Picnic Society and receive the latest news first.

3.2.2. Collaboration

> A good collaboration pushes the boundaries of both partners.
>
> Neil Blumenthal – businessman.

In the picnic park, gathered around the blanket, we not only talk but also feast: we taste, try, and share. When going on a picnic, we always have a little something in our basket: cookies baked yesterday, sandwiches, compote, or wine. When sitting around a particular blanket, we will always receive something and have something to treat others with. Maybe not always, but we will try to make it so.

At a Social Picnic, sandwiches and cookies are replaced by photos, presentations, texts, answers to questions, and information delivery, i.e., everything we can offer in more detail than what fits in the news.

If Communication is new, brief, and quick but often superficial, then Collaboration is broad, detailed, time-consuming, and profound.

Essentially, every Plaid becomes a gathering of experts on one or another topic. In reality, these experts can often be not very serious jesters or the most serious or best-informed about the matter. However they may be, Sharers, coming to one or another Plaid, expect to receive expert information, learn more, get material that they can later share themselves, and build their own expert reputation.

With the scent of fresh buns emanating from the blankets that spread across the entire park, some expect to taste those buns. At the NASA Plaid, people expect to receive reliable information about space; at the anti-vaxxer Plaid, those who want to support their opinion seek the latest anti-vaccination theories. The most appreciated are those Plaids that provide news and allow one to take something away, "put something in their pocket", save something on their computer and share it on their social media account.

Equally crucial to the "takeaway" part is receiving specific information interesting to a particular Sharer. This information can be referred to as personal collaboration. Often, a Sharer asks questions, and it would be a big mistake to ignore their questions. With every active Sharer, we must collaborate, constantly respond to the questions asked, and provide the requested information.

We should not forget that every Sharer (which is why they are called a Sharer) is a larger or smaller media outlet, a disseminator of information. Satisfied, having received what they want, they become loyal because they know that this Plaid responded to them, did not turn away from them, and paid attention to them. Therefore, just as in the past, responding to every journalist's call, letter, or request was essential, responding to every Sharer's desire or request is no less critical today.

Sometimes, even the most minor details are vital, as is paying close attention. One should never forget that every Sharer is, first and foremost, a human being, not just an email address or a profile. In practice, the question arises, "Is it worth it?" Is it worth it for a large corporation to engage with everyone who may sometimes appear too active, proactive, and demanding too much attention? I answer without hesitation – it is worth it. And although in the short term, the effect may go unnoticed, the efforts will be repaid in the long term. The statement born in the "Television" phase that a dissatisfied customer tells 11 people about it, and a satisfied customer tells 3 has not disappeared. Today, one could confidently multiply these numbers by a hundred.

Therefore, answering questions, sending information, and communicating is the minimum foundation that should be implemented constantly. However, in addition to that, today it is more important than ever to communicate in person, to meet not in the virtual space, to invite for visits, to show how things work, to let them try, to touch.

The increasing growth of virtuality does not contradict this, but rather quite the opposite. Trust is one of the main questions currently being addressed by the creators of the recently introduced "Metaverse" and cryptosystems. I do not expect that we will not have virtual deceits in the future, but trust in what we see on the screen or through glasses will proliferate. This is one of the main conditions for developing the future internet, the principle of "trust what you see". The more our lives and actions move into virtual space, the more we want to ensure safety.

However, no one is preparing to replace the real world with the virtual one. At least in the foreseeable future, the natural world will remain primary, and the virtual world will be an extension of the natural world, providing new opportunities. Real things will gain more value as the relationship with the virtual world grows. It may be that actual visits, meetings, and demonstrations will be essential and rare, which means they will be valuable. But we, PR professionals, are here precisely to discover what sets our Plaid apart from others, to make an impression, to leave a memory.

Attention is the new gold. Or better to say, it was always a bar of gold. It is just that the price of it has become much higher nowadays. English brewer and Conservative politician Richard Moss lived in the 19th century, but he already knew the greatest gift one person can give to the other. He said that "the greatest gift you can give another person is the purity of your attention". Since that time, the attention price has increased by many percentages. The more information we have, the more expensive attention becomes. Remember this next time you'll try to reach the attention of some particular group of people or one person. Do not write or call them – invite them to a meeting, dedicate your time and attention. You'll be surprised at the results.

I once was responsible for the communication element of a new factory. The construction of the factory caused much controversy within the neighboring community. Without delving into what caused this controversy, I will say that the factory was modern, clean, and necessary. It had professional employees who believed in the usefulness of their work. My goal was to inform the public about this, to answer emerging questions, and eventually eliminate unfounded fears.

I remember the evening when the first smoke was supposed to appear from the factory chimney. I was prepared for it and constantly monitored the social networks interested in such Plaids. I was confident that there would be a reaction as soon as the first smoke appeared at the top of the chimney. The smoke appeared late in the evening, and just five minutes later, I saw the first message on Facebook with a photo stating that the smoke was already rising and the factory had started its operation. The reaction to this post appeared after a few more minutes, and the woman who wrote it complained that she not only saw the smoke but also felt a nauseating odor that made her want to vomit. I couldn't argue whether she felt the smell that evening because people feel various odors in their environment, and some even cause them themselves. However, I was calm because no smell could spread from the new factory chimney as it was simply technologically impossible.

I monitored the Social Picnic space and reacted immediately, not allowing the discussions that had begun to escalate. In each discussion, I openly wrote my phone number and offered to immediately go to the factory and search together for the source of the unpleasant odor. I suggested going inside the factory, checking which way the wind was blowing, and determining where the smell was coming from. The discussion ended with a few "we know, we know" but no one appeared willing to go.

After a year or two, I had the opportunity to travel by train with the woman who had written the message about the smell, and we talked for almost an hour. At that time, she reminded me of the situation with the factory launch and my suggestion to go together, publicly providing my phone number. She said to me, "You know psychology well. When you posted your number, you knew no one would come, but without going, there would be no more discussion. With this action, you managed to calm us down, and, one could say, you built trust."

My knowledge of psychology is not that extensive. I was determined to go, even if it meant going with just one Sharer, and find the source of the smell.

This example emphasizes that one should not have initial assumptions and preconceptions about who is a significant and important Sharer and who is not worth paying attention to. It is never worthwhile to confine oneself within the framework of official communication. One should approach not theoretically or formally but realistically, believing in collaboration with everyone interested in the object of your communication. The principle of collaboration must be implemented constantly.

I refer to such situations as the best outcome achievable in building relationships and, through them, one's reputation. The result of PR activities is not about the quantity of articles or likes but rather about such meetings, evaluations, and conversations. They might be small and visible only to a small circle, but they are the most crucial.

Precisely, just like picnic-goers bring their sandwiches or wine to the park, some Sharers at a Plaid may come with their "sandwiches" or "wine" in the form of data, presentations, or photos. Some of this information can be new and useful, while others may contain incorrect information. However, attention should be given to both: proper information should be acknowledged, complemented with your own, and shared further, while for inappropriate information, you should engage in discussions, point out the inaccuracies, or refute them.

Indeed, the collaboration process, like communication, is mutual, and both participants in this process benefit:

- Their knowledge expands.
- New collaboration opportunities arise.

- Relationships are formed.
- Trust is built.
- Comfort is established.

However, it can also work the other way around – it can be established that the intentions of one party are insincere, seeking to deceive. Nevertheless, even in such a case, the collaboration process is beneficial – it helps understand what to expect from either the Plaid or the Sharer side. It is worth emphasizing that a Plaid or a Sharer can be perceived as trustworthy or untrustworthy not only in the eyes of the other party but also in their own.

Some Sharers or Plaids can be malicious actors or trolls who aim to harm and spread false information. During Communication and Collaboration, this can be quickly clarified, and once clarified, there is only one path – to distance oneself and ignore.

Collaboration is sharing what you have, know, and can do. Suppose we view accumulated knowledge as the sea. In that case, Communication will be each new wave, and Collaboration will be all the remaining water, from which we can draw at any time, give to those who ask, or pour in what others are sharing.

3.2.3. Education

> Education is not preparation for life; education is life itself.
>
> John Dewey – philosopher, psychologist, and educational reformer.

I believe you know that feeling when you come to visit someone or, if you will, to a picnic, and after tasting something new and delicious prepared by the hosts, there arises a desire to do it yourself, acquire it, and try it. We all seek to learn. Even that person who may not have been or is not the most advanced student in the class or university seeks to learn something new in one field or another.

The viewing of an unseen movie, presenting a new approach to phenomena discoveries, learning new skills, and sharing knowledge is Education. Not a single newspaper or television or radio show during the "Television" phase was without a topic that seemed to come out of nowhere: without the presentation of historical facts, without an explanation of scientific discoveries, without sections like "did you know that. . . .", "do it yourself", without the presentation of previously unseen information.

Similarly, during the "Network" phase, not a single successful Plaid can do without educating its Sharers. While continuously providing news (Communication) and sharing existing knowledge (Collaboration), it is essential not to forget to invite Sharers to seminars and conferences, or to organize lectures, courses, workshops, or other gatherings where Sharers can improve their knowledge.

The tools of the "Network" phase once again open up almost unlimited opportunities, even without having significant resources, sometimes even without having them at all. It is not necessary to do everything yourself; it is enough to be interested in what is happening, to connect to what is happening, and to offer to connect to your Plaid Sharers.

If you are interested in astronomy and have your Plaid on this topic, you can search for exciting people nearby willing to attend a lecture and share their knowledge. However, you can also constantly monitor the streams of NASA, ESA, or CSA Plaids and invite your Sharers to observe the new telescope's flight into space or participate in a lecture with hundreds of thousands of astronomy enthusiasts worldwide.

People enjoy learning. That is, they embrace innovations, especially when presented attractively. While learning, people feel they receive more expert information and become experts, often sharing what they have learned. And, of course, they remain grateful to the teacher subconsciously.

Therefore, without overestimating, it can be stated that Education is essential to the PR professional's activities, contributing to reputation building.

Each year, the Nobel Prize award ceremony is eagerly awaited news for many, and this is Communication. The stories related to the Nobel Prize about discoveries and people are Collaboration. Revealing the process of forging the physical Nobel Prize, explaining and demonstrating how a piece of metal becomes the Nobel Medal, is Education.

Every communicable phenomenon or object has these communication possibilities, i.e., it always has news, stories, and processes that can interest people interested in the topic or Sharers who can quickly disseminate that information today.

If your subject of communication is automobiles, there will always be news related to new models, stories, interesting facts from the history of cars, and education on how a car is made. If you communicate about costumes, you will have new models, materials, stories about fashion trends in costumes, and plenty of information to share about how to choose a costume correctly.

Each brand has within itself news, stories, and lessons it can teach those around it. Therefore, each, including Plaid, must adhere to the same model and, in one way or another, constantly prepare informational cocktails from Communication, Collaboration, and Education.

3.2.4. Entertainment

> A day without laughter is a day wasted.
>
> Charlie Chaplin – actor, filmmaker, and composer.

Even the most severe communication should have elements of play or humor. Humor is not only an excellent way to relieve tension but also one of the ways to convey information. Very often, highly complex messages are easily conveyed through memes, comics, or other forms of humor.

Let's return to the picnic in nature once again. Besides conversations, tasting new cookies, or learning how to bake them, there is always something more. Of course! That's the ball, cards, badminton rackets, or dominoes; in other words, games without which a full-fledged picnic is unimaginable.

And if we look at the last page of the "Television"-era magazine? We will find anecdotes, horoscopes, cartoons, tasks, and many other light-content items there. Why? So that everything seems manageable so that the reader expects not only what is on the first or fifth pages but also knows that a sweet ending, dessert, pleasure, and relaxation are still waiting for them. After reading even the most terrifying content in a newspaper that writes that the world will likely collapse tomorrow, the last page always remains with a crossword puzzle, calming words, and a guarantee that everything is okay. One can also make judgments and laugh, and have a guarantee that it will be there tomorrow as well.

A Plaid's communication at the Social Picnic should not be an exception, and humor should also have its place here. It is very healthy for Sharers to offer memes and funny videos related to the theme represented by your Plaid. Such humor always "blows off steam" and spreads the message about Plaid excellently. Plaid about cars can offer laughter about road situations; for Plaid about costumes, you can joke about peculiar ways of wearing them, and if Plaid is about food production, there will always be great jokes about failed experiments, and so on. Every topic, no matter how serious it may be, always has a funny side.

It is essential to remember that humor must not be expressed in a pure form. It can also be greetings, mentions of thematic anniversaries, professional celebrations, and historical event dates. Cartoons, caricatures, and unexpected discoveries also fit well here.

ConCrEtE is a formula that universally describes what needs to be done at the Social Picnic to draw attention to your activity and achieve your goals. Different Plaids have different relationships between these parts, and it would be hard to find a Plaid where the ratios of these parts are the same, i.e., Com (25%), Col (25%), Edu (25%), and Ent (25%).

If a Plaid is exclusively for entertainment purposes, then the ConCrEtE formula may look like this: 5:20:10:65. If Plaid is very serious, intended for political or business analysis: 30:30:30:10. If the goal of Plaid is education, popularization of science: 15:15:60:10. These ratios can be very diverse, but for every PR specialist, before creating a new Plaid or taking over a Plaid, it would be helpful to define this ratio and adhere to it.

I named this ratio the ConCrEtE Mix.

The ConCrEtE Mix is the foundation of each Plaid, the expectation of any Sharer who will visit your Plaid. Directly or indirectly perceiving or feeling the ConCrEtE Mix of each Plaid, the Sharer decides to stay with the Plaid constantly, visit occasionally, or turn away.

3.3. Rules

Rules are for the obedience of fools and the guidance of wise men.

Harry Day – pilot.

Whenever a new phenomenon arises, it almost always emerges without rules. Only when it starts to spread, highlighting its positive and negative qualities, do rules begin to be created for it. Money appeared long ago, and only after several centuries did modern monetary systems and international economic principles emerge. Newspapers appeared at the beginning of the "Television" phase, and only after a specific time did media ethics codes or laws exist.

In the early stages of the "Network" phase, with the emergence of the internet, no one thought of regulating it. Initially, the internet was perceived by a significant part of society as a space without any rules. At some point, the entire copyright-based industry would have gone bankrupt because content began to spread on the internet unrestricted, uncontrolled, and most importantly – for free. To a considerable part of the global community, even today, downloading a movie from the internet seems like a lesser theft compared to shoplifting a book from a bookstore. Some do not even perceive internet piracy as theft at all.

However, it is evident that as the "Network" phase evolves, rules and laws are being established. The emergence of non-fungible tokens, lawsuits against anonymous internet commentators, data leaks online, and similar phenomena are clear evidence that the internet strives for a similar level of security as in real life. Mark Zuckerberg, announcing the creation of the "Metaverse", identified security or, in other words, rules that must be followed to enjoy all the benefits of the "Metaverse" as the primary and fundamental task. In the future, we will most likely perceive trolls, who are still capable of achieving this and that today, as unwanted guests trying to enter our homes through the window.

In whatever form it may take, the internet will move towards more significant and sustainable regulation and easier personal identification. However, these rules will constitute a form of burdensome regulation that will be impossible to ignore, as otherwise, it would violate laws, regulations, or community standards.

However, as with all forms of regulation, there is another form of soft regulation. This regulation includes politeness, respect, and ethical norms. These things will most likely never be written down, but they exist and are crucial for reputation. A company leader demonstrating a lack of education will not be penalized even administratively, but it will cause considerable reputational damage to the company.

So, we have some unwritten universal rules in the Picnic Society that should be discussed. What is permissible and desirable at the Social Picnic, and what is not prohibited but undesirable?

In the "Network" phase, many global companies face the question of whether to allow employees to speak publicly on behalf of the company at the Social Picnic. Does this not contradict the decades-old "one company, one voice" principle? If allowed, it is as if one should monitor, see what the employee is doing, and observe whether they are doing it correctly. I remember these discussions well and have had the opportunity to participate in more than one and help leaders make decisions.

Indeed, this question is not as complex as it may seem at first glance. I always remember a statement from one of my clients in an information technology company about what was safer – the virtual world or the real. At that time, there was a discussion about people wanting to avoid submitting their annual income tax returns online because they believed it was unsafe. Someone could read them. At the same time, they were willingly sending them by mail.

So, my client suggested that I consider the peculiarity of this phenomenon. He said that one only needs to unseal the envelope to read a declaration sent by mail, or maybe even not that – one can replace the old envelope with a new one after making a copy of the document. Anyone, even an uneducated person, a child, can do that. But what if the declaration is sent electronically? Well, even if the file is sent completely unprotected, accessing it would require at least hacking into the e-mail server. Can anyone do that? Probably not. However, sending documents by mail still seemed safer to people at that time.

The same applies to the counterparts of all other natural phenomena in the virtual world, including communication. If an employee is dissatisfied with their employer, we may make the most tremendous efforts, but we will not find ways to stop their expressed opinion. They may not express it openly, but they constantly complain to family, friends, and colleagues. These activities will create a negative reputation, just as public speaking does. Perhaps even more vital, as silence from the company's side and rumors constitute a particularly potent communication mix.

So the answer is straightforward: free people speak, they will speak, and it would be best not to even think about silencing them. It is best to think about how to help those who want to communicate, advise, explain the processes taking place at the Social Picnic, the consequences of one or another step, provide information, and then allow everyone to do as they know best.

So many companies, without much thought, have devised rules recommended for adherence to the Sharers within the companies. These rules usually fall under Social Media Policies, which differ from one another not so strongly.

Let's briefly discuss what is written in many such sets of rules. I based my favorite set on the one created by the Sociallogical.com team. It was titled "The Common Sense Social Media Policy". I supplemented this set with my practice and what I found in various companies' social media policies. So, here is the Social Picnic set of rules that, I believe, every Plaid owner can use when communicating with Sharers. Essentially, anyone participating in Social Picnic events can follow them.

3.3.1. First Rule: Kindness

Kindness is the language which the deaf can hear and the blind can see.
Mark Twain – writer, humorist, entrepreneur, publisher, and lecturer.

Sometimes, people are afraid to be good. Even though everyone knows it's pleasant to meet a good person, it's nice to communicate with them, and the pleasant feeling of the conversation lingers for a long time. Kindness costs nothing but creates excellent value. This value is expressed in reputation points or units. A reasonable person always builds a much better foundation for the desired reputation.

There are many ways to express kindness at a Social Picnic. And it's much easier to do so than at a picnic in the park. In the park, you need to approach and find an opportunity to express gratitude, and gratitude can be expressed only to a minimal number of people.

At a Social Picnic, the most minor and common expression of kindness is the "Like" button or something similarly positive. When Facebook was created, Mark Zuckerberg resisted the presence of any button other than "Like" for a long time. Later, a few alternative buttons appeared, but "Dislike" was still absent. And although there is no shortage of negativity on Facebook, it is the position of the social network. This position does not negate negativity, but it also does not encourage direct competition between "Likes" and "Dislikes."

Kindness and politeness are potent factors in building a reputation. Kindness must contain within it "Action" and "Tongue" and "Style" – only then will kindness be not accidental but genuine and essential.

There is a folk saying, "A good person is not a profession." That's true. But it's also true that any profession without kindness is just a mechanical action, performing something you wouldn't otherwise do, but you do it to have something to live on.

When participating in a Social Picnic, it is essential not to forget that everything we release into the virtual space remains in the cloud in one form or another. Although that cloud existed even before the emergence of the virtual world, negativity also accumulated in the cloud, which constantly hung over bad people and occasionally burst; paradoxically, in the virtual world, this cloud materialized. All negative thoughts are no longer accumulating in the spiritual or emotional cloud but remain recorded in servers, constantly haunting the individuals, communities, Sharers, and Plaids who spread them.

I know several such instances, and I refer to them as revelations. I believe you may have noticed one or more of these revelations as well. You know someone from the real world, you occasionally meet them, and you know that they are representatives of one profession or another. Sometimes, you even greet each other, but you haven't interacted much. And suddenly, you meet this person at a Social Picnic. And you see a torrent of ugliness pouring out of them: contempt, gossip, insults. It feels like the person is constantly setting off explosives of negativity. Did that person change because Facebook appeared? Of course not. They have always been like that; their cloud has become visible to many. This revelation strongly and often irreversibly changes that person's reputation.

I have observed such "cloud color changes" more than once and have seen several drastic shifts in reputation among journalists, athletes, actors, and reviewers. Essentially, the profession here is not essential. What matters is kindness.

3.3.2. Second Rule: Identification

> I want freedom for the full expression of my personality.
>
> Mahatma Gandhi – lawyer, nationalist, and political ethicist.

I heard this somewhere: "Person first. Employee second." To me, that looks pretty accurate. Essentially, there is no such thing as the reputation of a company or corporation, or if there is, it is the sum of the reputations of the people working in those organizations. At the Social Picnic, the reputation of each Plaid is the sum of the reputations of the Sharers gathered around that Plaid.

I believe that, like me, you have seen the transformation of a brand when a large part of the company's employees change. A formerly strong brand weakens when a large part of the professionals leave the company. Similarly, it strengthens when the company hires strong and well-known specialists.

In systematically-building a reputation, every Sharer of each Plaid must publicly disclose their connections with one or more Plaids with which they are associated. If your Plaid is a company, you must identify this:

- Mark it in your profile.
- Link it to the company page.
- Provide contacts.
- Specify your duties.

Of course, most Plaids are informal, where there may not be formal positions, but at a Social Picnic, there are countless other ways to classify, identify, and connect yourself. Sometimes, it might be enough to do nothing, but the most important thing is not to have the goal of hiding, deceiving, or manipulating. If there is no such goal, ways will emerge to let other Sharers know who you are and what you do at the Social Picnic.

It is necessary to identify not only yourself but also your opinion. It is not necessary to write in every post that it is your personal opinion. Still, it would help if you made it clear to your audience when you speak as an individual, express your opinion, and present the organization's or Plaid's position. On the other hand, any of your opinions partly represent the organization's position, especially when it comes to values. It is hardly compatible to see public neo-Nazi behavior of an employee from an organization that nurtures human rights, openness, and liberal values.

The Social Picnic takes place on various platforms, so it's important not to forget that identification occurs across platforms as well. Although each platform has its rules and content specifics, you are unlikely to create a consistent personal or Plaid reputation if you are identified radically differently on different platforms. You can't appear rigidly professional on LinkedIn if your Facebook or TikTok profile is full of tasteless jokes that you might not even laugh at today, but they have remained there from five years ago. Before participating in one or another Social Picnic, it's worth considering whether you will have the time and desire to be there or if you're creating an account just caught in the impulse and will forget about it later. An abandoned Social Picnic account looks like an abandoned car, house, or even a neglected person. It looks pitiful.

Modern organizations encourage their employees to share corporate material. This activity achieves several goals – organization-created material spreads much better through personal channels, building the organization's reputation, and the employee, as a member, a Sharer, using the company's material, builds their reputation. It also strengthens the Sharer's identity, belonging to a certain Plaid.

Of course, this raises a crucial aspect of the Social Picnic – loyalty. Loyalty has always been important, but its significance has increased significantly in the Picnic Society. Loyal, satisfied employees will be the best spreaders of Plaid news; they will want to share the exciting content created by Plaid and will do so without any significant incentives. Therefore, one of the most essential reputational factors in the Picnic Society is the creation of loyalty and working conditions that employees would want to compete for.

By becoming Plaid Sharers of the organization, employees establish a direct connection with influencers, clients, and partners, expand their contacts, enhance their curriculum vitae, and lay the groundwork for their next professional step. The Plaid becomes a part of each of them, and the organization must consider this as a significant value, making the employee not only valuable as a specialist but also as a communicator. On the other hand, their public and continuous exposure is a sweet morsel for other competing Plaids.

The essence of this rule is not to hide, register in your name, constantly update your profile, identify contacts, affiliation with organizations (for a significant part of the audience, you are the voice of the organization), present a valid image, use corporate material to illustrate responses, and create a unified reputation across various Picnic Society platforms.

3.3.3. Third Rule: Listening

> I remind myself every morning: Nothing I say this day will teach me anything. So if I'm going to learn, I must do it by listening.
>
> Larry King – television and radio host.

From the side, some Sharers appear to be starving – it seems that they have not been allowed to eat for a long time, that is, to speak, and when the "Television" stage moves to the "Network" stage, suddenly there is much food, that is, opportunities to speak. Essentially, that's how it is – when transitioning from the "Television" to the "Network" stage, the world was flooded with almost limitless opportunities to express one's opinion freely. And people, of course, started to take advantage of those opportunities.

However, there is no way to communicate effectively other than the one that resonates with and matches the audience. And for that to happen, first, you need to listen, draw conclusions, plan your communication actions, and only then – speak.

Therefore, a Plaid or Sharer who consistently builds their reputation listens to more and shares less. I would even say that 90% of the time spent at the Social Picnic is spent listening, and only 10% is spent sharing. This way, one can avoid thoughtless actions. Here again, the analogy with food fits perfectly: you can fill your stomach with cheap and worthless food constantly, or you can be more interested in food, think, choose and eat, perhaps less often, but selectively and with value.

A crucial aspect of listening at the Social Picnic is that one needs to listen not only to what the environment and other Plaids are saying but also when someone posts something, one needs to monitor the reactions to the post attentively.

Many, especially popular Sharers or Plaids, are making a significant reputational mistake – they ignore the commentators on their posts. Ignorance creates an impression of arrogance. If your post has appeared in the public domain, be prepared to listen to reactions, respond to them, reply, and engage in discussions. In other words, don't run away from the discussion because, in terms of reputation, your action would be equivalent to starting a discussion by the bonfire at the park, attracting a large group of picnic-goers, and then suddenly disappearing. There might be situations where you intentionally planned such an escape, but in most cases, it is a reputational mistake.

A proper reaction to a post requires time, and time is found only by planning it. Therefore, before posting, don't forget to allocate time to react to the post and plan that time in your schedule.

Being prepared to respond and discuss doesn't mean engaging with trolls. When you reach a certain level of popularity, you might attract the attention of trolls. It is not necessary to engage with them because such discussions lead nowhere: the purpose of trolls is to troll and involve you in an endless discussion. However, determining who is a troll and who is not is something you can only do by listening carefully again.

The "Social media best practice guide"[1] from CIPR outlines the initial steps for crafting a social media strategy. It emphasizes the importance of listening to conversations about your organization, brand, competitors, industry, and stakeholders. Social media provides vast opportunities for online listening across diverse demographics and regions. One must consider employing suitable tools, techniques, and timeframes to embark on this.

Influential communication professionals should strive to comprehend the dynamics of who communicates what to whom, through which channels, and for what reasons. The crucial elements influencing strategy are understanding the various social media platforms, utilizing tools for managing and monitoring conversations, deciphering the language employed, and analyzing shared assets.

Furthermore, the guide underscores the value of your personal engagement with social media platforms. This hands-on experience is beneficial and integral to making informed decisions and developing effective strategies.

It can be put like this – if you don't feel confident about a post, don't post it. Regarding reputation, not posting is always better than an ill-considered post you will regret later.

3.3.4. Fourth Rule: Professionalism

> Making something simple is very difficult.
>
> Jack Dorsey – entrepreneur and philanthropist.

Professionalism consists of two parts: subject matter expertise and professional ethics. The first part usually raises no doubts, while the second part is often forgotten. And it doesn't matter where you are – at your workplace, in the park, or at the Social Picnic. The exact unwritten requirements for professionalism apply everywhere.

Expertise is best demonstrated in practice, of course. However, if you are a doctor or a teacher, you rarely can directly demonstrate your practice at the Social Picnic. However, your professionalism will quickly be revealed to a large audience through the dissemination of information. Therefore, if you have decided to be part of the Social Picnic, it is worth considering this.

If you know something well and want to build your reputation, share your knowledge systematically. Share a valuable article you've read or a video; it's not necessary to constantly create your content. It's not for nothing that the participants of the Social Picnic are called Sharers.

When sharing, avoid inaccuracies, and think about what your audience will immediately understand and what will require effort and immersion. Professionals often say that social media is shallow, superficial, and unprofessional. But then I always ask: are you contributing to making them more profound and professional? Social media is primarily media. That means it will primarily consume dessert, i.e., what is sweet. And that's normal – for many people, that's all they need. It's easy to create and share.

However, if a professional can turn complex content into something interesting, simplify it, and explain it, their reputation and the reputation of the represented brand are established.

A professional spreading knowledge must tell the truth, not be afraid to admit mistakes, be confident in what they say, and not disseminate old or unreliable, unverified information.

When building a professional reputation, it is crucial not to venture outside one's field. There are numerous examples of reputable professionals who, getting a taste of popularity, delve into areas where they are not experts. While this is not prohibited and is sometimes successful, it is a high-risk zone. I do not want to say one should be one-sided and avoid anything outside of one's professional field. Certainly not. However, before engaging in any topic, as mentioned earlier, it is essential to listen thoughtfully and understand its components and trends. Only then can one venture into a new arena. The effect of such action can be very positive, but it is worth being prepared.

The second part of professionalism is professional ethics. Abusing or boasting about knowing more than others does not create a professional reputation and creates a sense of alienation. It's not worth behaving disrespectfully towards those who know less or manipulating them. It is much more valuable, in terms of reputation, to explain, discuss, and provide examples.

3.3.5. Fifth Rule: Respect

> Respect for ourselves guides our morals, respect for others guides our manners.
>
> Laurence Sterne – novelist and cleric.

So, there are two types of respect: self-respect and respect for others. Without respecting oneself, it is impossible to respect others, as self-respect sets the rules by which we live, and those rules either dictate that we respect others or not.

Respecting oneself means respecting oneself as an individual, a Sharer, and respecting one's Plaid. Diminishing oneself, one's Plaid, or one's organization, humiliating them, or spreading negative information about one's employer will not help build a reputation for oneself or one's Plaid.

By respecting ourselves, we create rules for ourselves, specific boundaries, what we can allow ourselves in certain situations, and what is already a red line that we cannot cross. According to these moral rules, we live, and thus, each of our reputations is formed. At a picnic in the park, this is manifested in clothing, speaking style, and cleanliness. At the Social Picnic, it is in the care you put into maintaining your profile, your accessibility, and the content you distribute.

Respecting others entails our behavior towards others, manners, and communication. By belittling and mocking others, you may achieve some short-term goals, but reputation is not short-term, and such actions will harm it. Before allowing anything to go public, it's always worth considering: is belittling someone better than explaining, teaching, or showing another opinion? Diminishing others demonstrates anger, and anger creates a negative reputation. Always think about whether you want that.

3.3.6. Sixth Rule: Confidentiality

Confidentiality is a virtue of the loyal, as loyalty is the virtue of faithfulness.
Edwin Louis Cole – founder of the Christian Men's Network.

When communicating, people choose how much information to disclose to the other person and how much to keep to themselves. The more openly we communicate with another person, the more trust we demonstrate in them. And it is crucial whether the other person can keep what you wouldn't want to be spread more widely. They can understand what needs to be kept between you and what can be told more widely. If they can do this, over the long term, loyalty is formed, and ultimately, trust, which is the highest point of trust when one person completely trusts another and feels secure.

Therefore, confidentiality is a crucial foundation for any relationship and, of course, crucial for reputation because the more people you have who trust you, the stronger your reputation will be.

Disclosure of confidential information is a deadly blow to one's reputation. Once trust is lost, it is impossible to restore it thoroughly, and what's more, information about it spreads widely.

One should not confuse confidential information with covering up a crime. In the latter case, it is essential to understand that if you know about a crime and do not report it, you will become an accomplice, a criminal.

Distinguishing confidential information from information about criminal activity is not as difficult as it may seem in theory. In practice, among those engaged in positive activities, long-term relationships are usually formed, and the question of crime does not arise.

Confidential information is shared constantly, and it is often not something extremely secretive that only a few people know. Once, my client, a CEO of a large company, sent me a message that their mother was sleeping, and he had recently finished ironing clothes. The message was intended for his daughter but accidentally ended up on my phone. Well, it's neither highly confidential information nor something that must be hidden. Still, it's probably not the kind of information to share with your PR or legal consultant, employees, or spread outward. I informed him about it through a message as well, i.e., I warned him that his daughter most likely did not receive the message. Trust had long been established between us, and he could feel at ease knowing that even for humorous purposes, I would not spread such messages to anyone. However, if I had done so, it would hardly have had a positive impact on our relationship.

Social Picnic tools allow for a lot. Although photo collections and tagging are excellent, sound, and necessary functions, it is essential not to forget that each person's image and name are their property. And your views on what to do with this property may not necessarily coincide. Therefore, when publishing images of other people and tagging them, you should be entirely sure of their approval of this action unless these individuals are public figures, such as members of parliament, presidents, or other politicians, subject to different public standards.

I am often surprised by the behavior of some Sharers with the images of their families, especially their children. It can create the impression that some Sharers treat images of their children as their own. I understand the selfish desire of parents to show off their beautifully adorned little ones, but aren't these little ones separate individuals whose confidentiality is significantly violated without their consent? Perhaps sometimes there is asking, but not giving the right to refuse, as at this age, almost everything still depends on the parents' will. I leave it up to each Sharer to decide whether those little ones who will become adults in the future will be thrilled when the Social Picnic is full of their childhood photos. Or perhaps those delighted parents will separate and no longer want to see each other? In my opinion, violating children's confidentiality is one of the most widespread issues in the Social Picnic. It is likely that in the future, awareness among Sharers on this issue will increase.

The confidentiality rules of Social Picnic do not differ much from the confidentiality rules of the offline world. If there is a formal or informal agreement between two or more people not to disclose information, that is confidentiality. Confidentiality is the free choice of a free person – no one can force me to share what I know unless it is information about a committed crime.

On the other hand, the Social Picnic has significantly narrowed the boundaries of confidentiality precisely because Sharers themselves often willingly share what was previously considered highly confidential: photos from the workplace, used equipment, and various production processes today often become not only non-confidential but by showcasing them, various Brands strive to compete and build their reputation. Many of these things were highly confidential in the "Television" stage.

Many Sharers today also open up as versatile personalities previously known only in their narrow professional fields. Previously, the hobby of mountain climbing by the company's accountant was known only to his family members, perhaps to some colleagues. However, today, he shares it with his Sharers through his Plaid in the Social Picnic, and many participants in the Social Picnic are aware of it.

However, various documents remain confidential, such as contracts between business partners. The condition of confidentiality is usually included in their contracts. Whose business is it? How much do I sell my products to their buyer if not ours? My competitors don't need to find out about it and offer a lower price. They can do it successfully without knowing my prices. If both business partners believe that their agreement is confidential, two independent business entities desire to agree in this way.

Another important aspect of confidentiality is crises. During crises, every piece of information becomes several times more sensitive than it was before the crisis. Often, during a crisis, what was confidential before the crisis becomes public, new situations arise that need to be addressed promptly, and their disclosure can cause much damage.

Imagine a classic crisis in a large manufacturing company: a fire has broken out. The main task during such a crisis is to extinguish the fire and prevent casualties and pollution. During such a crisis, communication should be brief and precise, and efforts should be made to prevent unfounded rumors from spreading. Let's imagine that firefighters extinguishing the fire need to know whether there are people in the fire zone or not – the tactics for extinguishing the fire depend on this. If the company's manager knows that all employees are on-site and no one is left in the fire zone, that should be the information provided to the firefighters. Any other dissemination of rumors could change the tactics for extinguishing the fire and be devastating.

When preparing for crises, various organizations should explain in advance to their members and employees what is confidential not during a crisis but what becomes confidential in the event of a crisis and why.

Copyright is another relevant aspect of confidentiality in the digital age. The free sharing of information and easy accessibility create the illusion that there are no more copyrights – that everything is free. Unfortunately, in this case, ease is more likely to manifest as a more accessible opportunity to violate confidentiality or even commit a crime. Stealing a movie from the internet may be easier than from a store, but that does not mean the responsibility for it is less.

Copyright laws apply not only to clearly expressed creations such as films or music but also to posts and comments written by other Sharers. So if something strikes a chord with you and you would like to move it to your own space, don't forget to mention the author at least.

We should not forget about the technological aspect of confidentiality. It is often attempted to justify the complexity of privacy settings on social networks, claiming that they are difficult to understand. But it's the same as believing that no one will recognize you and openly go to a picnic in the park! If you have decided to participate in the Social Picnic, you should understand that no one else will take care of your account settings, no one will control what groups or pages you create, and what information will change there. So if you create open Plaids, create, but when providing information, don't forget that they are open. If you create closed Plaids, take care of their security and monitor the actions of Sharers who want to join.

Remembering how vital confidentiality is to reputation, we should only distribute what we are firmly convinced of. If you have doubts, do not distribute it; keep it for the future when you check, talk, listen, and gather more data.

When stating that a modern organization should allow its employees to express themselves in the Social Picnic freely, I certainly do not think that we should ignore what your Sharers are doing there. When we see harmful activity, we should stop it; when we see actions due to ignorance, we should educate, organize lectures, discuss various situations, and explain what is valuable to everyone and what causes harm. Confidentiality skills are acquired. The most important thing is to pay attention to this and start not with penalties but with understanding.

Let's never forget that in the "Network" stage, in the next few decades, we will all still be complete novices: some slightly more advanced, but very few. Therefore, making mistakes is and will be completely natural.

3.3.7. Seventh Rule: Accuracy

> Fast is fine, but accuracy is everything. You must learn to be slow in a hurry.
>
> Wyatt Earp – lawman and gambler.

I won't say anything new by stating that we live in the age of speed. Everything we see around us has become much faster than it used to be: transportation, news, work, and even leisure. Anything that does not fit the general trends is exclusive, expensive, and inaccessible to everyone. Today, it is the same with slowness and accuracy that goes with it. Being able to calm down, concentrate, and do something precisely is a great value worth acquiring or improving, especially if you are a PR professional.

In the age of short videos, one needs to find the necessary material, sometimes a long text, read it, draw conclusions, and communicate it concisely and clearly to the outside world.

Like a sniper, a communicating person must aim precisely. Aiming in communication means readiness, preparation, subject knowledge, observing the audience, and understanding their habits. Only then can the "shot" be accurate.

The Social Picnic is very fast-paced, with Plaids and Sharers emerging and disappearing, a large amount of information being disseminated, and constant information sharing. However, you, like me, probably noticed that quantity does not necessarily mean great success in Social Picnic. Some Sharers release dozens of messages into the public space per day, but their quantity means nothing. If there are many posts, but they are boring, about the same thing, only for the author's ego satisfaction – initially, perhaps, there is growth, but popularity quickly fades.

I wouldn't want to oppose speed on the Social Picnic over quality. It is certainly possible to find examples of a high-quality information flow in a large stream of information. However, ensuring such a flow requires considerable effort – understanding the subject matter, collecting data, summarizing it, and visualizing it. Therefore, for many Sharers and Plaids, this is not feasible.

Attention is essential not only in content but also in technological processes. In the previous Subsection, I spoke about confidentiality. It won't be easy to achieve it without ensuring the confidentiality and protection of your own and others' data. It is worth dedicating time and attention to various settings, limits, and rights; it is worth constantly monitoring them and being interested in whether the administrators of various Social Picnic tools have not changed them and reacting to the received notifications.

Acknowledging mistakes is also accuracy, which is an essential factor in building a reputation. If you have made a mistake, immediately acknowledge it, and once acknowledged, correct it. No one is free from mistakes, and those who try to appear infallible lose their reputational points. It is worth remembering that every entry in the Social Picnic is practically eternal, and uncorrected mistakes can "emerge" at the most inappropriate moment.

According to the "Social media best practice guide"[2] from CIPR, it is recommended to openly acknowledge and correct any mistakes made. Addressing online issues or crises prevents them from escalating. With effective social media monitoring in place, it becomes possible to identify emerging issues swiftly.

3.3.8. Eight Rule: Supportiveness

> Be strong, be fearless, be beautiful. And believe that anything is possible when you have the right people there to support you.
>
> Misty Copeland – ballet dancer.

Human beings are social, and therefore, each of us seeks recognition, support, and advocacy. We look for like-minded individuals, and even the most independent among us sooner or later yearn to be understood. Thus, it is entirely natural to have a desire to be understood and heard. Equally natural is to understand and listen. On the contrary, it is unnatural to ignore and see only what you are doing, to not become an ally to anyone. Therefore, it seems strange when Sharers or Plaids only care about one-way traffic in their Social Picnic communication, i.e., what they communicate, without paying attention to reactions or other Sharers or Plaids.

If you are a member of a particular Plaid, do not hesitate to react to your colleagues. If they are your collaborators, family, or members of a hunting group, this will not only help them on the Social Picnic but also create closer ties between you. Please write what you think about their post, support them, and share it. Always think about what you want in your colleague's place and do it for them. Do it sincerely and selflessly, and you will quickly see that it will pay off.

Respect your audience and avoid sneering at them directly or indirectly by presenting trivial information. Even if your Plaid's content is light-hearted, such as constantly sharing memes or humor, nothing will alienate an audience more than missing the mark on the usual style of humor.

The Social Picnic operates based on solidarity, i.e., when some Sharers and Plaids support other Sharers and Plaids. Solidarity should not be forgotten even when you achieve incredible popularity, which essentially is gained because someone noticed you, someone became close to you, or someone wanted to be like you. Therefore, please pay attention to those around you, support their initiatives, comment on their posts, participate in discussions, and share their content.

It is possible that you have advice for your colleagues or you feel that not everything they do is right. You have several options – either not pay attention to it, write a private message, or express your opinion publicly. Before doing this publicly, always consider not only yourself as the most intelligent person on the subject but also the common goal that you formally or informally pursue together with your colleague. If you think a public comment is necessary, do it, but do not forget there is always the possibility to remark privately. At least for the health of your relationship, this will always be the best choice.

If you are responsible for your Plaid's PR activities, for example, working in a large corporation with several thousand employees, remember that not every one of those employees has the same Social Picnic skills that you do. However, about one in three wants to be in the Social Picnic. Therefore, constantly organize meetings, training sessions, dialogues, and explanations about Social Picnic activities, innovations, trends, observations, and dangers.

Encourage employees at all levels to be active in the Social Picnic. Perhaps initially, people who haven't studied communication might feel uneasy and unsure about it. Still, they are your colleagues; they are free individuals and can express their thoughts as they see fit. You must show them how to achieve better results, what benefits them, and what could work against them.

Active employees who understand their actions and participate in the Social Picnic are a great help to both company management and PR specialists. The knowledge they disseminate is less polished but more authentic, so readers more readily accept it. After all, it is much more pleasant to read what my acquaintance Peter from Company X writes than just Company X, which is an impersonal source of information for me.

The company with which I have had the opportunity to work for several years, encourages its employees to be active on Social Picnic. Engaging with audiences and stakeholders across diverse social media platforms is integral to cultivating a brand presence online. Establishing both proactive and reactive content strategies and consistently participating in pertinent discussions are essential for fostering meaningful dialogue with stakeholders. It's crucial to have a clear understanding of the necessary resources, guidelines, and governance and security considerations.

However, there is another aspect of supportiveness – the help when trolls attack your colleagues, Sharers, or Plaids. Without delving deeply into what trolls are, for those hearing this term for the first time, I will offer the following example.

Most likely, in a picnic park, no one would think of bringing sound equipment that would overshadow the concert in the park with their blanket. Similarly, unruly behavior, annoyingly encroaching on other people's blankets if no one invites you there, is hard to imagine. Perhaps it does happen at one picnic or another, but picnics usually effectively manage this – they eliminate individuals who do not follow the general rules themselves or call for help.

The same thing happens in the Social Picnic. There are constantly trolls, those Social Picnic hooligans, who, for various reasons, can start encroaching on your personal or your Plaid's territory. In this case, it is also necessary to eliminate such hooligans from the Social Picnic or ignore them. Support from colleagues is also vital here.

There is much information on the internet and in books about identifying trolls and what to do with them.

However, speaking very simply, the Social Picnic follows one simple rule: if we react to a post, whether the reaction is positive or negative, we popularize it. If we do not react, its popularity decreases, and it quickly disappears (but does not vanish!) in the sea of information. Your beloved and respected colleague and the despised troll seek the same thing – to attract your attention. However, in the first case, it is worth and even necessary to do so, while in the second case, it is not worth it and is harmful. If the troll still managed to get your attention – use it only to block the troll.

3.3.9. Ninth Rule: Purpose

> Efforts and courage are not enough without purpose and direction.
>
> John F. Kennedy – politician.

While in the "Network" stage sitting in front of the television in the evening or even all day with a bag of chips and a can of beer in hand is often ridiculed as a symbol of meaninglessness in various memes, endless scrolling through social media for hours on end is a newer but no less vivid symbol.

Like any other activity, being in a Social Picnic must have a goal and direction, even if you are there because you want to spend your free time that way. Leisure time will also be good only with a purpose and direction. Sometimes, people say, "I would like to relax and do nothing." I always try to imagine what "doing nothing" might look like. The first thing that comes to mind is sleeping. Well, but sleeping is not "doing nothing". It is a significant activity aimed at resting and regaining strength. A book? Lying down and watching the clouds? A magazine? But all these activities are not "doing nothing" either.

For some, the constant scrolling that becomes a constant illness is also not "doing nothing". It is a constant stimulation of our brains with information that we don't need at all. Calling it rest is about the same as trying to put another piece of food into someone who has recently eaten well. Tired brains from the flow of information need to be without that flow, not to get that "extra piece".

So, any of our activities in the Social Picnic, like anywhere else, must have a goal and direction. If we are looking for information, i.e., we are passive on Social Picnic, we should know what we are looking for and at least roughly imagine where we should look. For example, if we want to learn more about space, we should tell ourselves that we will look for information about the James Webb Telescope, and this time, we will browse the NASA website about it. After doing this for an hour, we will know that we went where we wanted and found or did not find what we were looking for. You will avoid the feeling of emptiness that arises when you go online to search for "something".

Suppose you do go to a Social Picnic actively, i.e., not only searching but also posting, reacting, commenting, or discussing. In that case, you are directly shaping your reputation, and either you are doing it purposefully, or you don't feel it, and it builds up with every single "Like" you click.

While you are not yet strongly concerned about your reputation, you probably do not have a specific goal. Still, when you start doing it, you must clearly understand why you are taking a particular action in the Social Picnic.

Just as in real life, in the Social Picnic, if we do not think about what we are doing and the consequences, we have a result that forms spontaneously, or more precisely, according to what is encoded inside us by our parents. I leave this area to psychologists, but I am interested in purposeful action in creating a reputation.

In Chapter 1, I spoke about four basic types of reputation: leaders, professionals, scammers, and populists. I will remind you that the reputation of Leaders is formed when we have high credibility and high visibility. In contrast, the opposite is true for the reputation of scammers – when we have low credibility and low visibility. We should keep these four types of reputation in mind when setting our goal for our presence on Social Picnic.

Plan to have or help your client create a leader's reputation. You must have a considerable amount of quality content, share it, constantly react to current events in your field, and participate in discussions. The pace here should be significant, but the quality should not suffer.

Hardly anyone will ask for your help in creating a scammer's reputation. Still, it is essential not to forget that reputation forms entirely independently of whether you want it. Therefore, you can ensure that harmful types of reputation, such as Scammers or Populists, do not form for you or your client. For example, suppose your serious and professional client has a habit of participating in "brawls" in the Social Picnic in the evenings and commenting on various topics without doing anything to build a positive reputation simultaneously with your help. In that case, they should understand why market analysts do not highly value their opinion.

"Be mindful of the reputation you are creating," says Sociallogical.com. Let every action you take in the Social Picnic be influenced by the goal you are pursuing.

3.3.10. Tenth Rule: Uniqueness

> You are a human being and are allowed to be imperfect, and you are allowed to be flawed. There is a lot of beauty in your imperfections, in your uniqueness.
>
> Ileana D'Cruz – actress and model.

No copy, no matter how good it is, has ever surpassed the original. And if it did happen, then that copy is no longer a copy but has become the original itself. Therefore, it is very difficult or even impossible to create the desired reputation by copying someone else. The uniqueness lies in the charm, radiance, and attraction of every creation.

No person is perfect. If perfect people existed, they would resemble each other like two drops of water. If a society of perfect people existed, it would be a dull, uniform society where nothing happens.

Each person is unique, which means they have their imperfections and flaws. When you look at yourself in the mirror, you see many features that are unique to you:

- Hair that is not quite in place.
- One eyebrow higher than the other.
- A crooked smile.
- Some strange wrinkles.

If someone were standing on the other side of the mirror (similar to how it is in movies with criminals sitting behind one-way glass and being watched by the police on the other side), they would see a completely different image to what you see. Perhaps all, or even just some of what you perceive as your flaws, they would see as advantages that they would want to have, seeing them as unique traits that distinguish you, which no one else has.

It's the same with our appearance, our language, expressions, slang, and unique phrases that only we use. It's the same with our writing or any action we perform – each is unique if we don't try to imitate someone. When we try, we do not feel ourselves, and usually, after a while, we stop trying and return to our traits.

Behavior in the Social Picnic is just the same. We have to find our uniqueness and our style if we want to build a strong reputation. On the one hand, this seems very difficult (what new thing can I say? I certainly won't be as cool as this or that), but on the other hand, our uniqueness is within us; we don't need to create anything, we need to do what seems best.

Imagine being a surgeon performing multiple surgeries every day. You are a true professional, you know your job well, and you have accumulated much experience. If you occasionally participate in conferences, write something in the Social Picnic on medical topics, and the media seeks your opinion, you almost have a professional reputation.

However, if you want to become a leader, the person everyone thinks of when the conversation turns to surgery, you will need to put in more effort. You will need more communication; you will have to make yourself accessible in many cases when someone wants to know your opinion. You will have to participate in discussions and speak up actively. And in doing all this, you must be unique, i.e., have analogies, expressions, and humor that are unique to you. You might even try to plug your ears while listening to a recording of yourself because you will hear your mother or father in it. If this is the case, everything is fine. Remember that you hear your mother or father, but others hear a uniquely and interestingly speaking person.

Whether to follow the rules of the Social Picnic or not is entirely your free choice. They are there to help you achieve your goals in the Social Picnic and to answer questions if something is not going as planned and if something needs to be adjusted. For those independently building their reputation, these rules could become a plan for organizing their activities, an orientation on what to pay attention to. If a PR professional reads these rules, they will apply them excellently in evaluating their clients' behavior in the Social Picnic, providing advice, and planning various Plaid communication activities.

However, if you are thinking about purposeful reputation building, you should create your own rules and follow them.

3.4. Success and Value

Strive not to be a success, but rather to be of value.

Albert Einstein – physicist.

Let's move back to the picnic in the park. When does success visit us there? To answer this question, first, we should understand what success is.

Success – the achieving of the results wanted or hoped for (https://dictionary.cambridge.org).

In my firm belief, there is no single definition of success because there are no two people who have the same goals and achieve the same results in this life. If the goals and results are different, then success for each person is different. If a person's goal is a scientific discovery, then success will be the discovery itself, and failure will be an unsuccessful discovery. However, if the goal is popularity, success will be many admirers, and failure will be a small number.

People come to a picnic in the park driven by various goals – to socialize, to meet new people, to find new friends, to share their new cookies, to have a good time, and to be the center of attention. These goals are also valid for the Social Picnic.

Assessing the achievements of a particular Plaid or Sharer in the Social Picnic solely based on quantitative criteria at the "Network" stage is akin to evaluating the abundance of an advertising campaign at the "Television" stage. It is relatively easy to achieve the number of followers, likes, and engagement as it is to organize an advertising campaign – one needs a slightly larger budget, but the numbers will be reached. However, is this truly a success? If the goal of this action was to achieve those numbers, it is considered successful.

As we can see, success can be different. For the listener, success is to hear, while for the speaker, success is to be listened to.

Nevertheless, success alone is not enough. Something more is needed, and that "something" is value. If our scientist aims to make a scientific discovery, firstly, they seek that the discovery would have value and be significant, and only then can they expect success. Perhaps they also hope for success, but it is a small part of their motivation.

Value is a much broader, more meaningful, and long-lasting concept than success. Success does not ignore quantity, but it encompasses much more: content, a steady number of loyal sharers, and relationships.

Value – the importance or worth of something for someone (https://dictionary.cambridge.org).

On the internet and in literature, one can find various attempts to group the participating Sharers of the Social Picnic, and the number of such groups usually ranges between 4 and 12. I will not delve into a detailed examination of whether there are too many or too few of them here. Still, the purpose of the members of each group attending the Social Picnic is different. Their perception of success also varies; people use power and opportunities differently.

I have chosen six groups that seemed the most abundant to me. Two of these Social Picnic Sharers groups are passive, namely Ignorers and Spectators. Four are active, namely Joiners, Collectors, Critics, and Creators. There is an increase in the activity and engagement of Sharers in the Social Picnic activities, starting from Ignorers and ending with Creators.

Just as no pure representatives of any of these groups exist in this world, each Sharer can have characteristics of one or another group. Their presence in one or another group may change over time or depending on the situation. These models allow us to understand the different Successes achieved by Sharers and the Value created.

Let's look at the Success and Value of each group separately, starting with the two passive groups – Ignorers and Spectators.

3.4.1. Ignorers

> I don't focus on what I'm up against. I focus on my goals and I try to ignore the rest.
>
> Venus Williams – tennis player.

The most atypical group of Social Picnic participants, hardly considered a group of Sharers, is the most passive regarding their activity and the work done at the Social Picnic. These people ignore the Social Picnic and live as if it does not exist. And, of course, it is entirely their free choice and right. However, why do I still categorize them as Social Picnic participants?

Ignorers have a significant impact on other Social Picnic participants. They are silent observers of what is happening, and their minds are not directly affected by the informational flow at the Social Picnic.

This group is very diverse. It can consist of uneducated people who cannot use technology and professors who are too focused on their direct work and for whom any informational noise is excessive. Mothers and fathers, grandparents, and friends are also in this group.

One of my colleagues habitually shared stories about her grandmother through her social media account, including her perspective on what was happening around her, sometimes diversifying her posts with her grandmother's photos or videos. The popularity of these posts was enormous, and the grandmother became popular, influencing many people with her thoughts, but she did not directly participate in the Social Picnic.

A completely different example comes from the war in Ukraine. This book is being written as the war is ongoing. When a Russian warship approached Snake Island and demanded the surrender of the thirteen soldiers guarding the island via radio, the other side responded with what has now become a legendary phrase: "Russkij korabl, idi na hui!" This action took place without participating in the Social Picnic. Yet, it had a massive impact on the participants of the Social Picnic, as the phrase, with the help of Social Picnic Sharers, reached hundreds of millions of its participants within seconds.

In short, Ignorers, by being present and diving into a completely different informational flow, significantly impact the active Social Picnic participants, who communicate this in the Social Picnic Meadows.

What is the success and value of Ignorers? There are exceptions, and we might find Ignorers who intentionally seek popularity without participating in the Social Picnic. In this case, they would be more similar to Creators than Ignorers. When asked about their success, the vast majority of Ignorers will likely take pride in not being part of the Social Picnic, perhaps even looking down a bit on those who are there. Their success lies in their ability to resist, not create an account, not to use a smartphone, to behave as a true Ignorer does – to ignore.

The value created by Ignorers dramatically differs from their success. Their value lies in their achievements in the non-virtual world, their thoughts, phrases, lessons, and advice. They are like a breath of fresh air in a room often filled with carbon dioxide. Their success lies in their ability to resist the temptations of the Social Picnic and not participate in it.

3.4.2. Spectators

> If you want to see the true measure of a man, watch how he treats his inferiors, not his equals.
>
> J.K. Rowling – author and philanthropist.

The second passive group of Social Picnic participants is the Spectators. Due to their passiveness, they are not easily categorized as Sharers, but, like Ignorers, they are crucial to the overall flow.

From the name of this group, it is evident that, compared with Ignorers, what happens at the Social Picnic is very important to them. While we were still on the "Television" stage, many of us were Spectators because we didn't have the means to participate actively. Today, this group has significantly diminished but it hasn't disappeared. Most likely, each of us knows people who are well-informed about the ongoing processes of the Social Picnic, yet we have never seen them actively posting or commenting.

Some Spectators are such because they have difficulty adjusting to new technologies, while others do so consciously and, according to their nature, are inclined to observe rather than participate. The third group does this professionally to understand trends and monitor competitors, adversaries, and the market.

Suppose the first group, the less technologically savvy Spectators, has a similar impact on the Social Picnic as Ignorers, meaning they originally influence active Social Picnic participants. In that case, professional Spectators are more similar to active participants, as their reports, observations, and analyzes directly affect the actions of the active ones. This way, messages to competitors are formed, market proposals are made, or even military actions take place if the active Spectators are engaged in espionage.

It should be beneficial for every company to understand what customers, partners, competitors, or people, in general, are saying about them, as well as the emerging fashions, trends, and community opinions. Observing the Social Picnic allows one to draw conclusions about impending crises, which can serve as a source of ideas.

Quiet observation is crucial in today's fast-paced world because only an observer can see the big picture, the "bird's-eye view", and then plan and avoid mistakes, unlike a highly active participant.

If an Ignorer doesn't go to the park, then a Spectator practically lives there. The Spectator walks from one Plaid to another, gathers knowledge, and knows well which Plaid is interested in what. Walking in the park holds great significance in the Social Picnic, and we will discuss it in Chapter 4.

Professional Spectators are monitoring and analysis companies that can provide an excellent foundation for organizing PR activities. However, every PR professional must also be at least partially a Spectator, meaning actively observing and understanding what is happening, without directing the action.

Walking in the Social Picnic involves reading traditional and social media blogs, listening to podcasts, and following the right people. Walking is the ability to understand where it's worth going and where it's not, as it's simply impossible to be everywhere and observe everything.

The latter skill is essential because someone lacking this skill can quickly draw incorrect conclusions about which Plaids are important and which are not, relying solely on external factors such as Plaid name, official status, or size. In the Social Picnic, these attributes are not the main ones.

We can indeed have a Plaid with a bizarre name, as in the case of the group previously mentioned, South Smelltown Stinks, which gathers several thousand of the most active city dwellers.

We can even have an informal Plaid without clearly defined boundaries but existing as a network of supporters, managed by at most ten people. The value of this network can be significant because these supporters are key opinion leaders.

We should remember that the Social Picnic is a place where something can be monitored and a great source of ideas.

The success of Spectators lies in noticing, finding out, and sniffing around, while value is created through analytics that active social picnic participants can use.

The other four Social Picnic Sharers groups are active: Joiners, Collectors, Critics, and Creators.

3.4.3. Joiners

> You can't wait for inspiration. You have to go after it with a club.
>
> Jack London – novelist, journalist, and social activist.

The least active among the active groups are the Joiners. These are Sharers participating in Social Picnic, having their social accounts, but not knowing why they need them. Often, their motivation is that "everyone around them has it, so I need it too".

They are not very assertive participants in the picnic park. We see them walking and smiling but seemingly hesitantly approaching, asking, or starting a conversation. Such a sharer type is also present in Social Picnic.

Most likely, every Joiner has a secret dream of becoming a Collector, Critic, or Creator. Otherwise, why be a part of the Social Picnic at all? However, their lack of assertiveness holds them back.

In my opinion, two factors determine the lack of assertiveness in Joiners: technological unfamiliarity or introversion.

Less technologically-savvy Joiners often fear clicking and writing, as they are not confident that they will do everything well and won't make a fool of themselves. I think, in many cases, this is related to age. I do not underestimate older people and their ability to use information technology – many use it excellently. However, overall, older individuals tend to be more cautious and less inclined to use something they are not accustomed to.

Introverts are also not inclined to express themselves frequently in public. They ponder a lot and communicate less. But when they communicate, it is often significant information, at least for their small Plaid audience. Perhaps their most excellent created value lies in this – thanks to them, the Social Picnic is less cluttered because if everyone were in it and communicated, we would have much greater chaos than we have now.

Well, the success of Joiners is the rare reactions of their small audience, moments when they feel noticed and necessary, hitting the jackpot.

3.4.4. Collectors

> The greatest value of a picture is when it forces us to notice what we never expected to see.
>
> John Tukey – mathematician and statistician.

Like any collector, a Social Picnic Collector doesn't create content but collects it and aims to showcase it to others. The Collector's wall is full of shares on a specific topic, which helps you understand their personality.

Collectors have a permanent and limited audience and constantly present something new to them. They have characteristics of spectators, but their goal is not so much to find and capture something as to find and publish about it.

It can be said that Collectors are broadcasters, speaking in terms of the "Television" stage.

I must confess that I constantly oscillate between being a Collector and a not-very-active Creator on my personal Facebook profile. I enjoy noticing and sharing things that others might overlook. I carefully choose posts for my wall only from my favorite sources. And when I create, it's usually with images that I just can't pass by without being captivated.

The Collector does not create content and is, so to speak, a pure Sharer. There are professional and amateur Collectors, as with other Sharers. However, with certain exceptions, professional Collectors are likely to be concerned exclusively with their reputation. It's hard to imagine someone consulting solely on how to share content. Usually, such consultations are needed for content creation.

Amateur Collectors are the most widespread. Building one's reputation is relatively straightforward: observe specific channels and share the content from those channels with your audience.

People who don't pay much attention to their reputation often also find themselves among Collectors. It's common to come across Collectors who consistently post humorous content. However, they often forget that humor and its nature are the best reputation-building aids. The type of humor you share says a lot about you.

The Collector's wall is like an art gallery. Their success lies in finding good content. They create value through their reputation. If a person is well-known, an opinion leader, and a collector, sharing your Plaid content can become a new existential stage for your Plaid.

3.4.5. Critics

> A critic is someone who never actually goes to the battle, yet who afterwards comes out shooting the wounded.
>
> Tyne Daly – actress.

Criticizing is a reasonably convenient activity: You don't need to think much. Choose the correct targets, the most vulnerable or popular ones, and go ahead. The pure Critic doesn't create content but is a typical and active participant in the Social Picnic. You can find them everywhere, usually where the action is hot. The Critic often jumps from one topic to another and, at the same time, is an expert in virology, military affairs, and environmental protection.

Essentially, the Critic is a parasitic element in the Social Picnic, but in no way can we diminish its significance. This Sharer type is vital due to its prevalence, and often, precisely because of critics' activity, Plaids must change their strategies and react to criticism. Criticism in the Social Picnic can be compared to a park or a person going through life who is constantly dissatisfied with something. And although many know them and what to expect, sometimes they see things worth attention.

Critics constantly write comments, actively participate in discussions, share content, and express dissatisfaction with products and services but do not create content. And if their grumbling was barely audible on the "Television" stage, today, they, like all Sharers, have all the tools to express themselves.

Critics can be divided into three categories – the egotistical, the professionals, and the trolls. Most Critics are populists, simply seeking attention and are content with receiving it. They are often individuals with low levels of education, average individuals who feel good when they are essential. Today, they have the "Like" button to evoke that feeling within themselves, which interested people can press by engaging in their activities.

Professional critics have a specific goal, and they achieve it. In some cases, you can find professional PR specialists and communication strategists among them. For example, to highlight the damage the enemy is experiencing during a war, it may be necessary to comment and share on the Social Picnic as much as possible to spread that information widely. In this case, criticism can serve a positive purpose.

However, under normal circumstances, a PR specialist who begins to plan or implement campaigns based on criticism strongly risks crossing over to the dark side and becoming a troll. Trolls are extreme critics whose primary goal is to cause harm.

The success of Critics is as simple as their goal – to attract attention. Those Critics who do it professionally plan and measure their actions and achieve results. Those who do it for their pleasure enjoy the increased attention. The value created by Critics is the amount of damage done. If a critic not only manages to attract attention but also succeeds in influencing decisions to change established order, rules, and relationships, that is the main achievement of their activity, and at the same time, it creates value.

3.4.6. Creators

> Content makes poor men rich; discontent makes rich men poor.
>
> Benjamin Franklin – writer, scientist, inventor, stateman, diplomat, printer, publisher, and political philosopher.

And finally, the most active Social Picnic group – Creators. Perhaps, the most important group as well. What Spectators notice, what Joiners read, what Collectors share, and what Critics comment on is what Creators produce. If Creators didn't create content, Social Picnic would lose its meaning. In other words, what Creators generate becomes the foundation for other Sharers.

If, in the "Television" stage, Creators, with certain exceptions, essentially created content to sell it, the "Network" era shows that motives for creating content are much more diverse.

Some Creators in the Social Picnic create content professionally and make a living from it. However, many Creators create content for their pleasure because a specific field interests them or is close to them. The third group of Creators creates content for their popularity; the attention they receive pleasantly affects them, making them influential.

Content in the Social Picnic can be created very simply, for example, with personal photos or short posts. However, it can also require more effort, such as a longer analytical post or article, infographics, or explanations of processes.

Someone creates all the content we see on the Social Picnic. And that someone is a Creator. If you took a photo of a stunning sunrise this morning while walking your dog and posted it on your Instagram account, you are already a Creator, you have your Plaid, and most likely, you'll receive comments from Critics and shares from Collectors. If you wrote a random thought on your social account, you are a Creator. If you are a historian and just shared your knowledge about the Middle Ages on Facebook with illustrations, you are also a Creator.

Every Creator produces content; the more transparent, understandable, and accessible it is, the more resonance and popularity it will likely achieve. Of course, the value of the content varies wildly, depending on the intended audience of Sharers. The content ranges from sweet pictures of cats and flowers to more specialized topics like financial analysis, which not everyone might find palatable.

Creators aim to develop well-developed Plaids and gather Sharers around them. They have all the modern tools for content creation at their disposal: blogs, videos, photos, infographics, texts, and more.

Content plays a crucial role in reputation building. When creating content, and thus value, Creators can leverage all Four Pillars according to the ConCrEtE formula. It's essential to recognize that none of these pillars can be ignored in Social Picnic. It's not enough to have just the content itself; you need style, relevant topics, tone, empathy, and current news. With Sharers, it's essential to communicate and help, teach, and not forget about humor.

So, having acquainted ourselves with the six main types of Sharers, we have confirmed that each creates different success and value.

Table 3.2 Sharers' success and value.

Sharer	*Success*	*Value*
Ignorer	Ignoring	Help for active
Spectator	Notice	Help for active
Joiner	Little recognitions	Flow control
Collector	Discovery of quality content	Leveraging personal reputation
Critics	Getting attention	Amount of damage
Creator	Popularity	Created content

However, there are also common denominators of success and value for all Sharers. All types of Sharers are closely interconnected, and finding pure representatives of each isn't easy. In reality, a Creator can even become an Ignorer at certain stages. A Joiner can be an active Critic, and a Collector may engage in active Creator activities. In everyday life, all types are intertwined, and each Sharer has a balance of various characteristics.

The success of all Social Picnic participants lies in the fact that the Social Picnic is happening. The Sharers groups only empower this event, the largest communicative gathering in human history, leading to greater awareness, transparency, and a better life. The value created by all Social Picnic participants is the knowledge that, today, those born in Australia reach Kirkenes in northern Norway within seconds, and those born on the island of Niue in the Pacific Ocean reach London in the United Kingdom.

The profession that has known this event best from biblical times to the present day is "Public Relations", or as we agreed in the introduction of this book – "People Relations". Representatives of this profession are highly sought after today. They will be in the future because they are best oriented in relationships between people and Sharers, meaning they know the structure of the Picnic Society and the paths and byways of the Social Picnic the best. People Relations professionals are well acquainted with opinion leaders and various Plaids and their connections and can communicate in various languages, not just linguistically.

The foundation of the Social Picnic is discussion. There is no need to try to persuade; instead, it is essential to openly present one's knowledge, answer questions, and communicate. PR specialists excel at performing these tasks.

Today, PR specialists have various portfolio tools to offer their clients. A PR professional is the most important ally for any individual or organization concerned about their reputation.

CIPR notes[3] that as our society progresses towards greater openness, knowledge, and debate, the emergence of highly interactive communication tools such as social networking sites, blogs, and wikis necessitates a heightened focus on engaging in dialogue. This engagement underscores the importance of having PR professionals equipped with the requisite skills and training to manage these conversations effectively. By leveraging interactive communication skills, PR practitioners facilitate genuine dialogues – fostering two-way communication that cultivates relationships, enhances reputation, and builds trust. PR professionals play a pivotal role in ensuring that everyone within an organization understands their contribution to shaping its reputation. Trust, the cornerstone of our success, is essential for achieving our organizational objectives. It is you, our PR professionals, who establish and nurture this trust, thereby cultivating positive relationships that are crucial for our success. In contemporary society, trust isn't necessarily diminishing but evolving. Previously, blind trust prevailed; however, today, individuals seek clarification and engage in dialogue, particularly when confronted with information from various sources such as the internet or newspapers. This shift towards dialogue-driven trust should be embraced as a positive development, fostering informed decision-making and deeper engagement.

Notes

1 Social media best practice guide. CIPR, December 2013. https://www.slideshare.net/CIPRPaul/cipr-social-media-guidelines-final-2013 (accessed on 21-02-2024).
2 Social media best practice guide. CIPR, December 2013. https://www.slideshare.net/CIPRPaul/cipr-social-media-guidelines-final-2013 (accessed on 21-02-2024).
3 Demonstrating the value of public relations. CIPR, January 2013. https://issuu.com/cipr_uk_members/docs/demonstrating_the_value_of_pr (accessed on 21-02-2024).

4 Practicing a Picnic

Every new beginning comes from some other beginning's end.
Seneca – philosopher, statesman, dramatist, and satirist.

Every time you start something new today, whether you want it or not, you enter a new Social Picnic. In a new Social Picnic, you probably know almost nothing and have no idea about the relationships between its participants. However, one thing is always the same. Every Social Picnic operates by the same rules, stages, or steps. The goal of this chapter is to reveal them to you.

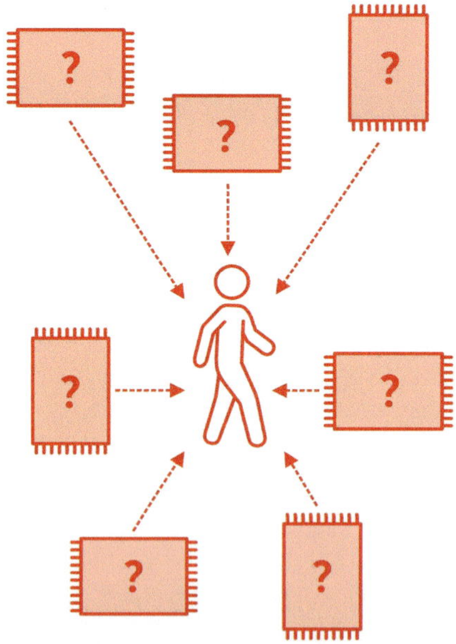

Figure 4.1 Looking at a Social Picnic from the outside, everything seems confusing and incomprehensible.

Figure by the author.

DOI: 10.4324/9781003466802-5

This chapter will discuss how to stroll in the park, i.e., in the Social Picnic: where to start and what characteristics are most important at each step. I have divided it into ten parts, or ten essential steps that must be taken for your Plaid to be liked, visited, and trusted. So – Ten Steps to Start Your Picnic.

Along with the theoretical description of each step, I will provide a practical example – from the construction of an imaginary waste-to-energy power plant – at the end of each step.

Let's imagine we are working together for an investor, Waste Killers (WK), which recently won a competition to build a waste-to-energy power plant in Smelltown, located in Blueland.

All technical construction details, of course, will be set aside. Let them remain with construction, investment, and architectural experts. To define the situation, I will mention that in Blueland, such a power plant will be the first of its kind, and its necessity is undeniable, as until now, Blueland has just been converting waste into landfill mountains. The new power plant will be a clean and state-of-the-art creation, implementing high-grade technologies and posing no danger to the environment and human health.

Of course, only one aspect of the construction of this power plant will be of interest – communication. Or more precisely, communication in the Social Picnic country, the community where the new facility will emerge.

Let's move forward.

4.1. Step 1 – Arrival. It Was Not You Who Started the Picnic, It Was Always Here

> We didn't start the fire.
>
> Billy Joel – musician, singer-songwriter, and composer.

Before taking your first step into the park where the Social Picnic is happening, think and realize one simple truth: you didn't start the Social Picnic and won't finish it. It was here before you and will be here long after you. You can only be a participant in it and create your Plaid or contribute to the creation of other Plaids. Everyone creates a Social Picnic, and no one has exclusive rights.

Therefore, the smartest thing you can do here is to find your place. Just like Crocs once found its place in what seemed like an overcrowded shoe market, just like mochi found its place in the overcrowded sweets market, you need to find your place in the Social Picnic market. In other words, you need to offer something a little different or from a slightly different angle. What this will be is entirely up to you, but first, to understand what new thing you can offer, you must know what is already happening.

What do you do first if you arrive at a picnic in the park on a sunny day and see many blankets, tents, and activities? You might not pay too much attention, but just lay out your blanket and settle in. But in that case, it's doubtful you can be called a true picnicker. In this scenario, you are most similar to an Ignorer.

After all, if your goal is to socialize, have fun, or even show something about yourself when you come to the picnic, it would probably be wise first to understand what's happening in the park. If you plan to give cookies out as treats or offer them for purchase, it's worth knowing how many of those exact cookies are already being offered. Perhaps even attend one or another picnic without doing anything else but observing and analyzing the action.

If we consider a picnic an investment, the first step is to research the market and understand the need. You can do this yourself or find those who know the market well. Some may think hiring consultants wastes money, but experienced investors do not see it that way because they know hiring knowledgeable people can save time and money.

Everything happens the same way in a social picnic. Before starting any activity here, the smartest thing you can do is observe and analyze. Or, find a consultant who will do it for you. A PR professional understands social picnics best. I wish everyone would find one whose competence they won't doubt.

Arriving in the park and analyzing the action requires specific skills. These include assessing the situation, strategic thinking, self-confidence, and the ability to assemble a professional team that can perform analytical work quickly and efficiently.

This step requires understanding who is who in the Social Picnic, starting to follow dominant channels, joining groups, getting acquainted with the activities of key opinion leaders, conducting various surveys, and subscribing to monitoring services. It's worth doing not only virtually but also in person, participating in events that take place in the physical world and have a significant impact in the virtual realm.

A social structure has already formed before you appear at a Social Picnic. Various Plaids have numerous ongoing discussions; some picnic participants know each other, share information, and comment on each other. Understanding these relationships is not easy initially, but understanding them is the key to later success.

It's important not to forget that genuine relationships, even in the "Network" stage, ultimately are not formed virtually.

A crucial part of this step is collecting the Plaids you need. This collection includes Plaids from several vital media outlets and government institutions, as well as key opinion leader Plaids, community Plaids, non-governmental organization Plaids, and competitor Plaids.

Relationships and connections have already formed among all these Plaids in the Social Picnic: some Plaids support each other, while others, conversely, may not like each other.

This step requires gathering all the information sources that are currently helpful and will continue to be so. These sources should be organized, subscribed to, joined, and constantly monitored. It's crucial to identify which are essential and influential.

Once you've identified the necessary Plaids, constant monitoring can be handed over to monitoring professionals or companies, and you can receive reports from them. However, that's not enough: to be in a Social Picnic, you must be there. Or at least have a very reliable colleague, consultant, or employee who is there.

In this step, there should also be a plan for moving forward. Go through the remaining steps:

- Get to know the Social Picnic participants (second step).
- Start creating your territory (third step).
- Decorate it (fourth step).
- Make friends (fifth step).

Arrival is just the first step, and taking the next steps is worth doing correctly. At the end of this ten-step journey, your goal is to feel comfortable and confident in the Social Picnic. For now, you are just observing, and at times, you may feel uncomfortable; the abundance of information may be overwhelming. However, this is temporary and normal.

Practical Example: Building a Waste-to-Energy (W2E) Power Plant – Step 1

So, the competition has been won, and according to the terms, actual construction is set to begin in two years. The documentation preparation period and project co-ordination are now underway. As the newly hired communications specialist, you join the Blueland Social Picnic and start your activities.

Blueland is not a very large country, with just about 5 million people. Therefore, the entire country's Social Picnic is like one big picnic where everyone knows each other quite well. Permanent Sharers groups, called Plaids, have formed over time.

This Social Picnic is easily distinguishable from all other global Social Picnics because its communication is almost entirely in Bluelandic. Occasionally, a post may be made in English or French, but most communication occurs in Bluelandic.

So, upon your arrival at the Blueland Social Picnic (BSP), life is already bustling. Politicians are participating in elections (or "concerts") and Sharers have gathered into various groups based on communities, hobbies, professions, and many other characteristics.

You arrive at the BSP and start wandering, observing, and searching for the Plaids that are relevant to you. How do we sift through this abundance and determine what is essential and what is not? The answer is obvious: you should select Plaids based on their significance and impact on your future activities at the power plant.

One important aspect here is that if the Plaids crucial for the functional operation of the power plant (project coordination, construction) are located farther away from the plant, such as those in governmental Plaids or controller

Plaids, then the Plaids closest to the plant, i.e., the community Plaids, are the most essential for communication activities.

Always start with the community, even though it may not seem the most pleasant practice initially. People might appear disgruntled and resistant to any changes. When constructing any industrial facility, especially one like the W2E power plant, you will inevitably have to engage with the community. It would help if you communicated with them to identify all the Plaids related to the surrounding communities. Join ongoing discussions, review the topics discussed in those groups over the past two years, and try to understand which communities are most concerned about environmental issues, transportation, or where leisure topics dominate.

You may come across closed groups. Try to join them as well. However, of course, do everything openly. Don't hide; introduce yourself and, if allowed, join the discussions.

Get to know the national and regional media in Blueland and the journalists. Many journalists today are individual opinion leaders, sometimes with more followers than the media outlets they represent. Conduct a retrospective media monitoring on waste topics, find out who has already written about waste-related issues, and understand their positions.

Don't forget that contemporary media can also be one person, sometimes reaching a much larger audience than the most prominent editorial offices.

At this point, I would like to pause and briefly discuss two terms that are often confused: "Influencer" and "Key Opinion Leader" (KOL).

While the term "Influencer" is undoubtedly more commonly heard today, and "Key Opinion Leader" might seem a relic of the bygone "Television" stage, I would like to rescue it. In my opinion, KOLs and influencers fundamentally differ, although, at times, they may coincide.

A KOL is an individual who, while being an expert in a specific field, is also a public figure, transparent, visible, and accessible, actively expressing their opinion. For example, it could be an immunologist actively voicing their opinion on vaccines and advising the public on immunoprophylactic matters. It might be a banking analyst frequently commenting on economic topics in various media outlets.

An Influencer is a person whose primary goal is popularity and, most often, monetising that popularity in one form or another. For instance, it could be a fitness entrepreneur constantly showcasing their photos on Instagram, garnering millions of likes, and later converting those likes into advertising revenue in one form or another. Or it could be a tech-savvy "science geek with big glasses", consistently reviewing and earning from the latest technologies.

The essential difference between KOLs and Influencers lies in the direct goal of earning from their popularity or the absence of such a goal, i.e., not selling their popularity. For a PR professional, of course, KOLs are more critical, as Influencers are essentially left to marketing teams.

Review the Plaids of public organizations in Blueland. Most likely, the Sharers who advocate for a healthy lifestyle and a clean environment will be vital to

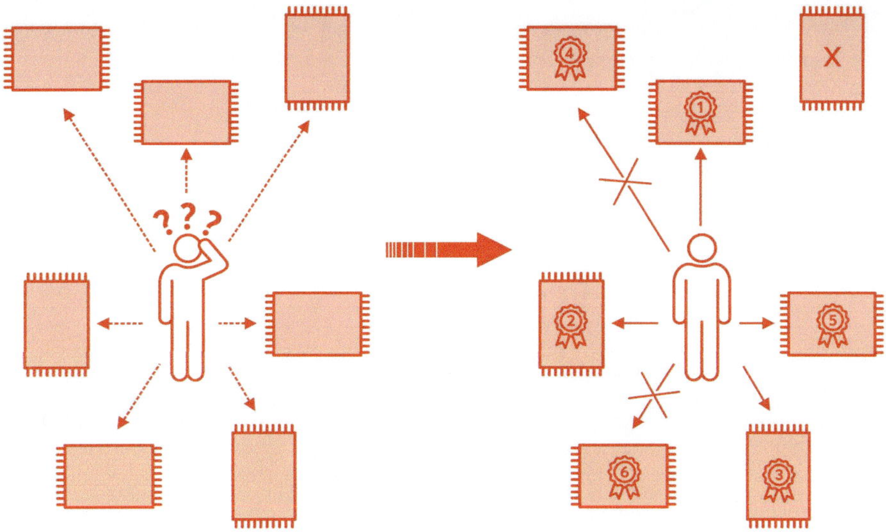

Figure 4.2 Arrival. The most important goal is to understand what is happening, decide what is essential, and prioritize effectively.

Figure by the author.

you, especially those within these organizations. Identify which of these Plaids are more radical and which are more moderate.

Another type of Plaid that will be important in this case are the Plaids of controlling institutions. Today, even traditionally "stern" institutions like the central bank, tax inspectors, or the police can and should have their Plaids because they understand the importance of direct communication.

Finally, complete your list with the Plaids of politicians. They are especially crucial because the prospective of your future work may heavily depend on their opinions. Try to understand the TOP 10 politicians who are essential to you, what they communicate externally, the topics they are interested in, and what matters to their constituents.

So, to conclude this step, the list of Plaids that must be important for the future Waste-to-Energy power plant includes communities, media and opinion leaders, public organizations, controlling institutions, and politicians.

4.2. Step 2 – Get Together. So Many Nice People Here!

> If you want peace, you don't talk to your friends. You talk to your enemies.
>
> Desmond Tutu – bishop and theologian.

The essential skills here are communication, self-confidence, and persuasiveness.

Simply coming to the park makes you a part of the picnic. Sneaking into the park is almost impossible – everyone is already familiar, and the appearance

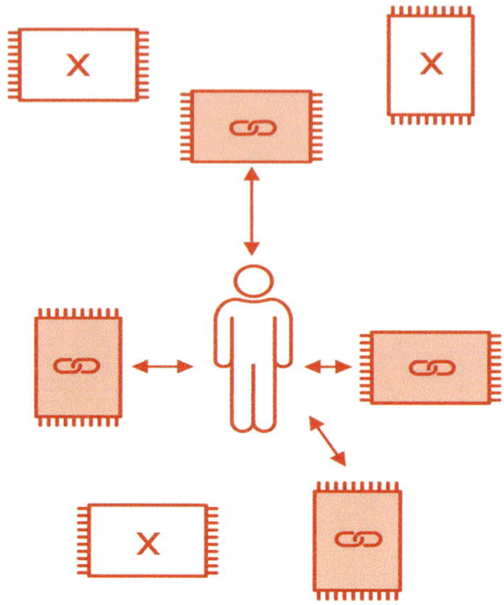

Figure 4.3 Get together. It's essential to establish connections with the most significant Social Picnic groups; the most crucial ones are not necessarily the friendliest.

Figure by the author.

of each new person, especially someone well-known, attracts the interest of various Plaids.

On the other hand, just showing up doesn't attract much attention: a new picnic-goer can calmly stroll around the park, observing and listening to conversations around various Plaids. At this stage, it's worth taking advantage of this comfort. There's no need to speak a lot or express your opinion. The most important thing is to walk around and listen attentively, understanding the formed groups and their connections.

Whether you represent a new organization entering the market or one operating for a long time, it is crucial to start with reconnaissance and understanding what groups and connections between those groups already exist.

If you have been in the market for a long time but are not yet part of its Social Picnic, joining is particularly valuable. You are likely very mistaken if you believe that your absence from the Social Picnic guarantees a peaceful life. There is probably already a lot of talk and knowledge about you in the Social Picnic, but you might not be aware of it. Market veterans often engage in self-deception, thinking they know everything because they have been there for a long time. However, the Social Picnic is a highly dynamic space – it constantly changes as generations, people, communication tools, and trends evolve.

If you haven't done so in the first step, list the most critical Plaids and try to establish contact with them.

In this second step, don't expect to form solid relationships, but you can introduce yourself and explain who you are and what you represent. Until you take the third step, you don't have your territory to invite Sharers to, but you can visit various other Plaids, interact, and find out what topics are currently most important.

Make sure to have a presentation, graphics, infographics, and photo and video material. Enhance new acquaintances with this material. Don't hesitate to invest in these visual elements – professionally prepared materials will make you feel more confident. Create small souvenirs as a way to start promoting your brand.

Find out the communication habits of each Plaid – the ways their members communicate, and the traditional and social media outlets, channels, groups, leaders, and websites that are important to them.

Initiate meetings with the Plaids. In some cases, meeting with a few members of the Plaid may be sufficient, while in other cases, meeting with the entire group might be necessary. Strive to secure their brief but personal attention.

Before and after meetings, gather all public information about new acquaintances. Visit their social media profiles and continue contact by thanking them for the meeting.

Social media contact is the new business card – it works much better and more extensively than the traditional one: each new contact will likely lead to more contacts soon.

Don't be afraid of hostile acquaintances or meetings. If you feel that a particular Plaid is hostile toward you or if you return from some meetings with not-so-positive emotions, don't underestimate them; it is all part of your knowledge-gathering in the Social Picnic. During such encounters, you will learn their arguments, allowing you to better prepare for future engagements.

Getting to know negative individuals should be proactive – take the first step, don't be afraid, and consistently seek dialogue. Listen to their arguments and understand the other side.

You can perform this work yourself, but like all other communication tasks, you can entrust it to a PR professional. Entrusting the work to a professional will save you much time. You will still need to participate in some meetings, but you won't have to worry about which ones.

Practical Example: Building a Waste-to-Energy (W2E) Power Plant – Step 2

The Plaid list is ready – it's time to start connecting with important Plaids. However, before doing so, review your social media profiles. Particular attention should be given to professional social media, such as LinkedIn.

If you haven't done so already, tidying up information about yourself is essential. Look at how your life description, photo, and accurate, up-to-date contact information appear. When you start making acquaintances, Sharers will visit your profile to seek more information about you, and they must find what you'd like them to find. So, start your acquaintance with new clothes, i.e., your appearance at the Social Picnic. According to appearance, one gets acquainted, and based on intellect, one says goodbye, as my country's folk wisdom goes. While it might not be an absolute truth in today's times, people haven't changed much – the initial impression often does a significant part of the work. However, the place of this impression has significantly shifted – if, in the past, preparing for a meeting meant putting on a suit or a dress, today, a more critical factor than clothing is a good, detailed, and representative profile on social media. It doesn't determine everything, but it will undoubtedly help you in your further steps in the Social Picnic.

Once the profile is organized, start making acquaintances. Regularly visit the Plaids that are important to you. As mentioned earlier, please start with the Blueland communities, identify the leaders of specific Plaids, and get to know them virtually and over a cup of coffee. The most important thing at this stage is not to make a fundamental mistake: don't pretend to be something you're not. While getting to know people, you don't necessarily have to reveal your project to the most minor details, but describe it in general terms and don't hide it.

Prepare for an adverse reaction – you will likely face opposition. Finding a community that wants a waste-to-energy power plant in its vicinity would be challenging. In many people's eyes, such an object is like a giant mountain of burning trash, polluting everything around it and emitting a terrible odor.

When getting to know community leaders, try to discover the community's way of life, sincerely inquire about their problems, and attempt to identify issues where you could potentially help find solutions.

Continuously monitor community activities on the Social Picnic, react to disseminated information, introduce yourself, and communicate. Remember that the worst thing for people is to see an object or construction and not see the people behind it. When people witness significant changes in their neighborhood, they need to know whom to turn to if they have questions or concerns. They must be able to ask, communicate, and receive information informally. Feedback builds relationships.

Please get to know the Blueland media and join their Plaids. Just like with community leaders, try to acquaint yourself virtually, participate in media-organized events, and introduce yourself during these events. Find out what topics interest media representatives and see if you have information that journalists might need.

Don't forget that your company likely belongs to some international associated structures, such as the W2E Association. Such structures usually gather information about the situation in various countries and regions. You can offer this information to the Blueland media. Obtaining this kind of information should not be difficult for you, but it might not be easily accessible to the general media, so you will gain trust and build relationships through this.

Similar rules apply to public organizations, controlling institutions, and political Plaids. Don't try to save on time for personal contacts – create a network of contacts with people you meet in person, and be not just a profile but also an easily accessible person, an expert whom one can turn to when needed.

4.3. Step 3 – Your Own Territory. Just One in a Million

If you have a garden and a library, you have everything you need.
Marcus Tullius Cicero – statesman, lawyer, scholar, and philosopher.

The garden in the time of Cicero, is the Plaid today. The library is your knowledge, your know-how. You have the Plaid; you can invite guests. However, until then, some work needs to be done.

The critical **skills** at this stage are creativity, originality, team-building, insight, and graphic perception.

The third step is the first step into the Creators' space, the beginning of creating your Plaid, spreading your information, and maintaining a consistent position.

Perhaps you've already seriously engaged in various conversations and acquaintances in the second step, but to continue your effective activity on Social Picnic, you must create your Plaid. Discussions in other neighborhoods by other Plaids are not bad. Still, effective participation in a Social Picnic requires moving as many discussions as possible to your neighborhood, to your Plaid, i.e., where you are the host and so can control the process and give it your direction.

Your Plaid is your editorial, website, blog, social media account, open or closed group, or channel. You set the rules, privacy settings, and communication style and decide what is desirable. In other words, you behave just like you would in your own home: you probably don't invite everyone in, and not everything that happens there needs to be public.

When creating your Plaid in the Social Picnic, you prepare for future meetings and conversations. Therefore, you must strive to make it comfortable for

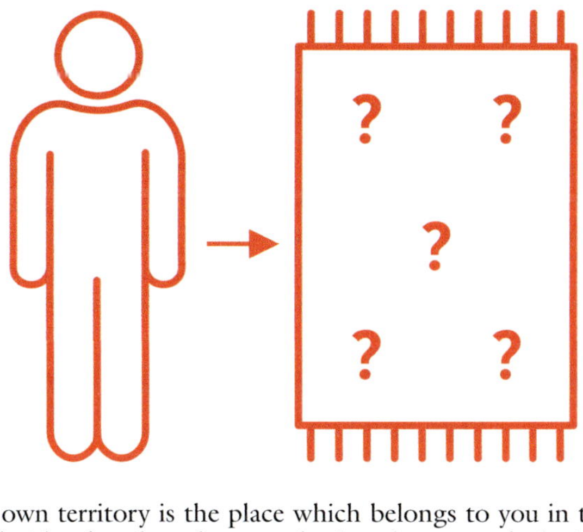

Figure 4.4 Your own territory is the place which belongs to you in the Social Picnic. You decide what the rules are, who is welcome, and who is not.

Figure by the author.

your desired Sharers. At this stage, the creation of your dialogue begins – not the dialogue itself, but the preparation for it.

When creating your territory, your Plaid, carefully consider how many and what kind of Plaids you want in your Social Picnic. Although it may seem easy to create your account, often the ease turns into creating many accounts, and there is no longer time to care for all of them or attend to their hygiene.

Consider how one account will interact with others and what information you share on Facebook versus LinkedIn. Think about the names and how they should relate to your website addresses.

A significant factor for non-English-speaking countries is the language used in communication on the Plaid or whether bilingualism or multilingualism will be allowed.

Each social media platform has its requirements and rules, and although they may often seem standard, it is essential to follow them carefully. A social media tool may often temporarily block an account in the heat of a Social Picnic.

It is worth paying attention to the account details: provide as much detailed information as possible in sections like "About". Specify contacts, addresses, and website addresses. Although perhaps Sharers do not use this information very often, it does affect the reputation and accessibility of your Plaid. I call the completion of these tasks communication hygiene. Like an unclean area at a picnic in the park, an incomplete profile on Social Picnic raises suspicions, distrust, and other factors negatively affecting reputation.

On the other hand, it's important to remember that social media platforms tend to standardize and make all Sharers somewhat similar. Therefore, it's worth not overdoing it to stand out. The rule here is simple – your territory must be created according to the specific rules of the social media platform, not by trying to break them. This rule applies not only to social media but to any form of participation in a Social Picnic. The "Television" stage requires shock, and the "Network" stage requires content. And although we often hear today that we are "drowning in content surplus", that "information chaos reigns", and the like, we still live in the age of content, and content is crucial in the Social Picnic.

So, create your territory by thinking about how you will spread content, and only then think about how it will look. And, of course, don't forget hygiene: your Plaid's reputation will be much healthier if it is clear to whom it belongs, how to connect with it, and it has a properly resolution main image, rather than a strange "no name", whose owner is unclear and origin is unknown.

Practical Example: Building a Waste-to-Energy (W2E) Power Plant – Step 3

It's time to create your Plaid's base on the Social Picnic. Carefully consider the channels you will use for communication. Suppose you've decided that your communication will require the following social media platforms: Facebook, YouTube, LinkedIn, Instagram, Wikipedia, and Google Maps. Let's discuss each one separately.

Facebook

Facebook is probably the universal social media platform chosen today by businesses, politicians, neighbors, and many others. Like all universal tools, it lacks specific features, but it encompasses the widest audience.

Despite its critics, Facebook is the most popular social media platform globally, with almost 3.01 billion users.[1] So, one would need strong arguments to justify why Facebook should not be in your toolkit.

When creating your territory on Facebook, consider the sources from which you will gather information. Your accumulated diverse material from presentations, what you have spoken about or heard at conferences, and the material held by associated structures can be excellent sources. Don't forget that social media is a platform for sharing, so content often doesn't have to be constantly created; in many cases, you can share it. Therefore, if you belong to an association and the association has its Facebook page – here's one excellent source for your content stream.

Also, come up with and always have several topics in advance; prioritize them if relevant news arises. Plan the frequency of your Facebook posts, monitor reactions, and by no means leave any unanswered questions.

YouTube

YouTube is the second-largest global social media platform, not far behind Facebook, with about 2.49 billion[2] users). It is much more specialized and exclusively tailored for video content.

Do you have a wealth of video content about waste-to-energy, or do you know where to find it? If so, great; create your territory on YouTube. Of course, if your available material is limited to just a few videos, it may not be worth doing.

YouTube can be used as an archive for video content and live streaming. It is a reliable platform for accumulating liked videos.

YouTube doesn't require constant updates, so you don't have to worry too much about not having video content for a long time. A well-maintained channel can be comfortably kept as a reserve until it is needed again. On the other hand, when you find good video content about waste-to-energy, always include it in your YouTube playlist – you will help the Plaid that created it and promote your YouTube Plaid.

LinkedIn

While LinkedIn falls behind the major social media platforms, it is still a network with around 0.9 billion[3] users. It is significantly more specialized than Facebook and YouTube. Plaids here are somewhat different; you may rarely find communities, but you will undoubtedly find decision-makers, partners, and competitors.

Like Facebook, it's worth planning your strategy here, but be sure to gather all the Plaids that are important to you. Ask employees to list your Plaid as their workplace and share the information you spread. Generally, LinkedIn users are willing to do this because it helps build their Plaid's reputation and that of their company.

The Social Picnic on LinkedIn is much more serious. So, adjust your content accordingly, but don't overdo it. The ConCrEtE formula works here, too, as only having serious information can become dull over time.

Instagram

Yes, waste-to-energy plants can also be here. Say what you want, but waste mountains, while not beautiful, are undoubtedly impressive. On the other hand, well-managed waste is a beautiful waste. You will also undoubtedly have impressive industrial views from construction sites, completed structures, and sunsets, which someone might catch glimpses of while climbing the plant's chimney.

Instagram is more specialized in age demographics; there are fewer older or even middle-aged Sharers here. However, this app has at least 2 billion[4] users on their phones.

Wikipedia

Be sure to take care of your Plaid in the global encyclopedia because: a) if you don't do it, someone else will, probably not quite accurately, and then you'll have to correct those mistakes; and b) Google often highlights Wikipedia in searches, so when Sharers start searching for information about you, this is what they will get.

Wikipedia is like a silent Social Picnic: public discussions don't occur there, but the information presented works silently but reliably.

Google Maps

Do you know where your drivers will first look when transporting equipment to your new plant? Yes, you guessed it – Google Maps. And if your location is not there or is mismarked, they'll be confused.

So, when starting your Social Picnic, take the time for Google Maps: try to upload the best available photos and list all necessary contacts. Then, you can forget about Google Maps. After a few months, you'll be surprised when you receive a message from Google saying that your location has been viewed for the 10,000th time, then the 100,000th time, and so on.

4.4. Step 4 – Design. It Is Still Possible to Be Unique

> The details are not the details. They make the design.
>
> Charles Eames – designer, architect, and filmmaker.

Although in the third step, I wrote that it's worth thinking about content first and then about visuals, the importance of your Plaid's appearance never disappears. An excellent visual complements good content and creates stylistic coherence.

Therefore, when taking a step towards styling your Plaid, it is vital to have the following **skills**:

- A detailed and general visual perception.
- A sense of taste and style.
- The ability to write and create visuals impressively.
- An understanding of communication hygiene.

The majority of the Social Picnic, of course, is made up of social media tools. Social media tools create their standards to which Sharers must adapt. It's a fascinating phenomenon in a world that shines with originality, individualism, and a reluctance to conform to systems. Social media tools seem to say, "Be original in content; form doesn't matter." Today, we have perfect tools to express form – projectors, 3D glasses, curved screens – but our content is precisely defined by the number of pixels in Facebook or LinkedIn images or symbols in a Twitter post.

These limits are not a coincidence. After all, it probably wouldn't be much trouble for Facebook to allow users to style their profiles more than is currently allowed. However, users are still limited to one main image of a standard size and one round profile picture. Why? The main focus here, as in the Social Picnic, is content.

Does this mean that the significance of design will be less critical in the future? I would say not. However, I must also acknowledge that before the end of the "Network" era, there was often an excessive focus on design, with content frequently overlooked. So today, everything is simply returning to normal proportions.

Plaid design is essential. Sharers are drawn to tasteful Plaids; they enjoy seeing clean, high-quality, informative images with coordinated colors, changing visuals, and uncluttered pictures. If all of this illustrates quality content, it is the foundation of each Plaid's success.

With the advent of the "Network" era, information design has experienced a new qualitative rebirth. Not too long ago, it was possible to be impressed by a unique website that didn't work. Everything in it was beautiful but non-functional. Conversely, it was also possible, and often still is, to compel users to use certain online services simply because those services have no alternative. This situation is well illustrated by the websites of some government institutions, where the design aspect was forgotten in the development process.

Social Picnic Sharers appreciate beautifully and tastefully presented content – infographics, timelines, videos, and photos harmonized with the overall Plaid concept.

Figure 4.5 If tasteful Plaid design illustrates quality content, success is guaranteed.
Figure by the author.

The Social Picnic's design returns to the fundamental function of design – presenting content conveniently, originally, impressively, and tastefully.

Simple text and images without content are no longer engaging; there is a need for synergy between content and design, resulting in uniqueness. And there are still many untapped opportunities in existing platforms and those that await us in the future.

If Mark Zuckerberg's "Metaverse" dreams become a reality (and he's probably not the only one dreaming), think about the design and content each Plaid will need! Even if it doesn't happen, we still move in that direction. Today's habit of staring at black squares (smartphones and monitors) will become quite amusing in the future. We'll likely laugh about it in the future the way we do about fax machines or landline phones today. But that's a topic for Chapter 5.

Practical Example: Building a Waste-to-Energy (W2E) Power Plant – Step 4

Return to the selected social media platforms: Facebook, YouTube, LinkedIn, Instagram, Wikipedia, and Google Maps.

Of course, we must first consider the basic building blocks of the Social Picnic design: profile pictures and main images.

It's important not to forget that many logos may not fit specific social media platform standards. For example, if your power station's logo is strongly horizontal, it will appear very small and practically indiscernible on Facebook. Such subtleties demand specific design solutions, which may not have been anticipated in your power station's brand book, or, if one is currently being developed, designers might have overlooked the fact that a specific, round and tiny logo would be needed. It's worth supplementing the brand book with solutions tailored to each social media platform.

In short, the logo must be adapted separately for each social media platform and should never be automatically "inserted". In the case of a power station, instead of the logo, you can use a chimney, a stack of pipes, or various energy symbols – sometimes, it might not even be a logo but a different symbol that fits your Plaid. For instance, if your Plaid is a vegan restaurant Plaid, instead of a logo, you might use a soybean or a radish. Or they could change depending on the season or the menu offered.

Another crucial element of a Plaid is photos or other visuals, especially the main image, which is essential on some social media platforms. For example, on Facebook or LinkedIn, the main image is essentially the sole visualization of the entire Plaid, aside from the logo. Therefore, a Sharer coming to your Plaid sees it as the main focal point of your visual communication.

Photos and visuals look different on various social media platforms. They need to be specially prepared for each platform, so it's worth paying attention to this and not leaving this issue unresolved but organizing it thoroughly. For example, the main image on Facebook must be in a 1640 x 720 pixel format, while on LinkedIn, it should be in an extended format of 1128 x 191 pixels. These minor details mean that simply cropping any image or photo won't work; here, the skilful touch of a designer is needed to create visual consistency for your Plaid.

Photos also need to be "equipped" for Google Maps because if you don't do it, someone else will, and they may not be of high quality. Don't hesitate to allocate time and resources consistently for photos and their uploading to various social media platforms. High-quality and up-to-date photos work for you constantly and reliably because they are what Sharers see about you.

Create a visualization or a photo shoot for the future power station or the already built one – industrial design can be stunning and exciting.

4.5. Step 5 – Friends. Like Always – They Best Describe You

> Old friends pass away, new friends appear. It is just like the days. An old day passes, a new day arrives. The important thing is to make it meaningful: a meaningful friend – or a meaningful day.
>
> Dalai Lama – spiritual leader.

Well then, you're already a part of Social Picnic, you have your Plaid, it's visually well-maintained, and you're navigating nicely among various Social Picnic Plaids, visiting them, and constantly receiving information from Plaids that matter to you. It's time to invite some friends!

With the advent of social media platforms and Picnic Society, the term "friend" has changed significantly. Many people still find it confusing.

When Russia started the war in Ukraine, I received a reproach from a well-known activist who stated that a prominent pro-Russian figure was among my Facebook "Friends", and that this cast a shadow on my reputation.

It is just one example, but many people think this way. It's understandable because the term "Friend" strongly misleads them, as it signifies a close and dear person to them.

It can be a mistake, and a different term should have been coined to define friendship in social media from the beginning. This confusion raises concerns for regular Social Picnic participants and judges in the highest courts. However, the situation is what it is, and we must live with two types of "friends" – real and virtual.

In my view, the concept of "Friend" in the Social Picnic is nothing more than a "significant Plaid that I want or need to follow". Although I know that pro-Russian individual personally, he is in my "Friends" not because I have warm and friendly feelings towards him. He is there because I need to monitor his actions on the Social Picnic – it's essential for my professional activities, my clients, and my understanding of the environment and what's happening.

What will "Friends" be if we imagine a Plaid as a media outlet from the previous "Television" stage? The answer is straightforward – the number of "Friends" is the circulation of your personal media outlet. And although some social media platforms distinguish between "Friend", "Follower", or "Network", the essence remains the same – it's a list of people important to us. It could be both a friend and a foe.

So, what would be the most suitable name for what is currently our Plaid "Friend", "Contact", or "Follower"? We already discussed this in Chapter 3. It's a Sharer! Every Plaid in the Social Picnic strives to have as many Sharers as possible.

However, in this fifth step, it is crucial to gather those Sharers most similar to one's real friends and buddies. Why? There are several reasons.

Firstly, the information we disseminate must begin to spread. The spreading is best achieved by Sharers who are loyal to us, friendly, and supportive of the information we share in our Plaid.

Another not less important reason is that while Plaid is still in its infancy, it's crucial to receive support and approval rather than negativity and criticism. Here, an appropriate analogy with a baby is quite fitting. Initially, love and care are essential, not disdain and rejection. A baby, and similarly a Plaid, has much more chances for successful existence when allowed to develop safely.

So, try to have as many real friends among the first hundred Sharers of your Plaid as possible. To attract them, act in a friendly manner. The most crucial skills at this step are charisma, empathy, listening, and paying attention.

The first friends are critical. Like at a picnic in the park, ensuring they feel good here is essential. Invite your Plaid close ones, well-acquainted people, partners. Please try to get them to share information they wouldn't get anywhere else and could share through their Plaids.

The circle of first Sharers and recommendations is a powerful impulse for other Sharers. The initial recommendations and ratings are like water for a recently planted plant. If there is too little, the plant will wither, and reviving it will require much more effort than consistently providing ample nourishment.

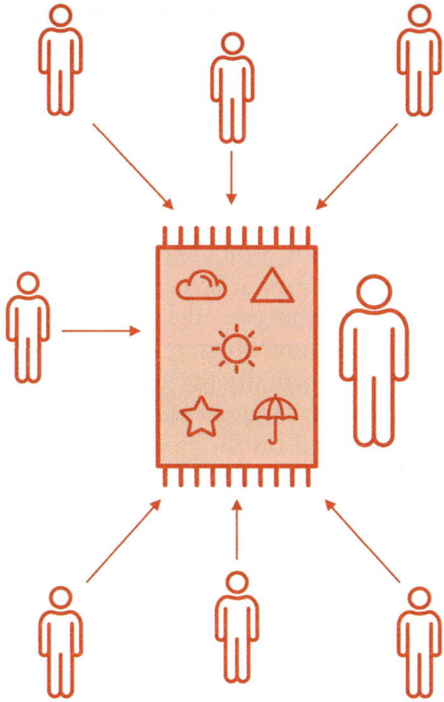

Figure 4.6 Please pay special attention to your first friends because they are the water for your newly sprouted plant (Plaid).

Figure by the author.

Don't hesitate to pay attention to your first Plaid friends. Thank them, respond to their comments, meet them in person, communicate, inquire about topics relevant to them, and respond to the information received through your Plaid.

Always imagine that your Plaid is unique; there's nothing quite like it, and along with all your Plaid Sharers, you are the only one of its kind in the world. No one else is as deeply invested in your topics as you are. That's true, but it's crucial to feel that way as well.

Again and again, check your essential Plaids and try to find one or a few Sharers in each of them whom you could attract to your Plaid. Strive to make the most critical individuals among your first Plaid Sharers be those who participate in the Social Picnic. Once you've correctly gathered the first hundred Sharers, it will work like a snowball effect in the following steps: the ball will keep growing, and adequately chosen initial Sharers will act like a magnet, attracting other vital individuals to you.

Although forming such a circle is as old as humanity, a Social Picnic is unique because it happens during days, sometimes hours, instead of the old months or years. With a reasonable effort, you can form the right Plaid Sharers circle in just a few weeks today. High speed is a unique feature of the Social Picnic, which we can use for the first time as representatives of all humanity.

Practical Example: Building a Waste-to-Energy (W2E) Power Plant – Step 5

Let's imagine what our new powerhouse's best Friends and Sharers are. As I mentioned before, at the beginning, these concepts are very closely related to each other.

Firstly, I suggest taking a look around you. Here, you will find dozens, if not hundreds, of employees bustling around you. These are your first and most loyal Sharers. Stroll around the office, through the construction site, and take photos. Send the pictures to your colleagues. Many will thank you because they will have the opportunity to "share themselves" with their Sharers. Ask if those who express gratitude or react positively in other ways would allow their photos to be shared on the new powerhouse's Plaid. Many will agree and appreciate it. Play creatively with this information, expand it over time, comment on it, and establish connections.

When contacts with your employees start working, perform similar actions with partners and contractors' employees, reach out to the PR people of your partners, and share information with their companies' Plaids and the associations they belong to. After these actions, your Sharers circle will approach the first 100.

Tapping into the wells of employees and partners doesn't mean you should forget about them later. Move on to representatives of government institutions who have already supported your activities. For now, limit your engagement to bureaucrats, as politicians might wait a bit because your initial steps may attract them very enthusiastically for their benefit. This fact may not necessarily be detrimental to you, but each politician usually closely observes the actions of others, and this can prematurely involve you in a political show. I by no means want to say that the opinions of politicians are unimportant or should be ignored. On the contrary, I believe that their attention will be very beneficial at a later stage, and with their help, you can gain more popularity. However, it's advisable to avoid it in the initial stage.

At this stage, make an effort to invite non-political representatives of ministries, municipalities, and representatives of regulatory authorities to your Plaid. These institutions and individuals likely have their own Plaids for the Social Picnic. It's worthwhile to initiate shared activities with them.

4.6. Step 6 – Walking. Nobody Pays You for That

> Everywhere is within walking distance if you have the time.
>
> Steven Wright – stand-up comedian, actor, writer, and film producer.

When I was very young and inexperienced, starting as a public relations specialist, it sincerely seemed to me that the most important thing was to perform everything needed for a specific task as accurately as possible, meet only with those people who were explicitly needed at any given time, and thus move from one task to another.

It is essential, but not the most important. If an engineer is building a large object, the most important thing is to have a good plan and move forward; our profession is a bit different.

Today, I can confidently say that all the contacts and clients I have, all the acquaintances and colleagues I've gained throughout my life, are from those professional moments you can't classify as precisely planned.

A PR professional has to dedicate much time to what may not seem so important at first glance. For example, I have to choose a client who is about a four-hour drive away next week. Four hours there, four hours back – it's already a whole working day. Most likely, I'll need to stay overnight. The travel and accommodation will incur costs.

The task that requires me to embark on this journey is straightforward. My client, a manufacturing company, is organizing a safety week: they will meet with their employees, and there will be training on providing first aid.

My alternative is not to go anywhere, get photos from the training, and conduct the meeting using the Teams platform.

So, to go or not to go?

The answer for me today is obvious: if there is an opportunity – go. Yes, I could get photos without traveling, but if I participate, I can take them myself, see emotions and reactions, and feel the collective mood. When I sit with everyone in the room, I can joke together; there will be a coffee break with one or another colleague, and we'll exchange a few words about the news. Relationships will ignite and refresh; we will feel each other.

These small, seemingly insignificant things are the most important to a PR professional. Nothing else is as crucial as emotional connections, which, perhaps, sometimes tire, sometimes rejuvenate, but most importantly – they build trust.

The best client for a PR professional is the one who allows them to "stroll". By strolling, I mean participating in conferences, coffee meetings, lunches and dinners, and other gatherings.

Once, a colleague of mine, whose words I always remember and use to encourage myself when it seems I'm doing something wrong, taught me a lesson. The lesson happened during a conference we both attended, and we didn't go back to the room because we found our interaction more valuable. So, he said that conferences are mainly not for what many expect, i.e., learning and gaining knowledge. That is also very important. However, the most crucial part of conferences is what happens before, after, and during coffee or lunch breaks. That's when every PR professional's leading and most important action takes place – building or renewing relationships and connections.

The most critical **skills** at this stage are communicability, courage, politeness, and continuous improvement.

It's paradoxical, but Walking continues, forming the essence of a PR professional's activities and professional development, yet it's rarely directly paid for.

A PR professional must engage in as much communication, travel, speaking, and networking with diverse people as possible. They should read a wide range of literature, stay well-informed about global events, and understand history and economics – essentially, they must be versatile. I call this entire process Walking.

Walking begins when we start our PR career and, for many, ends when life ends; for some, it ends when their professional activities conclude. Walking is an uninterrupted process. If you imagine yourself as a charged element, Walking is the state when the element is charged.

In creating relationships, it is essential to charge up, and this charging is done with knowledge, acquaintances, communication, observation, and innovations. Social Picnic Walking is carried out by walking and observing various Plaids, interacting with their Sharers, and sharing information.

All this charging and gathering is later utilized when advising the client. The client pays not for the charging but what you can do when fully charged.

Therefore, most often, Walking must be done by oneself, with one's funds. Charging for flying, living in hotels, and attending conferences, etc., is an investment, no different from other investments. It can either pay off or not. However, only after making it can one try to sell it to the client. Like any other

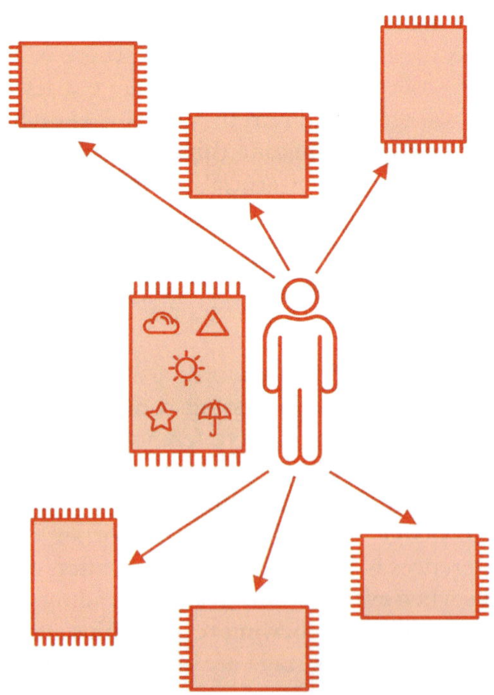

Figure 4.7 Walking is an investment that every PR professional must make for themselves. Figure by the author.

investment, investments in Walking have a cost. If they are reasonable and justified, they yield profit.

Walking in a Social Picnic requires much time. And time is the most significant value we have. Therefore, it's worth walking responsibly because it's straightforward to squander that value. Responsible Walking requires calm and consistent planning. And once again, that means – time.

An experienced PR professional understands that well, while a beginner often does not. To a novice specialist, it often seems that Walking is unimportant or only necessary to accomplish one specific action, such as organizing an event.

However, the true purpose of Walking is not explicitly expressed. It is charging, fulfilment and improvement. If the Walking process is carried out consistently, calmly, well thought out, and planned, every meeting with a client, consultation, media release, strategy, and event becomes more mature and meaningful, which means it is more valuable.

Finally, Walking is essentially nothing new. We have been doing it throughout our entire professional history. Only the form of Walking has changed slightly. If in the past, Walking was expressed exclusively by physical presence somewhere, going somewhere, today, without forgetting the old Walking traditions, a significant part of Walking must also be dedicated to the virtual space. Today's Social Picnic is essential, necessary, and beneficial for the entire society and the PR professional.

Practical Example: Building a Waste-to-Energy (W2E) Power Plant – Step 6

So, if you haven't done it yet, start investing. Whether you're an experienced PR professional or just starting, you'll need to make new acquaintances, you'll need to walk and become part of the Plaids of energy professionals and waste managers, and you'll need to connect with opinion leaders and community members you haven't met yet.

Find out about various conferences, seminars, and workgroups; gather information about closed and open community groups. Start attending them, engaging in conversations, establishing connections, sharing your opinions and positions, and participating in discussions.

Don't forget about international practices; don't confine yourself only to your country's Social Picnic. Explore international arenas, seek opinion leaders beyond your country's borders, communicate with them, invite them to your Plaid, and visit them.

This activity will energize you, provide a wealth of new knowledge and material, broaden your horizons, and significantly strengthen you professionally. However, you must perform many of these actions, i.e., invest in them.

4.7. Step 7 – First Meeting. Unforgettable But You Aren't Married Yet

> Let us always meet each other with smile, for the smile is the beginning of love.
>
> Mother Teresa – nun and missionary.

So, everything is ready: known Plaids and Sharers, your territory, organized just as you want it. The goal of this step is to start proactive, solid activity. Although we mainly talk about the Social Picnic, which takes place virtually, the first meeting, the initial spark, doesn't necessarily have to happen virtually.

The First Meeting can be but doesn't necessarily have to be a specific event. It marks the beginning of proactive activity, which can start with a big boom. Still, the boom can be replaced by a series of events, informational solid knowledge, virtual events, or events.

After this step, you must start actively participating in various discussions and events, sharing your knowledge, giving interviews, and becoming visible as an expert in your field.

The most critical **skills** at this stage include organising, initiating, communicating effectively, knowledge of your target audience, and hospitality.

However, the main goal of all these efforts is to attract Sharers to your Plaid.

The arsenal of PR professional tools today, compared to the situation 20–30 years ago, is very extensive. We can organize video conferences, hybrid meetings, conduct continuous live broadcasts, share video material and photos, co-ordinate joint reviews, events, and groups.

However, the most crucial factor remains content as it was 20–30 years ago and at any time before. All these tools will assist and yield the desired results when you have content that resonates with sharers, and none of them will be effective if you lack such content.

Therefore, from the first meeting, it is essential to focus on content and plan for the upcoming weeks and months.

I always suggest categorizing content into two groups: timely, ad-hoc, reactive, and evergreen, always relevant, and filler content. The goal of the first is to constantly demonstrate that you are not falling behind on current affairs and are responsive to what is happening. The second goal is to fill the void when nothing specific occurs.

I recommend creating content plans in advance and organizing the flow of content to avoid congestion and empty streets. Flexibly push content, adapting it to the constantly changing environment, but always have prepared content you can publish at any time.

The initial meetings for your new Plaid are crucial. Depending on the type of Sharers you initially attract, you will shape the circles of others joining Sharers. Therefore, pay special attention to your first friends.

Monitor who joins your Plaid after the initial meetings, who shares your material, and who comments. Engage with these people, respond to their comments, and supplement their statements with your information. On the other hand, ruthlessly weed out trolls. It might initially seem problematic, considering they are also Sharers who have noticed your Plaid, but experience shows no benefit in dealing with them. In truth, the damage is not significant either, but if you have many trolls, you'll constantly spend valuable

Figure 4.8. The first meeting can be virtual or not, or it may not happen at all, as a series of events could replace it. However, the most crucial aspect here is content.

Figure by the author.

time contemplating what to do with them. Frankly, there isn't much to consider – trolls must be removed and ignored.

Practical Example: Building a Waste-to-Energy (W2E) Power Plant – Step 7

Today, in your hands, is what was available only to large organizations for a substantial amount of money 20 years ago. I remember my first virtual press conference, during which we streamed video on the internet, and since the internet speed was too slow, we transmitted the audio over the phone. Ultimately, the video with sound from the press conference differed by 20 minutes. Today, in the era of Teams and Zoom, that sounds quite amusing.

Make your new facility presentation a hybrid event. Invite people to the company premises and give them a tour. Please encourage them to take photos and videos and actively promote them. Please take pictures and videos of them yourself and later share the footage with them. Also, live stream everything and create an event on your Facebook page, website, and YouTube channel. Perhaps you can offer this video material to media outlets and opinion leaders.

Prepare for such a meeting thoroughly to ensure it runs smoothly and visually appealing. Dedicate maximum attention to the technology's proper functioning (consider utilizing professional videographers' services) and content preparation.

Actively respond to all comments, monitor whether all participating Sharers have joined your facility's Plaid, see what material they shared, and don't forget to click the Like button on those shares.

The material you create during such a presentation will serve you for a long time, residing on your YouTube channel and Facebook page. Whenever questions arise in various Social Picnic discussions for which the answers are in that material, provide Sharers with links.

You can make a series of meetings instead of a single one, categorizing participants by audiences: organize one meeting for the community, another for politicians, a third for energy specialists, and a fourth for students.

Instead of a meeting, you can organize and promote live and virtual tours virtually. You can also hold open house days and concerts. All these methods may seem somewhat familiar, but nothing new. Indeed, the Social Picnic adds an extra layer of reach, publicity, and interactivity to each of them.

4.8. Step 8 – Walking. This Activity Is the Main One and You Can't Stop It

> The greatest gift you can give another is the purity of your attention.
>
> Richard Moss – brewer and politician.

It is not a mistake; the eighth step is "Walking" again. "Walking" is the core activity in the Social Picnic. It must continue constantly, i.e., as long as you are in one or another Social Picnic. If you stop, you'll fall behind, the picnic will move forward, and you'll be left not understanding what's happening, what news is currently relevant, what's "on the wave", and where you need to be.

To prevent this from happening, you need to walk, communicate, see each other, discuss, be visible, and make new contacts.

And continue to choose the most important ones, sparing no attention to them, personal relationships, and your time. A PR professional is a Social Picnic Walker, investigator, expert, collector, familiar with many Social Picnic participants, and known by many.

The most critical **skills** of continuous walking are communication, courage, politeness, the ability to embrace innovations, and the willingness to improve.

If you feel that a particular Plaid is especially important to you, pause by it longer, engage in a conversation while looking into its eyes, and feel the spirit flowing from that Plaid. Building relationships takes time and attention. It's an unchanging constant throughout the entire history of humanity.

The most crucial "currency" in today's relationship building is the purity of your attention. Therefore, as you walk, choose where to spend it. Focusing your attention on a particular question or showing attention to specific individuals can move mountains. In today's world, where many people struggle to concentrate and divert their eyes from their phones while interacting, sincere attention may seem like a significant surprise or a different kind of activity to some. If you discover an area that, in your opinion, deserves more attention, always consider what you can do to get the most out of that area. Remember that to receive, you must first give. And giving should be without expecting to receive. Then, attention becomes sincere.

Every PR professional's job comprises two parts: the performance of technical tasks, such as writing, distributing, organizing, and Walking, which involves building contacts and relationships, gathering information, and consulting. If we were a battery, in the first case, we would discharge, and in the second case, we would recharge. Remember this when everyday tasks become dull and routine starts to set in; know there is about 10–20% battery left. Then, remember Walking and go for a walk: visit interesting Plaids, read, participate in conferences, communicate. When you feel that the battery is approaching 100% again, return to your routine.

However, Walking also has its limits, just like a fully charged battery – if you continue to charge it, there won't be much benefit. Therefore, although Walking is one of the most essential, fundamental activities shaping the know-how of a PR professional, charging them with knowledge and experience, it only makes sense when that knowledge and experience can be used.

Therefore, I advise you not to play around with Walking and always remember that this action must have meaning, benefit, and contribute. If, at the beginning of your professional activities, it's worth participating in almost every thematic conference, making new acquaintances, joining professional associations, and doing a fair amount of volunteer work to build up, then, as you progress a bit and reach the midpoint of your career, it's worth looking at this activity much more refinedly. Choose the unheard-of, the unexplored, perhaps deepen your knowledge in more specialized events and seek connections where little attention has been paid.

Practical Example: Building a Waste-to-Energy (W2E) Power Plant – Step 8

Today, you work with a somewhat hostile community towards your power plant. You try to understand why there is hostility and where the fear comes from. Many rumors arise during the construction of the power plant.

Get in the car and drive to that community. Walk around the town, read announcements, buy a local newspaper (yes, they still exist), talk to people in the store, visit the market. Join community accounts on social networks, listen to what people are talking about. If there's an event mentioned, go and participate in it. Perhaps all these actions may seem unnecessary, not directly related to what you do, but that's a mistaken perspective. Even having lunch at a local restaurant, not rushing and listening to how two "locals" converse is of golden value to a PR professional. Unconsciously, by interacting with another community member or their group, you will incorporate the community's issues into your speech and, just as unconsciously, become one of them. These are very subtle but incredibly important aspects of our work.

When you next receive a complaint from a community member that your heavy vehicles are raising much dust near his house, and he and his children can't go outside, try to do what you can:

- Talk to the logistics manager and see if the route can be changed and if the dusty road can be watered.
- Sincerely do what you can and go personally to inform that community member about your actions.
- Along with the information, bring him an exciting tulip bulb; as you know from social media, this man is very interested in growing flowers.

And even if you don't hit it off very well with that tulip bulb and see that the bulb you brought is already the 101st among the existing hundred, you will always hit it off differently because that tulip bulb will never be forgotten. Your attention and sincere interest in one specific person will do the job.

Every person likes to be noticed and remembered and wants to connect. When you react personally, giving all your attention, spending lunch or a day with one person, you perform work that several official events or texts cannot accomplish.

4.9. Step 9 – Storytelling and Advertising. Yes, Advertising

> Humans think in stories, and we try to make sense of the world by telling stories.
> Yuval Noah Harari – public intellectual, historian, and professor.

Walking continues constantly, but for effective walking, you need to have stories and be able to tell them compellingly. The most essential **skills** in this step are marketing knowledge, creativity, storytelling ability, and intellectual insight.

In every human encounter, we do two things – we listen to stories, and we tell them. Otherwise, we would sit in silence.

In gatherings with friends, we share what happened while we were apart, often recounting amusing incidents. We negotiate or strive to reach a mutually beneficial agreement in business meetings. In community meetings, we share what we know from our practice, exchange experiences, and persuade. However, the foundation of all this is various stories and narratives about what was, is, or will be.

Therefore, a PR professional must have a plethora of stories. Accumulating these stories is only possible by constantly being curious, participating, engaging, and reading. Of course, one can physically collect and record these stories in various ways; everyone can do it in the most convenient way. However, the most crucial stories reside in the mind and emerge when needed. The mind is filled with them only through the oldest and still unchanged method – the intellectual act of listening and reading.

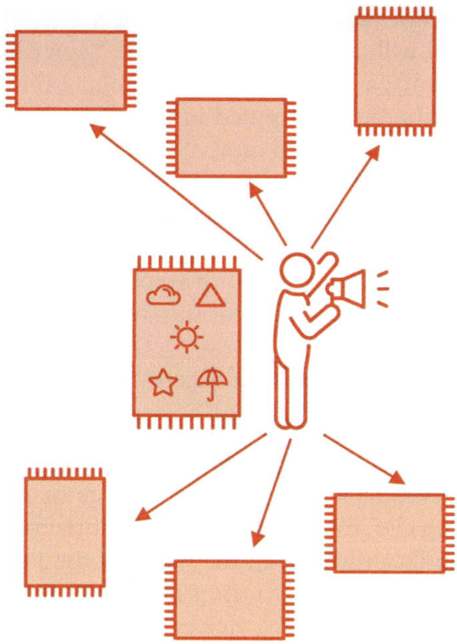

Figure 4.9. How you accumulate stories is up to you, but you must have them.

Figure by the author.

Stories also require technical dissemination. While social media allows us to spread our stories more widely without marketing assistance, it is, in many cases, still necessary.

Many social networks operate commercially, meaning their main goal is profit-making. This goal implies that they will try to structure things so that your stories, especially those related to a brand, won't spread too widely without financial injections.

Therefore, in this step, it's also worth taking care of your Plaid advertising. Marketing knowledge will come in handy for that. In summary, when you already feel confident in your Social Picnic: you know the necessary Plaids, your Plaid is well-organized, you have your Sharers, and you have walked around quite a bit – it's time to create stories and make an effort to give them maximum visibility.

In the "Network" stage, advertising gradually returns to its original functional state, meaning less and less advertising is shown through beautiful but fundamentally unhelpful images, and more advertising money is spent on promoting good content.

Good stories in the Social Picnic need to attract attention, meaning you have to speak a little louder than others and appear more vivid and distinctive. Many social networks don't allow you to stand out. They put everyone in standard frames and let you compete in terms of reach, meaning the amount of money determines not which advertising creator you will hire or what kind of beautiful image you will create (as it was in the "Television" stage), but how many Social Picnic participants will see your content. I think this is a qualitative advertising step from the bubble formed in the "Television" stage towards the core function of advertising – to sell more. Selling in a Social Picnic is not just a direct action where the buyer purchases something directly from the seller. Selling in a Social Picnic includes increasing the Sharers' circle, the number of Likes and Shares, and all the other effectiveness metrics that have become common.

So, if you've already reached the ninth step – create good new stories and make an effort to invest money in promoting them.

Practical Example: Building a Waste-to-Energy (W2E) Power Plant – Step 9

Every field has an abundance of stories. It's just that until the "Network" stage, the media had drilled into our heads that only what is attractive to the media is interesting. The media finds what is attractive to the majority of its consumers interesting. Everything else, the media said, is only interesting to you. It must be admitted that this significantly clipped the wings of the PR professional.

Today, we can bring all stories to the surface and test their appeal by presenting them directly to our readers, viewers, and information consumers.

Here is a list of stories that you would almost never see in the mainstream media during the "Television" stage, but in the Social Picnic, they have a good chance, and you can confidently give them a try. Of course, since we are building a power plant, all of them are related to this field.

List of stories:

- Today, our high-altitude drone climbed into the chimney in the morning and witnessed breathtaking views of the flowing sun, taking several photos.
- Yesterday, the power plant was shut down, and next week, the men will climb into the boiler, which will undoubtedly offer views even more impressive than stalactites.
- We sorted through a truckload and calculated the weight of various types of waste. We can provide data on what makes up the majority of waste in our city.
- Our office employees are growing pineapples, and they recently sent photos. We can share them.
- Yesterday, a truck full of contraband cigarettes was brought to us to be incinerated. We have great visuals.
- Our operational personnel manager recently attended an international conference showcasing films from various W2E power plants worldwide. These films are freely accessible to everyone; we can share them.
- Our basketball team participated in the city's amateur basketball tournament.
- Talented high school students are currently interning with us, and they have created a project on how electricians could organize their tools more conveniently.
- Yesterday, students from Australia visited us, took part in a tour, and interacted with power plant employees.

Each field has such and similar stories; it's worth just looking around, collecting them every day, and using the Social Picnic. Employees themselves can significantly contribute, but not being PR specialists, they often forget to share these stories. It's worth constantly reminding them and showing interest in what they do every day, and gradually, the flow of information from within the company to your side will increase. This way, you will always have something to share on your Plaid's Social Picnic.

4.10. Step 10 – Cosiness and Publicity. Everyone Thinks It Is Out of the Blue

> Timing, perseverance, and ten years of trying will eventually make you like an overnight success.
>
> Christopher Isaac Stone – entrepreneur.

And here is the final step: you are no longer a newcomer to the Social Picnic. You feel comfortable and confident, have a large circle of loyal Sharers, and maybe even are a celebrity in the Social Picnic world. Many people think you are a lucky person for whom things worked out.

However, only you and your team know how much effort it took. The journey in the Social Picnic can often take several years, and in exceptional cases, even up to ten years.

The most critical **skills** at this stage are professionalism, understanding, attentiveness, and reliability.

There is nothing new – just continuous, planned communication activities and work. Technology and a changing environment, speed, and tools do not change the fundamental basis, i.e., content. To have professional content, we must be professionals in a particular field. Suppose you are a professional in the energy sector, for example. In that case, you will naturally be able to provide insights and forecasts, and the PR professional working alongside you will easily create exciting content. The same goes if you work in medicine, the military, biotechnology, or any other field.

Even the most advanced technologies won't help you if you have nothing to say. However, if you are deeply immersed in a particular field, information flows to you, from you, through you – that flow is uninterrupted, and something new is happening daily. Then, all you have to do is choose the best available tools today to present that information interestingly.

Consistently step into any Social Picnic, and you will always be guaranteed success. Today's communication doesn't require any booms. Today, Sharers want to receive reliable information on time. If you have it – try to be an exciting and attractive source of information, occupy your narrow niche or a few niches, and feel comfortable. The Social Picnic belongs to no one and belongs to everyone, so it belongs to you too. The Social Picnic is currently the most perfect form of human communication until we have something better.

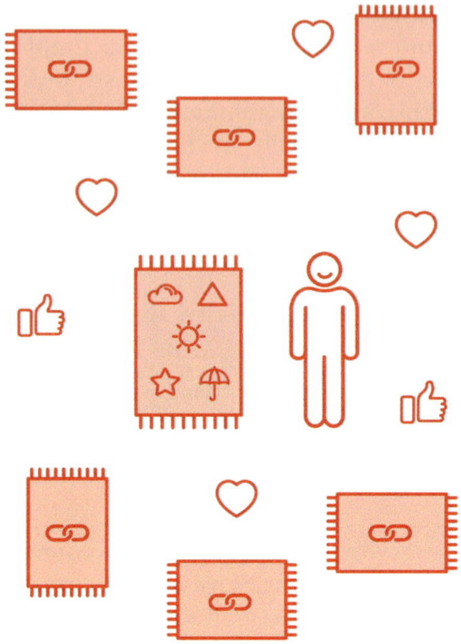

Figure 4.10. You have completed all ten steps if you feel at home in the Social Picnic. From the outside, everything seems to be going well for you.

Figure by the author.

If you've reached this step, continuously repeat individual steps and improvise: observe emerging Social Picnics, gather new Sharers, engage in discussions, update the design, and organize meetings. The Social Picnic never ends; it's a constantly awake, global, real, and virtual city.

Practical Example: Building a Waste-to-Energy (W2E) Power Plant – Step 10

I assume that since you are already here, your Plaid is a well-known place for all your neighbors, energy specialists, politicians, partners, and everyone else interested in your activities. You probably participate in events organized by other Plaid members, receive various internal information from your colleagues, and handle a large amount of exciting material through your hands.

Maintain your Plaid style, keep the flow of information, delight your Sharers with unheard news, and remember that a significant part of the information can be shared without the need to create anything. The Social Picnic is unique in that everyone contributes to the content, but the effort required for a specific content creator is much less.

Like any other picnic, being at a Social Picnic is more of a game than work. Work is necessary, but it is carried out constantly while playing, improvising, and jazzing. The Social Picnic is a collective creation of all of us, so everyone can and should improvise here.

However, like in any improvisation, it is essential to know the basics to perform it with quality and professionalism. You can confidently start improvising if you have taken the ten Social Picnic steps.

Notes

1 Number of monthly active users in January 2024. https://www.statista.com/statistics/272014/global-social-networks-ranked-by-number-of-users/ (accessed on 21-02-2024).
2 Number of monthly active users in January 2024. https://www.statista.com/statistics/272014/global-social-networks-ranked-by-number-of-users/ (accessed on 21-02-2024).
3 Number of LinkedIn users in 2023. https://www.linkedin.com/pulse/important-linkedin-statistics-data-trends-oleksii-bondar-pqlie/ (accessed on 21-02-2024).
4 Number of monthly active users in January 2024. https://www.statista.com/statistics/272014/global-social-networks-ranked-by-number-of-users/ (accessed on 21-02-2024).

5 Future

> Learn from yesterday, live for today, hope for tomorrow. The important thing is not to stop questioning.
>
> Albert Einstein – theoretical physicist.

It's time for imagination. We have discussed what has happened in the past and what is happening in the present. In this section, I will try to organize my thoughts about what awaits us in the future.

Sometimes, I catch myself thinking that what we have already achieved seems like a completely perfect world – all that's left is to fix what is not yet fully fixed, for example, eliminate hunger wars and address the reckless use of resources, and we will live almost in paradise. However, if that's the case, it means the end of development, a halt to progress, stagnation.

Then, my gaze turns to space, and I realize that, for now, we have achieved almost nothing. Well, okay, we have achieved a lot, but only recently were we able to launch a telescope that would show us the limits of the space in which we live. Are we alone? How do we overcome distances measured in parsecs and connect with other forms of life, whatever they may be?

We will most likely see and understand the significant things only in the future, and talking about them is beyond my capabilities for now. Therefore, here I would like to discuss what today seems unnatural and should change in the future. Of course, I am only referring to PR matters here. I leave questions of nutrition and health to those who know them best.

I'm not a prominent expert in science fiction. However, what else can we rely on when talking about the future if not on fantasies?

One of my favorite science fiction writers, the palaeontologist and social thinker Ivan Yefremov, in his short story "The Bull's Hour", claims that currently (he lived and wrote in the 20th century), humanity is living in The Era of Disjoint World.

If we were to follow Yefremov's thoughts further, we would see that The Era of World Reunion lies ahead of us. The transition from one era to another involves a major global war that almost decimates humanity, and brings

DOI: 10.4324/9781003466802-6

significant ecological degradation, pollution, and the resulting diseases and global epidemics.

The Era of World Reunion dawns when people realize that fighting among themselves is senseless, especially considering the cosmic future, and they create a new society, fundamentally a world without states, at least in a competitive sense. It is a world where humanity is united, possessing and striving towards a common goal, for example, initially cleaning, improving, and beautifying the Earth. The fantasist calls this The Era of Common Labor.

Yefremov foresaw two more eras, but I'll leave these for you to explore independently. In this book, I am more interested in the periods closer to us, namely, the one we currently live in and the one we are heading toward.

It's evident that, for now, we live in The Era of Disjoint World, although our era is further subdivided into smaller periods. So far, everything we fundamentally aimed for is to divide the world, i.e., compete with each other and have better technologies, resources, and territory. Our ancestors understood this very straightforwardly and sought to conquer as much land as possible. When all the free territories were occupied, the goal shifted to conquering and taking territories from each other.

The culmination of this process, of course, was the Second World War, during which almost 4% of the human population, or about 85 million people, were annihilated. After the war, dictators continued to inflict harm on people, and this process has not ceased to this day.

However, simultaneously, another process, one of unification, was unfolding. Starting on July 4, 1776, known today as Independence Day, the United States, then 13 colonies, declared their independence. The United Nations, NATO, the European Union, and many other unification projects are gaining more influence worldwide and borders are becoming more open. People can speak various languages and travel freely. If we look at the world, we will see that from the beginning of the 19th century until now, the number of democracies has gone from 0 to more than 60. This process will inevitably progress because progress requires creativity and only free people can create.

The transformation of societies from authoritarian to democratic is a shift from the old to the new. Even in democracies, resistance is often to what is new, unknown, and untested. Various radical actors in democracies try to cling desperately to the old, manipulate history, roll back a country that has moved forward, and argue how things were good in the past and are now wrong. These actors are nothing new; history is full of examples of how progress was hindered by those who were more resistant, less enlightened, and more fearful.

While such attempts to cling to the past fundamentally change nothing, they can, unfortunately, often pause, slow down, or even significantly delay progress. Just think about where we would be if it weren't for the two world wars, Hitler and Stalin's barbaric theories and practices, and the Cold War period. But perhaps that is the cost of development; humanity must go through all stages of development and cannot skip the most brutal, animalistic ones to understand what should not be allowed and done.

Humanity is moving forward in both these times and all others, and no obstacles will stop it.

I don't know if additional Yefremov-predicted world wars and epidemics are necessary, but if we consider that the two world wars, the near descent to nuclear war during the Cuban Missile Crisis in 1962, Russia's ongoing war against Ukraine, and the COVID-19 pandemic are enough for the world to cleanse itself from regressive and criminal elements, at least on a planetary scale, we can see several signs that we are moving towards The Era of World Reunion or even The Era of Common Labor.

Of course, I'm not such an optimist who believes that all threats have disappeared and that COVID-19 was the last pandemic that will take place on Earth. Far from it. I think we still have a lot to do for that to happen. There are 195 countries worldwide, meaning that only 30% live in democracies today. Non-democratic regimes still control nuclear weapons, and viruses and bacteria emerge not only in nature but also in malevolent laboratories. However, we are still moving in the right direction, and those who succeed pull along those who are not doing well.

And those who succeed, with seven-league strides, move towards The Era of World Reunion. How can you find out about it? Well, it's even visible without particular knowledge. Isn't the consolidation of democratic countries in organizations like the European Union and NATO an example of that? What about a common European currency? What about the internet, social networks, and cryptocurrency projects? What about joint space programs: the journey to Mars, lunar exploration teams, solar drones, and the recently launched James Webb Space Telescope, which may soon tell us where we all came from? What is all this, if not steps, towards The Era of World Reunion?

And let's think about moving toward a cleaner world, concern for climate change, the visible end of fossil fuel use, and the rise of renewable resources. It seems more like The Era Of Common Labor than The Era of World Reunion. Humanity will never cease progressing; the human mind is so designed that it constantly creates and discovers something new. And yet, before us lies the entire cosmos.

All these projects will be most effectively implemented when the world considers them its main goal and engages in as little internal strife as possible. Inter-country conflicts are essentially as outdated as the muskets we can see in museums. However, they will only end when good triumphs over evil, i.e., when the entire world becomes democratic.

Transitioning from one era to another is always a long and undulating process. More developed countries move into the next era faster; they must help those less developed and have mechanisms of self-protection to prevent evil from dragging them backwards. All of this requires time, effort, and resources. However, the goal is entirely clear.

I have divided my fantasies about the future into seven parts and named each one separately, giving each name a bit of mystery. Just as it should be in true fantasies, please forgive me if some aspects seem unreal, perhaps impossible, and may not come true. Fantasy is a genre that allows you to dream without getting bogged down in various thoughts about what will be and what will be, but differently. Here it is – about that.

One thing that seems indisputable to me when considering the future, is that humanity will develop for the triumph of good over evil. History clearly shows that good prevails over evil, no matter how banal it may sound. Or perhaps it sounds banal precisely because it is so familiar that it seems impossible to be otherwise? Even the darkest nights end, and dawn always breaks. Of course, much is sacrificed for this to happen. Still, everything that happens afterwards unfolds differently, protecting, improving, and figuring out how to make the future brighter, more beautiful, and most importantly – allowing progress and moving forward, discovering more and increasingly incredible things.

Humanity still has a lot ahead of it, and we live in a time when changes are gaining momentum. Technologies are changing at an unprecedented pace, and they will continue to evolve in the future. However, the foundational values on which they are built remain the same. It is called goodness. With respect and gratitude, we remember those who created something for the sake of goodness, to live better, safer, and more comfortably, and for the sake of continuing to create. We remember these people's Action, Tongue, and Style, i.e., their reputation. It was important then, remains so today, and will be important tomorrow. These three fundamentals are the foundations that do not change if we think on a civilizational, not cosmic, scale.

5.1. Starry Night: Alone or Not?

> Look at the sky. We are not alone. The whole universe is friendly to us and conspires only to give the best to those who dream and work.
>
> Avul Pakir Jainulabdeen Abdul Kalam – aerospace scientist and President of India.

Humanity is constantly working. In my opinion, work is the very first skill humans perceive, enabling survival. On the other hand, there is a saying that all inventions are made out of laziness, meaning that humans strive to survive and live more comfortably. From the primitive stages, humanity has invented a lot, but probably, we are still in the primitive stage when thinking about what awaits us in the future.

In the future, it is clear that space awaits us. We are already beginning to understand what is happening here on Earth. We will soon arrange it so that living here will be good and comfortable; we will clean it. Of course, when I say "soon", I mean decades or even centuries. However, in terms of civilization, that is fast.

Nevertheless, the most significant discoveries about space are still ahead of us. There, we are just beginning to move, just beginning to understand, just beginning to explore.

Planned missions to the Moon and Mars, human colonization, new cultures, plants, organisms, theories, and technologies. Hundreds of people, primarily scientists, are working on this today, but the communicative work is also clearly visible.

Every discovery, invention, and new step requires more communication, explanation, and understanding. Each new step needs justification and funding; humanity must see meaning in those steps.

And what if, imagine, life in the Universe was discovered? It would be a significant explosion in society, as well as in the work of PR professionals. How many new theories, methods, and attempts would emerge?

However, the most important thing is that humanity, progressing, seems to climb stairs, reaching higher and higher levels. The inhabitants of lower levels (the past) created the foundations for the inhabitants of the higher levels. Without the first levels, the higher ones would be impossible. Man discovered electricity, without which electrical devices could not have been invented.

All new scientific and cosmic discoveries made today are because someone in the past invented something, i.e., created the foundation for inventing what is being invented today and what will be invented in the future. Google, Amazon, Facebook, and other terms that have almost become common today are known to us because electricity and the internet were discovered in the past.

And today, we are laying the foundations for the inhabitants of higher levels. Future space public transport will fly because today, the first commercial flights into space are being made, and people are modeling these flights based on journeys to the Moon or Mars.

The sparkling sky promises us an immeasurable future and a distant development. Therefore, in the future, space communication will be one of the most progressive branches of communication science and practice.

In the future, we will discover a lot in space, profoundly changing our lives on Earth.

5.2. Black Square: It Is Weird, Isn't It?

> Everything great in science and art is simple. What can be less complicated than the greatest discoveries of humanity – gravitation, the compass, the printing press, the steam engine, the electric telegraph?
>
> Jules Verne – novelist, poet, and playwright.

Do you remember the landline telephone? How about the telegraph? Do you still read paper newspapers, or do you remember that your grandparents used to read them? And your great-grandparents probably traveled by horse-drawn carriage?

All of these technologies that we no longer use today – why? Well, because we have invented better ones.

Often, looking at the screen of a computer or phone, I think that in the future, this habit will seem just as strange as talking on a landline phone today. No matter how advanced computer technology may seem today, being attached to the black square (computer or phone screen) is neither a natural nor comfortable state for humans.

Gradually, and with the help of the COVID-19 pandemic, we are freeing ourselves quite rapidly from the confines of the office, and only commuting to them to perform work that couldn't be done otherwise. Today, black squares allow many of us to work anywhere and anytime. This change is already a significant step towards freedom, but I believe that in the future, we will also free ourselves from the "slavery" of the black squares themselves.

So another change awaiting us is the disappearance of computers and smartphones with screens. It's just a matter of time before we can comfortably see and work without screens, and still feel natural in how we interact with people during dinners, meetings, or picnics in the park.

This prediction is essentially already coming true. The Metaverse speaks to the same idea – the internet is expected to transform into a three-dimensional, tangible, sensory, emotional, and intuitive space. Just imagine the new possibilities opening up for PR professionals and the kind of Social Picnic that will take place here!

In the future, we will break free from black square frames and live much more naturally in virtual space.

5.3. Playing Child: The Best Feeling

> My parents said that sitting at home playing video games all day won't bring you anywhere in life.
>
> Felix Arvid Ulf Kjellberg (PewDiePie) – YouTuber, online personality, and content creator.

In 1859, young people in America caused a moral panic by playing chess, which was viewed as a waste of time.

I remember when I was a child, and the first time an automatic washing machine arrived at our house, I couldn't take my eyes off it. I could sit for a long time by its door, watching the laundry start to spin, the water filling in, the bubbles appearing, and so on. Similarly, I could watch the fish swimming in the aquarium for a long time. Do you also remember how, in childhood, you would play with figurines or dolls so intensely that it was hard to stop and sleep? Or how would you get so engrossed in reading a book that you'd almost make it to morning, and your eyes would close themselves? Does it still happen now? Do you ever find yourself doing something that you can't stop? If so, congratulations – there's still a little child inside you who can dream and create.

"Panem et circenses!" (Bread and circuses!) cried the crowds in ancient Rome, expressing their demand to the authorities and clearly stating what they needed. On the one hand, these are the needs of controlled crowds, and on the other hand, the most elemental, basic needs of any human. Don't give a person a meal for just one day; they'll become sad, gloomy, and dull. Turn their work into a boring routine, merely a means to earn food, and the result will be the same.

We all strive to be well-fed and live interesting, non-monotonous lives. Only when we are satisfied and happy can we create, i.e., express ourselves – write, sing, dance, and make scientific discoveries. Or in other words, move forward. Of course, we can find various exceptions in history, but 99% of us are just like that.

All this means that the natural state of a human is to seek wellbeing for oneself and others constantly. Therefore, "Panem et circenses!" has never disappeared; we still want and will want bread and circuses in the future.

And what if the conjunction "and" didn't separate bread and games? What if obtaining bread was combined with playing games? Isn't that already the case for many people? Have you noticed how many various routine activities have become, if not games, at least infused with elements of play?

As we go about our day, we tally points; the washing machine plays a tune when it finishes its task; the Waze navigator is filled with cheerful icons of fellow drivers; under Social Picnic posts, we collect likes, hearts, and other emojis; staying in hotels or traveling earns us points; shopping in stores accumulates stickers or grants various discounts. There are numerous game elements in our lives today compared to 50 years ago.

The term "gamification" emerged in the early 21st century and is associated with the internet and computerization. However, the underlying need is much older, I believe, and dates back to the beginnings of humanity.

And although, like all processes, gamification has its drawbacks, I believe it's only a matter of time before many more routine tasks will become more gamified. The Social Picnic is no exception and already resembles a game – we react, share, discuss, aim for more incredible popularity, and monitor the spread of shared knowledge. Some Plaids become paid, and in some, we become Sharers "with honors". In others, Plaids are appreciated for their work, and we are given volunteer or other status.

In the future, as content becomes increasingly independent of advertising, gamification will only grow. Authors will want direct payment from their readers and viewers, so more platforms for this will emerge. We can already see hints of this today in various crowdsourcing platforms.

In the future, a significant portion of work, mainly routine tasks, will become a game. Working will be more enjoyable overall.

5.4. Bizarre Marriage: The Divorce Is Inevitable

> Half the money I spend on advertising is wasted; the trouble is, I don't know which half.
>
> John Wanamaker – merchant and religious, civic, and political figure.

Everyone in a free country is entitled to their own opinion, and I don't seek to change the opinions of those who think differently. However, in my view, looking at it broadly on a global scale, advertising can be seen as a waste of resources. If that's the case, every form of waste sooner or later comes to an end.

It's worth considering how much paper, plastic, and other materials are discarded on Earth to prove that we need something! And how much energy do we consume today, gigawatts of it, to receive junk mail electronically? Advertising is perhaps the most significant waste of resources on this planet, directly and indirectly compelling or commanding us to buy things we often don't need – items that often end up unused and discarded. While this is done voluntarily, the freedom of choice for many people isn't as significant as it might seem.

However, in this section, I am interested in a narrower, more PR-related type of advertising. It's the kind of advertising that, by exploiting our illusion of getting content for free, is constantly inserted next to the content, claiming that without it, we wouldn't receive it. It's a significant lie spread by those who make a living from advertising in the media.

I believe that at least such brazen advertising will disappear, where you must watch at least three ads to read an article. More and more people worldwide are willing to pay for quality content, not only because it's not expensive but because they have begun to understand that accessible content is manipulation – payment is made not with money but with the time and attention taken by advertising. And these values are becoming much more precious than money today.

I see the media and advertising tandem as the best example of a marriage for money. Like many similar unions, they are destined to fail. For a certain period, we allowed the media to trade our attention, as if we quietly agreed to transfer the rights to manage our attention, and in return, they provided us with free or cheaper content.

While our attention was relatively cheap, this situation satisfied both parties. However, as attention becomes more valuable, this situation is much more profitable for the media than us. Therefore, we are starting to disagree with it.

I think several factors should altogether terminate these marriages in the future.

The first factor is technologies that allow content creators to be independent of advertising revenue. The desire to earn money directly for one's work will be both a future preference and a matter of self-respect. This future has already begun: in some cases, we willingly, and in others, are obligated to pay for content. This trend will strengthen.

The new generation of technology users will have no difficulties or reservations about paying directly for content, and the content's quality, uniqueness, and independence from advertising will determine the price. This generation will have no qualms about paying for something they cannot physically grasp – information will be an inherently understood value.

Paying directly for content is a fair and accessible agreement between creators and users. Advertising has only temporarily taken on the role of a not-so-honest intermediary. The time has come to renegotiate the terms.

The second factor is the new generation's intolerance of advertising, as they are on the verge of entering an independent world. The new generation is entirely social, shaping their fashions, trends, and interests exclusively based on the examples of opinion leaders or influencers. Advertising is fundamentally strange and incomprehensible to them. In a world where trends of eco-friendliness and waste reduction are spreading, environmental pollution by advertising will be entirely unacceptable.

If the current generation of payers tolerates it for now and only gradually begins to understand that behind "free content" lies the payment of millions for their attention and time, the growing Generation Z will be much less tolerant of this phenomenon. They will certainly not tolerate trading their time without their knowledge or consent.

For this pragmatic generation, anything done through coercion is fundamentally unacceptable. When these young people need information, they seek it quickly and only want what they are looking for; they are much more selective about the content presented to them. Considering their technological savvy, deceiving them and slipping in hidden advertising will be increasingly difficult. Suppose today we call hidden advertising what is defined by laws and deliberately concealed. In that case, it's likely that in the future, the new generation will give a completely different meaning to the word "hidden".

"Hidden" would mean something that pops up when they've accumulated enough views and are reading an article that interests them or something that blinks when they want to view video material that catches their interest. Such entirely legal advertising today will likely become undesirable and, quite possibly, prohibited by laws tomorrow. I think it could already be done freely now because any blinking or flashing, unwanted by me, is a blatant violation of my rights. And if we were to add the impact of such advertising on pollution and start calculating how much energy is wastefully spent to show it to those who don't want it at all! After all, fundamentally, advertising, no matter how targeted and no matter what its advocates say, is shooting with a shotgun to hit a fly.

According to the new understanding, sponsors of "hidden" advertising will risk damaging their reputation in the long run.

The third factor is gamification. This phenomenon is seeping into many areas of life, and the media is no exception. Why do people collect points and compete with each other or themselves in activities such as running? Because it's interesting and exciting, it makes you stand out in a particular area and be recognized among peers. People compete in wine tasting, climbing mountains, swimming, reading, and collecting points. Therefore, the future belongs to those media outlets that offer the most exciting and attractive gamified content, those that can attract financial streams and distribute them interestingly among those who create content and those who use it most effectively and purposefully.

In the future, advertising will disappear, and future generations will view media outlets abundant with advertising as interesting relics of the past.

5.5. World Reunion: Everyone Is Reachable, Everyone Is Safe

> In a democracy there will always be a tension between security and privacy.
>
> Keir Starmer – politician and lawyer.

Privacy and accessibility contradict each other, at least for today. Imagining a wholly private or open person is also practically impossible. There is always a certain balance between privacy and accessibility: for some, the scales lean more towards privacy, while for others, towards accessibility.

Although the emergence of social networks and other technologies may have significantly reduced the amount of privacy, I believe this is a very superficial perspective. It's just a misleading impression because we easily observe many people willingly giving up their privacy, creating the impression that it is the norm.

However, even those who seem to share aspects of their lives easily only show us what they want to show, and often, they significantly embellish the presented image. Apart from them, some do not share much or share very rarely. Once, I tried to count the percentage of those actively sharing their personal lives versus those who don't share or share very little in my surroundings. I was surprised to find that the latter make up the absolute majority. Of course, I don't claim this observation to be part of any objective research, but this section is not about that.

This section is about the future, that is, about fantasies of how everything will be in the future. I wanted to illustrate the competition between accessibility and privacy as fundamental, as a problem that we have constantly addressed and will continue to solve in the future.

However, I believe that we will resolve it.

I believe that everyone has been in such a situation or a similar one. You visit your parents, children, friends, or other close people, the conversation is already underway, you're enjoying being together, and suddenly, it all comes to a halt due to a phone call. The host "apologizes" and disappears for about 15–30 minutes. Then you wait, staring at the wall, perhaps inspecting the kitchen utensils or browsing your phone. Then the host returns, and everything should seemingly return to the initial vibes, but it doesn't. Initial vibes do not return because during your host's phone call, a part of the atmosphere was transferred to another space and started "living" there, and upon returning to you, it hasn't fully returned yet; it is still influenced by what it recently heard or saw. Perhaps you have already become interested in some topic on your phone. It takes time for everything to return to the initial vibes. It's even better if, upon return, there is no new incoming call.

Is it good? Probably not. Who is to blame for this? The inability to fully use technology and habits. Over the decades of landline telephones, our parents and grandparents ingrained in their blood what an unanswered phone call meant. It meant absence at home, loss of contact, and lengthy explanations to the boss about why they couldn't find you when needed. And even though the generation of the 2000s doesn't remember landline phones anymore, habits and traditions persist. I have heard arguments from representatives of this generation that a lack of an instant response to a notification signifies ignorance, anger, and the loss of a relationship.

In short, people with such habits sacrifice their privacy for accessibility. The caller or the person sending a message a priori becomes more critical than the person sitting opposite at the table. For some, these habits can be so ingrained that they won't even allow a moment of peace to go to the bathroom. Most likely, at some point, we'll hear a complaint from such people that supposedly "technology has destroyed privacy".

However, the truth is that it's not technology that creates or destroys something; it's people, and whether they know how to use technology or not. Technology makes things easier to do. Technology is an extension of ourselves, an addition, a prosthesis, if you will, that we control. Blaming a prosthesis for not moving in a specific direction would be odd.

Mark Zuckerberg, presenting the Metaverse concept in 2021, stated, I believe, two crucial things – the Metaverse would significantly emphasize security and privacy. It might even be the foundation of the Metaverse. And, in my opinion, this is very important.

Whatever technologies are developed in the future, they must prioritize security and ensure privacy. Security and privacy mean that in the future, IF WE CHOOSE TO, we will be completely accessible through all possible means. Physically being thousands of kilometers apart, or even on different planets, we will feel a closeness to the person with whom we want to be. Furthermore, we will be sure to interact with that person, not with some impostor or deceiver, ensuring accurate visual representation. Technology will guarantee this.

Conversely, IF WE CHOOSE TO, we will instantly find ourselves in complete privacy without causing any stress to ourselves or others. We will be able to exist in our private bubble without the possibility of being reached at all, or we will be accessible only to those we choose to be reachable.

This accessibility or inaccessibility will be much more sophisticated than it is now when either we receive a heap of messages and struggle to manage which ones we want to receive and which ones we don't, or we "don't raise the flag" and trigger a cascade of thoughts from "something must have happened to her/him, probably very bad because she/he can't even respond" to "she/he doesn't love me because she/he can't even find time to respond". Our bubbles will indicate to the world in every possible way the nature of our accessibility or inaccessibility, and no one will have any questions about it. I believe that shortly, we will see privacy bubbles like "focused", "in a business meeting", "completely inaccessible", "in a class", and so on.

This process leads us towards the Era of World Reunion described by Yefremov[1] and we are only taking the first steps in it. Through the creation of the internet, social networks, and the global Social Picnic, we have already entered this era. Through concepts like Metaverse, we will continue to progress and deepen the integration of the entire world. In this era, it becomes meaningless to fight for what humanity has fought for since its inception - fighting for land and territory. Being a leader in the global Social Picnic will not depend on the specific point on Earth where you are. Values will become the virtual "territory". People will find and appreciate each other not based on nationality, citizenship, skin color, language, or sexual orientation. They will form groups based on virtual values, thoughts, actions, and ideas. Due to the circumstances, I cannot ask the sci-fi author precisely what he had in mind and what he would say today, but what we are heading towards seems most similar to The Era of World Reunion.

We will have technologies that allow us to achieve complete privacy or openness in the future. The most important thing is that we will learn to do it ourselves.

5.6. Awesome Sound: Aren't We All Singing?

> If you talk to a man in a language he understands, that goes to his head. If you talk to him in his language, that goes to his heart.
>
> Nelson Mandela – revolutionary and political leader.

One day, I was sitting in a business meeting next to my client, and on the other side, another colleague was seated. I was on the left side of my client, and my colleague was on the right. I knew there were tense relations between my client and my colleague; they didn't like each other as they were very different people. Whenever my colleague started talking, my client wouldn't say anything. He wouldn't even move or change his sitting posture, and I, sitting next to him, wouldn't even look at him. However, somehow, through vibrations that I couldn't understand, I could feel how he was boiling inside and wanted to silence or contradict but remained silent. Conversely, when my colleague stopped talking, I could sense how the tension, the energy emanating from the person sitting next to me would ease.

We communicate with each other through language, gestures, or facial expressions and in some emotional and sensory way. You've probably been in a situation where, even without anyone speaking, there is a thick tension in the room, and it feels like a mere whisper or a click could cause it to explode as if it were gas. The more empathy a person has, the more they feel, and the more such communication occurs.

So here on Earth, we communicate with different verbal languages and some unified language based on feelings, emotions, and empathy, where sound is not essential. We can fall in love without understanding language; we can hate without speaking; we can sense the right places in an entirely unknown city, create tension, or, conversely, create a good atmosphere for people sitting at a neighboring table without communicating or looking at them.

Language is a crucial part of national identity. Being well-acquainted with the issues in post-Soviet countries and having experienced the transformation from Soviet dictatorship to democracy, I see the significant role language plays.

In countries where the native language was not forcibly suppressed, crushed, or destroyed, traditions quickly recovered. The Russian language, imposed for many years during the Soviet era, just disappeared from public life and gained the status of an ordinary foreign language.

Conversely, in countries where attention to their language was lacking or couldn't be given, where their language was pushed aside, belittled, called rural, or poor, the recovery process has been, and continues to be, slow, with setbacks, obstacles and resistance.

However, if we look at language from a different perspective, through the ability to communicate with the world, we'll understand that multilingualism isn't necessarily a straightforward advantage. Well, if we simplify, there's no convenience in figuring out how to ask or order lunch after flying for several hours. These are minor inconveniences, but there are more severe issues like politicians being unable to communicate, scientists being unable to understand each other, and business miscommunications. And, of course, it's natural that people strive to eliminate these communication barriers and understand each other.

If you've ever had the chance to observe the work of the European Parliament and the bustling interpreters, you've probably thought that it resembles something of a madhouse. The European Union currently has 24 official languages, and the European Parliament must use them all. In practice, this means that any Member of the European Parliament (MEP) from Bulgaria, Finland, Germany, or any other country can speak in their language during a session. Meanwhile, any MEP from Ireland, Italy, Lithuania, or another country can receive a direct translation into their language. This requirement also implies that should be 576 interpreters capable of translating directly from Bulgarian to Finnish, German to Italian, Lithuanian to English, and so on at every session. Today, there are 720 MEPs.

The number of interpreters is, of course, challenging to grasp, especially when considering that each interpreter needs a separate booth and also requires breaks. In practice, this is addressed by performing double-synchronous translations, where the speech is initially translated into a few main languages, such as English, French, or German, and then translated into the remaining languages. You can imagine the quality of such synchronous translation, especially when the conversation delves into more specific topics. Therefore, a significant portion of MEPs opt to speak and listen in a few main languages, as it helps to understand the essence of the matter better.

The European Union (EU) has embraced the principle of multilingualism, which is highly democratic and emphasizes the fundamental principles of the world's largest union of countries. And it is true that the diversity of languages is lovely, and that when we speak, we sing. We sing in different styles, with different sounds or intonations.

However, I believe we will part with language diversity in the future. It may not happen very quickly, but humans solve and do everything in a way that is more convenient for them, and the inability to communicate is not convenient. Whether in the future we will speak some artificial language, or it will be English, or if machine translation will improve so much that we won't have to worry about what language we are speaking – we will see. However, one thing is clear – we will have something that everyone will understand, and we won't need another person next to us for that understanding.

It is essential to understand a straightforward thing and discard the dogma ingrained in us by nationalism and traditions. For instance, language is an invaluable asset, and we should strive to preserve languages and the only way to that is to use them. On the other hand, we should accept that we need to have one "world" language if we want smooth communication around the globe – and even beyond!

We all sing in unique and beautiful ways, meaning we speak various languages. However, as we delve deeper into space, when the need arises to communicate with beings from light-years away (I'm not even talking about finding a civilization similar to ours), we won't be bothered by language anymore – we'll use the one that is most convenient to use.

5.7. Endless Creativity: We Are All Too Deep Into Work

> Free time is there for you to exercise your creativity.
>
> Yoko Ono – artist, singer, songwriter, and peace activist.

Have you ever tried doing nothing for an extended period? Like, for example, lying in bed and staring at the ceiling? I tried, and I couldn't last more than two hours. I know there are various meditation techniques, and you can go for longer, shut off your mind, and achieve various deeply relaxing states. It's essential, necessary, helpful. I'm personally taking steps towards that, and I believe that's where what we call happiness lies. Modern people have freed themselves from many obligations they had in the past. They no longer need to hunt a mammoth to make a fur coat for warmth and, after that, eat the mammoth to satisfy hunger. We don't need to go to the bank and stand in line to pay utility bills – we can do it with a few clicks in our black rectangles. We had to allocate time for every action we had to perform in the past to survive.

Each new invention freed up that time, meaning the time we used to spend going to the bank, standing in line, and returning, we reclaimed from the bank and returned it to ourselves.

However, the most important thing is not whether we return it to ourselves but what we do with the reclaimed time. Not much has changed if we just replace standing in the bank with more extended TV watching or aimlessly scrolling online. Suppose it resulted in more time for books and loved ones – great. Well, if you started creating more and realizing yourself – you are a modern, happy person with endless dreams, aspirations, and activities.

It can be said that the modern person is much more accessible than ever before. Many tasks can be done from anywhere efficiently, allowing for large amounts of free time, the distribution of which depends solely on each of us. All human inventions are made just so that people have more time.

In the future, even more time will be liberated: we will work less yet accomplish more. We will have excellent opportunities to earn a living by working a tiny part of our time or employing robots circulating in our environment. The mind, free from existential concerns, will be able to create peacefully, and as a result, the collective creativity of humanity will flourish. This freedom will lead us to unprecedented horizons that we dare not even dream about today.

To use liberated time as you wish and not squander it, you need to be able to plan time and continuously develop those skills; but that is already the subject of another book I plan to write.

Finally, however much time we may have, wherever we travel, we will always need to have our most crucial anchor – our reputation. Remember? "We will be known forever by the tracks we leave." And "tracks" are creations. It's what we leave behind.

Note

1 Yefremov I. (1970). *The Bull's Hour*. Moscow: Molodaya Gvardiya.

6 Final Remarks

Every new beginning comes from some other beginning's end.

Seneca – philosopher, statesman, dramatist, and satirist.

I feel like I've summarized everything accumulated over the years of my professional career. However, I don't feel finished or that I have thoroughly explored this topic. I sense that this is just the beginning, and I believe that either I or others will have the opportunity to develop the ideas presented here further.

The most significant impact on this will come from the changing world and the emergence of new tools and possibilities. Even very shortly, tools will change rapidly, but the essence and values of PR will remain unchanged until artificial intelligence partially takes over this field from us. However, even when that happens – and I believe it will – we still need to educate artificial intelligence. Proper education for artificial intelligence will still have to be based on the same unchanging fundamental factors that make up a reputation: Action, Tongue, and Style.

Writing this book, I felt that I extracted something from within me and handed it over to the screen. It seemed like reliving my professional life and gradually purging what had accumulated over many years. Writing this book was an arrangement of my experiences into pages, into a system, and a presentation to the reader. Every sentence written here is a life stage experienced and felt at one time or another. Therefore, I don't claim absolute truth or a precise theory. The most important thing for me was to describe what I had accumulated and felt. I feel renewed and am accumulating thoughts for the next stage, perhaps for another book.

I sincerely hope that in professionally clearing myself on these pages, I have presented not chaos but systematically organized thoughts arranged on shelves. I hope these thoughts will not become a burden to the reader but rather be of assistance when needed most.

Once, I participated in one of those abundant and communication-rich public relations conferences, where it seems even the food breathes dialogue during breaks, and I met a colleague. Unlike everyone else, he stood facing the bar, calmly eating with a plate in hand. I approached and asked him why he was

DOI: 10.4324/9781003466802-7

having lunch in such an unusual way. In response, he said that after 20 years of public relations practice, he finally realized that he is, after all, an introvert. It not only amused me greatly but also made me think. I thought that I felt similarly. Why is that? Are all public relations people, being the most communicative part of society, truly introverts, having learned to communicate professionally?

Communicating with my colleagues and recounting this incident repeatedly, I formed an opinion as to why I feel this way. My answer lies in overstimulation. No, as public relations professionals, we are not introverts, and many of us genuinely enjoy communication. But like anything enjoyed and done constantly, it has its limits. Therefore, the best rest for me, a person engaged in constant communication, is in silence, without haste, within myself or in my small, close circle of loved ones. I constantly notice that large groups of people start to bother me.

The coronavirus pandemic was a major global disaster, but it also had positive impacts. One was the opportunity to communicate less, pause, slow down, see fewer people, and spend more time at home. The pandemic also allowed technology to showcase its power, which existed before but was not fully utilized. The pandemic was cruel, but it was also a unique experiment in how people would feel when their ability to communicate directly, be with others, and replace face-to-face communication with remote interaction was restricted.

I derived from this experiment what suited this book. My conclusions are as follows:

1. Humans cannot avoid communication.
2. Remote communication can replace a significant portion of face-to-face interaction.
3. Engaging in remote communication makes people miss direct interaction, causing them to value it more, and use it responsibly, sparingly, without abuse.
4. Despite appearing almost perfect, current technologies are still very primitive and unnatural; we will see many much more advanced ones in the future.
5. The Social Picnic, as a new concept in people relations, will become more apparent, widely used, and developed.

I eagerly await what the future holds. Let's enjoy the ever-expanding possibilities of communication that unfold daily. Let's use them and appreciate and respect every participant in our Social Picnic, even if their opinion seems vastly different to you. Together, you are all part of this global communication flow; without you, this flow wouldn't be possible.

Together, we have already created an immense amount. We could create even more if we were less destructive. Let's strive in the future to create as much as possible and destroy as little as possible. If we all focus on creating, we will witness amazing things.

Thank you for being with the Picnic Society and, simultaneously, with me.

7 Thank You

> There are two basic motivating forces: fear and love. When we are afraid, we pull back from life. When we are in love, we open to all that life has to offer with passion, excitement, and acceptance. We need to learn to love ourselves first, in all our glory and our imperfections. If we cannot love ourselves, we cannot fully open to our ability to love others or our potential to create. Evolution and all hopes for a better world rest in the fearlessness and open-hearted vision of people who embrace life.
>
> John Lennon – singer, songwriter, and peace activist.

Fear never motivates; it only compels. Love allows you to feel safe and liberated, enabling you to spread your wings and accomplish much, as if effortlessly, without coercion, naturally. It's strange, but I only recently understood this, and once I did, I could embark on writing this book. Until then, I was afraid, and in my fear, I always found reasons to wait and not to write.

Now that I see this clearly, I understand that throughout my entire life, I have been surrounded by, and continue to be surrounded by, only two types of people: those who evoke more fear or those who love more.

When I was a little child and then when I was learning and starting my professional journey, people who instilled fear significantly impacted me. I feared those who spoke sternly, yelled, and were angry or rude. And, of course, as long as I was afraid, I held myself back. What if I'm wrong? What if it's foolish? What if I make a fool of myself? These questions are the result of what fear-inducing people instil in us. They directly or indirectly raise these questions for us, and these questions prevent us from moving forward, obstructing our path and forcing us to curl up and cower. Now I understand that people who instil fear in others are the unhappiest in the world, and instilling fear is a way of covering their wounds of inadequacy. We should pity those who instil fear, help them if possible, and if not, pay no attention and ignore them.

However, in this world, love has much greater power than fear. When we face a significant threat and are afraid, that fear diminishes when a loving person appears by our side, extends a hand, embraces, and assures that everything will be fine. The threat diminishes, weakens, and sometimes even disappears altogether.

DOI: 10.4324/9781003466802-8

I am very fortunate because, although I waded through the river of fear for a long time, there were always so many people around me who loved me that at least one person would extend a helping hand in any abyss. Without them, this book would not have existed; it would have drowned somewhere in the backwaters of fear.

However, it did not sink; you are holding it in your hands, which means I am infinitely grateful to everyone who, at one time or another, held me by the hand and, with their love, helped me overcome fear.

A few years before the dawning of the 21st century, my mother, Laima, and I founded Lithuania's first public relations agency. At that time, hardly anyone here knew such a term, and a green business studies student, I suspect, seemed amusing to more than one client and collaborator. Therefore, I carried the professional weight behind a firm backbone; as oddly as it may sound, my mother, who had already been the head of the public relations departments at several banks, had a vast network of connections and appeared much more reputable. Although we often passionately argued about various things at that time, today, I believe those disputes stemmed from my fears and lack of experience. I am very grateful, Mom, that you held on, always supported, and knew we were on the right path.

The profession has given me many wonderful, sensitive, and loving people, many of whom have become colleagues and friends.

First and foremost, of course, is Igor Sokolov. When we first met in a hotel lobby in Vilnius, I couldn't imagine how important this person would become to me and how much he would help me on my professional path. All the people we meet can be divided into those who remain acquaintances, "stick around", and those who do not. Igor and I became close immediately, although we haven't done significant work or earned money together. However, he somehow managed to say things in a way that my professional self-esteem seemed to grow several times higher. When I talked to him, I regained balance and understood that I was thinking correctly, that this was how it should be, and that I was not making things up. And it happens constantly; it never stops. I can confidently say that Igor is my professional soulmate, a spigot constantly replenishing the glass when the professional elixir is running low. Igor contributed a lot to the creation of this book. Thank you very much, and I am infinitely happy that we crossed paths in this life.

My second professional companion is Meelis Kubits. When I first wanted to meet him at a joint partner event in the park, I didn't know what he looked like. Colleagues who already knew him advised me to look for someone with red shoes. And that's how he has been for me ever since – a person with red shoes: bold, insightful, active, and constantly aware of everything happening in his field of attention. Although our acquaintance and friendship developed almost immediately, Meelis seemed to be somewhere a bit higher for a long time, somewhere I might have already missed the opportunity to climb to. I listened to his stories and some were so incredible they seemed like they came from comics. However, later on, I realized that he is not just a person with red shoes but also a friendly and loving person. Although my professional achievements are much less significant, I constantly feel Meelis's support, attention, and friendship. Thank you.

In the professional jungles, just like in the real ones, I would probably have been devoured long ago if not for my professional colleagues and partners, a significant portion of whom I can confidently call friends, and each of whom has been crucial to me. Of course, directly or indirectly, they have all contributed to the creation of this book. I believe that the thoughts of everyone met in this journey are somehow embedded in this book. Therefore, I want to express my gratitude to every one of them.

Index

credibility 38–41, 47–50, 80, 186

For Product Safety Concerns and Information please contact our EU representative GPSR@taylorandfrancis.com Taylor & Francis Verlag GmbH, Kaufingerstraße 24, 80331 München, Germany